The Myth of
WILD
AFRICA

The Myth of WILD AFRICA

CONSERVATION WITHOUT ILLUSION

JONATHAN S. ADAMS
THOMAS O. McSHANE

UNIVERSITY OF CALIFORNIA PRESS

Berkeley · Los Angeles · London

University of California Press
Berkeley and Los Angeles, California

University of California Press, Ltd.
London, England

First Paperback Printing 1996

Library of Congress Cataloging-in-Publication Data
Adams, Jonathan S.
    The myth of wild Africa : conservation without illusion / Jonathan
S. Adams, Thomas O. McShane.
      p.   cm.
    Originally published: New York : W.W. Norton, 1992.
    Includes bibliographical references and index.
    ISBN 0-520-20671-1
    1. Wildlife conservation—Africa—Philosophy. 2. Animals and
civilization—Africa. I. McShane, Thomas O. II. Title.
[QL84.6.A1A33 1996]
333.95'9'096—dc20
                                      96-17658
                                         CIP

The paper used in this publication meets the minimum requirements of
American National Standard for Information Sciences—Permanence
of Paper for Printed Library Materials,
ANSI Z39.48-1984. ∞

FOR NAOMI AND ERICA

CONTENTS

▼ ▼ ▼

ACKNOWLEDGMENTS

▼ ▼ ▼

The idea for the collaboration that led to this book came more or less simultaneously to three people. The one not listed on the title page, Robert J. McCoy, Director of Publications at World Wildlife Fund, may be the person most directly responsible for the book's existence, for without his encouragement we may never have actually put pen to paper. We are also indebted to him for choosing a title that early on helped crystallize the ideas we were trying to express.

Richard Bell, David Cumming, and Holly Dublin read all or part of the manuscript, and their enthusiasm, comments, and insight into conservation in Africa were invaluable. Any errors that remain are, of course, the responsibility of the authors.

Amy Cherry and Ed Barber of W. W. Norton showed great faith in two untested writers, and then provided skilled and patient editing. Their persistence vastly improved the quality of this book, and for that we are deeply grateful.

Many people contributed to this work with kindness, information, and assistance. We thank the following, with the understanding that the names of others who were no less helpful will occur to us when it is too late; those we thank as well, with our apologies: Issa Amadou, Richard Barnes, Abdi Omar Bashir, Olivier Bilala, John Boshe, Watson Botha, the staff and students of the College of African Wildlife Management, Ted Dardani, Jean Hubert Eyi-Mbeng, Horace Freeland Judson, Assetou Kanoute, Joe Kioko, Richard Leakey, Alphonse Mackanga, Matthew Matemba, Rowan Martin, Costa Mlay, Rob Monroe, John Mphande, Simon Munthali, Marshall Murphree, Henri Nsanjama, Sylvie Nkoussee-Evinah, Joyce Poole, George Pangetti, and Bill Weber. Joseph School, director of Cartographic Services at the University of Maryland, Baltimore County, provided the maps.

Finally, a special thanks to Russell E. Train, Chairman of the Board of World Wildlife Fund, for his wisdom and for kindly granting us the use of his spectacular collection of Africana, and to Phyllis Yearwood, for enabling two authors to complete a book even though they were often on opposite sides of the Atlantic.

INTRODUCTION

▼ ▼ ▼

On the second floor of New York's Museum of Modern Art hangs a large canvas entitled *The Dream,* by the French painter Henri Rousseau. *The Dream* depicts a fantastic moonlit jungle in shades of green, with brilliant splashes of blue, yellow, and orange. On the left, tucked neatly among ferns and orchids, a naked woman reclines on a Louis-Philippe couch, her out-stretched arm reaching toward a dark-skinned man, clad in a brightly striped loincloth, playing a flute. Even more arresting than this remarkable pair, however, are two eyes, wide black circles rimmed with yellow, that peer out from the bush and bring the viewer up short: a lion crouches in the grass. Closer inspection reveals a lioness as well, and then a serpent, two birds, a monkey, and, finally, deep in the jungle, the eye and huge ear of an elephant.

What is one to make of this? The woman lounging in the jungle—Rousseau called her Yadwhigha—is not in the jungle at all, he once explained, but at home, dreaming of wild places, perhaps of paradise. *The Dream* portrays an ideal wilderness beyond the reach of Europe, and in so doing it captures a vision of Africa that has persisted for over five centuries.

Rousseau had similar dreams. He was called the *Douanier,* or customs inspector, a title that implies a knowledge of the world beyond Paris. Rousseau, however, was not a *douanier* at all but rather a *gabelou,* an employee of the municipal toll service. He never set foot outside of France. He found his jungles at the Jardin des Plantes, his wild animals in the pages of the encyclopedia and in his imagination. In this Rousseau resembled most of his generation, which came of age in the last half of the nineteenth century. Although few Europeans of that era had firsthand knowledge of Africa, many conjured up visions of exotic jungles filled with animals. Rousseau gave the visions form and color.

Images of Africa among Rousseau's contemporaries grew from stories told by explorers and travelers like Mungo Park, Richard Burton, and David Livingstone. From these and others came tales of the Dark Continent, the world's last great wilderness. The heroic figures from the golden age of African exploration searched for the sublime and found it; here was a refuge from industrial, despoiled Europe. To an eager audience steeped in romanticism, and to the generations that followed, the tales of the explorers created an Africa that was both paradise and wilderness, a place of spectacular but savage beauty.

Europeans invented a mythical Africa, which soon claimed a place of privilege in the Western imagination. We cling to our faith in Africa as a glorious Eden for wildlife. The sights and sounds we instinctively associate with wild Africa—lions, zebra, giraffe, rhinos, and especially elephants—fit into the dream of a refuge from the technological age. We are unwilling to let that dream slip away, and perhaps appropriately so. The march of civilization has tamed or destroyed the wilderness of North America and Europe, but the emotional need for wild places, for vast open spaces like the East Africa's Serengeti Plain, persists.

European explorers wanted to believe in a virgin land, unsullied by human hands. Yet, this Africa never was. Indeed, nowhere does the vision of Africa depart further from reality. Man has been an integral part of the African landscape for over 2 million years. That people lived in Africa, however, was irrelevant to the West; what mattered was the wilderness. Wild Africa was considered so important, in fact, that people in Europe and North America organized a movement to save it.

Once Africa's wilderness began to shrink, countless individuals, whose motivations ranged from true altruism to rather obvious greed, sought to exploit the frightening notion that the continent's animals were about to vanish. Nothing plucks the heartstrings better than a lion cub or a baby elephant. Thus, over the last one hundred years, we have found ourselves deluged with books, lectures, and now television shows and movies about Africa, some explicitly trying to raise money, others designed to win converts to a cause. More people have probably got their first taste of Africa from public television—with "Nature," "Nova," and specials produced by the National Geographic Society—than from any other source. "Nature" alone has several million viewers every Saturday night. Although well made and reasonably accurate, such programs have a serious flaw: they return over and over again to the same images of East Africa, primarily Kenya and Tanzania. It is thus hardly surprising that in the popular mind, Africa consists entirely of wide grassy plains and wild animals.

The myth of wild Africa has changed since Rousseau's time. Ask someone to paint a picture of Africa today and it would resemble not Rousseau's dreamy jungle but rather the Serengeti of "Nature": thousands of wildebeest marching nose-to-tail in a line a mile long, while several well-fed lions laze under a flat-topped acacia tree nearby. In the background, the modern Rousseau would paint vultures picking at what little remains of last night's kill, while hyenas slink off to their dens with the bones.

The Dream, completed in 1910, seems to portray a tropical Anyplace, as the fluteplayer resembles the Tahitians favored by Rousseau's contemporary, Paul Gauguin. The more recent vision of Africa, on the other hand, springs from a real place, inhabited by real people. The Maasai who live here call it *siringet*—the endless plain.

The Serengeti has such great emotional appeal that for many people it has become Africa, a feat of mental gymnastics that collapses a fantastically diverse continent onto the head of a pin. A typical question put to a traveler returning from safari is, "What language do they speak in Africa?"—implying that the continent is one country and one people, rather than a jumble of some eight hundred ethnic groups and over one thousand languages and dialects.

Africa is the poorest region on earth, and it attracts thousands of well-intentioned Western governments, international banks, conservation organizations, and other institutions and individuals seeking to fill the continent's urgent needs. Many of these would-be benefactors arrive with the simplistic image of Africa as baggage, and that image sets the ground rules for their actions regarding both wildlife conservation and human development.

Wildlife conservation has become one of the most visible and contentious areas of contact between Africa and the West. The effort to save Africa's natural heritage has, justifiably, been seen as an unquestioned good, practically a moral duty for the developed world. Many people have dedicated their lives to saving at least small slivers of wild Africa, and their sincerity cannot be doubted. Some of Africa's leading conservationists and scientists—among them George Adamson, Jane Goodall, and, most recently, Richard Leakey—are now hailed as heroes, after decades of working in relative anonymity. Their commitment has helped pull species back from the brink of extinction and preserve unique wild habitats. The methods these and other conservationists have often used, such as establishing parks and putting armed rangers in the field—the basic elements of an approach called "preservationism"—date from the early colonial era, and they remain important tools.

However, they can no longer stand alone. Despite the accomplishments and the goodwill, as long as conservation operates on the notion that saving wild animals means keeping them as far away as possible from human beings, it will become less and less relevant to modern Africans. Parks and other protected areas will eventually be overrun by people's need for land unless the parks serve, or are at least not completely inimical to, the needs of the local population.

The method for establishing parks has hardly changed in over a century. The process has always involved the expensive operation of removing those people living on the newly protected land. In almost all cases, the result is a park surrounded by people who were excluded from the planning of the area, do not understand its purpose, derive little or no benefit from the money poured into its creation, and hence do not support its existence. As a result, local communities develop a lasting distrust of park authorities, in part because of the glaring lack of attention those authorities, supported by conservationists, have traditionally paid to the link between park ecology, the survival of wildlife, and the livelihood of the displaced people.

Countless African societies historically co-existed successfully with wild animals, but throughout the last two centuries they have been perceived as threats. African hunters have been branded "poachers," a word laden with value judgments about the supposed heroes and villains of conservation. Rural Africans have become increasingly wary of conservation efforts. Common sense would seemingly dictate a new approach. Yet for decades each new park was hailed as a conservation triumph.

The man leading the cheers for the parks throughout the 1960s and 1970s, in Serengeti and elsewhere, was one of the towering figures of African conservation: Professor Bernhard Grzimek, president of the Frankfurt Zoological Society and former director of the Frankfurt Zoo. Grzimek embodied the traditional approach that still plays a large role in shaping conservation efforts in Africa.

In 1959, Grzimek wrote:

> Africa is dying and will continue to die. Old maps and rem-
> nants of settlements and animals show that the Sahara has ad-
> vanced 250 miles northward on a 1,250 mile front during the
> last three centuries. In that short time 390,000 square miles of
> good land were lost. . . . So much of Africa is dead already,
> must the rest follow? Must *everything* be turned into deserts,
> farmland, big cities, native settlements, and dry bush? One
> small part of the continent at least should retain its original
> splendor so that the black and white men who follow us will be
> able to see it in its awe-filled past glory.
>   Serengeti, at least, shall not die.

That the Serengeti lived at all was because the Maasai and
their predecessors understood man's place in the savanna—a
point Grzimek missed. In fact, for Grzimek the Maasai "had
no business" in the Serengeti at all. "The Maasai were the
cause of all our hard work," he wrote. "A National Park must
remain a primordial wilderness to be effective. No men, not
even native ones, should live inside its borders."

Grzimek followed a long line of conservationists who envisioned a system of national parks in Africa modeled on that in
the United States. The mold never quite fit. While Yellowstone, Yosemite, and the rest were intended to protect mag-
nificent landscapes, parks in Africa were created to protect
large mammals. The first areas set aside were remote, largely
uninhabited, and frequently disease-ridden. They fit the Western definition of wilderness, and colonial governments and
then independent African states steadily enlarged upon them.
As the protected areas grew larger, they collided with areas
long inhabited and used as hunting grounds, pasture, or farmland.

Where park meets non-park in Africa, the seemingly obvious distinction between wilderness and civilization collapses.
For Europeans and Americans, wilderness lies "out there,"

distinct from daily life and readily identifiable. In Africa, however, it is often impossible to say with certainty where the wilderness begins. Does the region patrolled by park rangers in the Serengeti—otherwise uninhabited bush—qualify as wilderness? By some definition, yes; but the Maasai and other indigenous peoples like the Wata or Wadindiga feel quite at home there. The Western notion of wilderness does not hold in Africa, because man and animals have evolved together in the continent's diverse ecosystems.

Classic conservation methods sometimes serve neither man nor animal. In the Serengeti, where such methods had their truest test, the creation of protected areas for wildlife—along with the expansion of commercial agriculture—has forced the Maasai and other settlers to reduce some parts of the savanna to desert as they destroy trees and ground cover disappears with overgrazing. Both Maasai cattle and wildlife have less food available. The breakup of the Maasai's communal areas has also led to a deterioration of the tribe's social structures. The Maasai culture is dying, and with it a value system that has sustained a community and an ecosystem for generations.

The entire modern conservation edifice rests on the ideals and visions of people other than Africans. The great majority of Africans now active in conservation were trained in the traditional Western methods of wildlife management, thus perpetuating a system created in Europe at the turn of the century and inhibiting the growth of an African conservation ethic. This raises the question of whether Africans, without Western influence, would develop a conservation ethic similar to the familiar European version. Probably not: Europeans created their conservation ethic based on the experience of nearly destroying their environment through industrialization. Africans, while they face real challenges to their environment, seem unlikely to follow the same path. Africa does not have to mimic the environmentally destructive practices of Europe and the United States before a homegrown approach to conservation takes hold.

Some conservationists maintain that the majority of Africans cannot be trusted to conserve their wildlife resources. Put in such bald terms, this attitude would garner little support, yet it is the unspoken belief that underlies many current conservation programs. The author Roderick Nash in a speech to an international conference announced that if Tanzania could not prevent poaching in the Serengeti, "we will just have to go in and buy it."

Conservation has long operated on the comfortable belief that Africa is a paradise to be defended, even against the people who have lived there for thousands of years. The continuing reluctance to accept the link between vigorous indigenous culture and the survival of wildlife has led to conservation programs doomed to eventual failure because they depend on building barriers of one sort or another between people and wildlife. Such persistent blindness is tragic, given the effort that has been put into scientific research on both animal and human societies in Africa. The Serengeti, for example, is perhaps the most intensively studied ecosystem of its size in the world, and few cultures have attracted more anthropologists than the Maasai. With reams of data in hand, conservationists, biologists, and ecologists have succeeded only in documenting, in often grisly detail, the decline of the Serengeti.

Conservationists and scientists apparently have gone about their business with blinders on, ignoring each other as well as the people affected by their decisions. While anthropologists have been busily collecting information on these same people and coming to understand their relationship with the land, and economists have developed new models of natural resource utilization, their work has only begun to be recognized by conservationists. So far, the products of seminars and colloquia have barely moved out of the academy, and have had little if any impact on the lives of individuals or on the conduct of conservation programs.

Without doubt, conservation as practiced in Africa is more sophisticated now than it was twenty-five or even five years ago. The question is whether the refinements represent changes in the basic attitudes and values of conservation, or simply the application of modern techniques to old-fashioned ideas—a new coat of paint slapped onto old. If that is the case, eventually the cracks will show through.

The most tenacious of all the old-fashioned ideas among conservationists holds that development is the enemy because of the technology it produces—roads, dams, irrigated farms, and the like. The unspoken message is that for conservation to succeed, it has to hold back the clock. That approach had some success before human population growth and human needs began to press in on even the remotest areas. To their credit, many conservationists now realize that erecting barricades from which to make a last desperate stand against development will fail. Success lies instead in understanding that conservation and development, long at loggerheads, are two parts of a single process. Conservation cannot ignore the needs of human beings, while development that runs roughshod over the environment is doomed.

The integration of conservation, science, and development has begun in earnest across Africa, from Zimbabwe in the south to Gabon in the west to Tanzania in the east. As with any pathbreaking efforts, these projects have proceeded in fits and starts. Failures may outnumber successes for some time to come, but there is simply no other choice. Conservation will either contribute to solving the problems of the rural poor who live day to day with wild animals, or those animals will disappear.

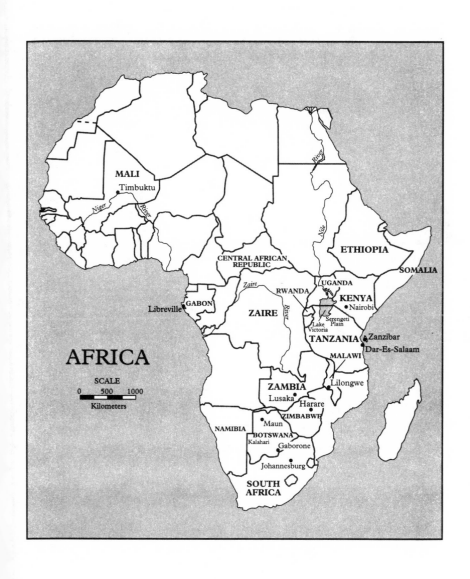

AFRICA

SCALE

0   500   1000

Kilometers

MALI
Timbuktu

Niger

River

Niger

Nile

River

CENTRAL AFRICAN
REPUBLIC

ETHIOPIA

SOMALIA

Zaire

RWANDA

UGANDA

KENYA

Libreville

GABON

ZAIRE

Nairobi

Serengeti
Plain

Lake
Victoria

TANZANIA

Zanzibar

Dar-Es-Salaam

MALAWI

Lilongwe

ZAMBIA

Lusaka

Harare

NAMIBIA

Maun

BOTSWANA

ZIMBABWE

Kalahari

Gaborone

Johannesburg

SOUTH
AFRICA

The Myth of
WILD
AFRICA

CHAPTER I

▾ ▾ ▾

A MYTH IS BORN

. . . Geographers in Afric-Maps
With Savage-Pictures fill their Gaps,
And o'er inhospitable Downs
Place elephants for want of Towns.
　　　　　　—Swift, *On Poetry*

The first European image of Africa grew from legends of the Pharaoh's Egypt and the spectacular fertility of the Nile Valley. Europe would slowly learn that the rest of the continent—particularly south of the Sahara—bore no resemblance to the Nile floodplains. The Romans broadened Europe's perceptions to include all of the Sahara, as they built garrisons across the desert from the Atlantic to the Red Sea, establishing a province they called Africa and pulling the region into Mediterranean commerce and civilization.

Yet most of Africa remained hidden. For centuries many Europeans simply called the entire continent "Ethiopia," from the Greek, meaning "land of dark-skinned people." Africa gradually revealed itself through its products—ivory, spices, perfume, gems, gold, and slaves—which flowed north along ancient Saharan trade routes to the Muslim states that ruled North Africa following the fall of Rome, and through the stories these Arab traders told of the interior.

No European would reach sub-Saharan Africa until one thousand years after the first Roman contact with the continent. The Portuguese succeeded where others had failed in pushing south of the great desert because they knew the winds and currents off their long Atlantic coast. In 1444, Portuguese sailing for Prince Henry the Navigator reached the significantly named Cape Verde—the "Green Cape"—with its lush vegetation. By the end of the century, Vasco da Gama had rounded the Cape of Good Hope, sailed up the East African coast, and crossed the Indian Ocean.

Portugal sought gold and slaves, commodities readily acquired through existing African political and commercial structures. Since the Portuguese were interested in commerce, not territory, they had little impact on African history. The Dutch, who seized most of Portugal's African territories in the mid-seventeenth century, also had little interest in Africa itself, being more concerned with controlling the East Indian half of the spice trade by means of a colony on the Cape. The experience of the Portuguese and Dutch commercial ventures, however, opened the door for the aggressive exploitation of Africa by European powers.

The colonization of Africa did not follow the pattern of North America, southern South America, Australia, or New Zealand. According to the historian Alfred W. Crosby, these places became "neo-Europes," dominated by people of European descent along with their crops, animals, and diseases. In his recent book *Ecological Imperialism,* Crosby argues that Africa, the Amazon, and Southeast Asia were not conquered until the late nineteenth century because "the ecosystem was simply too lush, too untamed and untameable for the invaders until they added more science and technology to their armaments. Europeans did not have the gear or the concepts equal to the Pleistocene challenge of the rain forest."

European crops rotted in Africa's steamy climate, or fell victim to insects or animals—with the exception of the Cape Colony, which flourished in a temperate environment that resembled the one the colonists had left behind. In the equatorial colonies, even if the crops survived the humidity, insects, and abundant wild animals, the unvarying length of the tropical day gave them no clue about when to blossom or seed, and they died or produced no fruit. Domestic animals from Europe stood little chance against African parasites and diseases, particularly foot-and-mouth disease (which remains a problem in much of Africa today). Most devastating, however, was Africa's vast range of deadly or debilitating human ailments, such as malaria, yellow fever, dengue fever, sleeping sickness, and the diverse parasitic worms.

Europeans eventually established lasting colonies in Africa, but they never brought the continent fully under their control. This fact played an important role in shaping the relationship between settlers and wildlife. Africa's ecosystems were not overwhelmed more or less at once by disease and exotic species from abroad; instead, they remained intact and supported the large numbers of animals that provided a lasting attraction for hunters throughout the nineteenth and early twentieth centuries.

Europeans could easily have pictured Africa as a land of pestilence and death. Yet many explorers believed they would find a glorious garden in the interior, if only they could push past the coastline. João de Barros, one of the Portuguese *marinheiros* who explored the West African coast in the sixteenth century, put Africa's biological impenetrability in mystical terms: "But it seems that for our sins, or for some inscrutable judgement of God, in all the entrances of this great Ethiopia that we navigate along, He has placed a striking angel with a flaming sword of deadly fevers, who prevents us from penetrating into the interior to the springs of this garden, whence proceed rivers of gold that flow to the sea in so many parts of our conquest."

Where de Barros saw angels guarding paradise, others saw a wilderness. Curiously, in both historical and contemporary discussions of Africa the ideas of wilderness and Eden seem interchangeable, sometimes even colliding and forming the phrase "wild Eden." "Wilderness" and "Eden," however,

mean quite different things. "Eden" is paradise and man's do-
minion, where all the earth's creatures do his bidding. Our
emotional response to a vision of Eden never wavers.

"Wilderness" exhibits a more complex character. The
deeply rooted concept of wilderness lies at the heart of the
myth of wild Africa, and accounts for its lasting resonance. We
are as ambivalent toward the wilderness as we are certain
about Eden. The notion of a place beyond human control,
where order breaks down, stems from sources as diverse as
Beowulf and the Bible, and it evokes responses ranging from
fear to awe to delight.

The equivalent of the word "wilderness" does not exist in
Romance languages. As Roderick Nash points out in his *Wilderness and the American Mind,* Romance languages usually
express the concept by a phrase highlighting one of the several
attributes associated with wilderness, such as the Spanish *falta
de cultura,* or the marvelous Italian *scene di disordine o confus-
ione.* Wilderness lies beyond Eden's walls, it is where man
must go when he is cast out of paradise. The word "wilderness" is Teutonic in its origins, and its roots tie the wilderness
to the Northern European tradition, in which horrible beasts
were found in primeval forests.

The rise of cities, however, led to a growing appreciation of
wilderness. The Romantic movement coveted the wilderness
qualities of solitude, mystery, and chaos, and felt that wilderness favored the sublime. Romanticism also emphasized a ho-
listic view of nature, which stressed the importance of living in
harmony with the earth. The ecologist and philosopher Henry
David Thoreau, one of the leading voices of romanticism, saw
unity in the entire animate world. "The unsympathizing
man," Thoreau said, "regards the wildness of some animals
. . . as a sin; as if all their virtues consisted in their tamable-
ness."

The dark side of the Romantic view of the wilderness was the
equally powerful idea that man should subdue nature, and that
the world could be a man-made paradise. In his book *Nature's*

Economy, the historian Donald Worster suggests that this ethic of domination emerged from the work of Charles Darwin. Darwin redefined the benign natural world of the Romantics to include a violent, ongoing competition for survival. As the Romantic age slid into the Victorian, nature took on a malevolent aspect.

The Darwinian portrait of a fallen natural world led Victorians to defend civilization as, in Worster's words, "the necessary, rational management of nature." History, the Victorians believed, would thus define a long ascent from chaos to perfect managerial control. The favored metaphor for this ethic was the garden: civilization within the walls, Darwinian jungle without.

In the United States, the conflict between the Romantic view of untamed nature and the notion that man must control his environment played out as a battle between two men, John Muir and Gifford Pinchot. Muir, the founder of the Sierra Club, spoke eloquently of the inherent values of wilderness and sought to preserve intact as much of it as possible. Pinchot served as Theodore Roosevelt's Chief Forester and in 1905 organized the U.S. Forest Service. For Pinchot, conservation meant "the development and use of the Earth and all its resources for the enduring good of men."

The utilitarian Pinchot and the mystical Muir serve as emblems for a lasting debate over preservation versus use that remains fundamental to conservation in Africa today. They also embody the gulf between two sets of values, between Eden and the wilderness. To subdue wilderness was to establish order and perhaps to recreate Eden, while to feel awed was to celebrate wilderness in its own right. Muir and Pinchot were products of these conflicting ethics, as were nearly all the most influential British travelers and explorers of Africa. The explorers often set out with uncertain motives. Raised in the Romantic tradition, they saw inherent value in wilderness, but many were also driven by religious zeal—the missionary David Livingstone provides the classic example—and by national-ism, simple greed, and the love of conquest.

The African explorers did more than simply travel to exotic lands. They also communicated their impressions to an eager audience in Europe, and the language they used helped create the myth of wild Africa. While the explorers' writings have received little attention from modern scholars, their role in shaping the relationship between Europe and Africa places them at the center of any understanding of conservation in Africa. The explorers' books—the most lasting artifact of their journeys—provided those seeking to colonize Africa with the same tangled, contradictory images about wilderness that the explorers had carried with them from Europe. The early set-tlers thus had an ambivalent relationship with the wilderness, and that ambivalence permeates much of modern conserva-tion as well. From the beginning of the colonial era, Africa was seen both as a place to be tamed for the good of man and as a reminder of our savage past, to be held in trust for future generations.

Oddly, this double vision, reminiscent of the ancient Roman personification of Africa as a woman holding a cornu-copia and a scorpion, would grow stronger as Europeans learned more about Africa. The persistent belief in the gardens of Africa was built on faith: no European penetrated the inte-rior of sub-Saharan Africa until the 1770s, when a now gener-ally forgotten Scottish explorer named James Bruce traveled in Abyssinia (Ethiopia) and claimed to have discovered the source of the Blue Nile (he was close, but didn't quite reach Lake Tana, the river's true origin). Bruce's wildly exaggerated tales—he boasted of eating a raw steak cut from the flanks of a live buffalo—were ridiculed by no less an authority than Dr. Johnson, and most critics dismissed him as a fabulist. He pub-lished nothing until 1790, nearly seventeen years after his re-turn to England. When it finally appeared, his massive five-volume work *Travels to Discover the Source of the Nile* was a critical failure but a popular success, though some people read it as romantic fiction rather than science.

Bruce was active during a crucial period in Europe's relationship with Africa. Prior to the late eighteenth century, the demand for slaves in the Americas drove European interests in the continent. Portugal, Spain, the Netherlands, and England all fought for slaving outposts along the West African coast. In 1807, however, the British, who carried nearly two thirds of the slaves taken from West Africa to the Americas, abolished their slave trade. The entire trans-Atlantic trade ended by midcentury, radically reshaping the relationship between Europe and Africa. Without slaves, Africa came to be seen in new ways: as a source of "legitimate" commerce, as a tropical paradise suitable for Utopian social experiments, as fertile ground for spreading Christianity, and, eventually, as open land ready for imperial conquest.

The last years of the eighteenth century mark the beginning of the great age of African exploration. For the first time, Europeans ventured abroad with the sole purpose of collecting specific, scholarly information. Philip D. Curtin, a historian who has analyzed the roots of European perceptions of Africa, calls these early adventurers "enlightened travellers." Their reports attracted increasing attention at home. Compared with the later explorers, who were selected by the Royal Geographical Society and other sponsors primarily on the basis of their ability to survive an arduous journey, the first Europeans to travel in West Africa came from a broad educational background and with a universal curiosity. Their purpose was limited—to collecting botanical or zoological specimens from a single location, for example—but they also observed African culture, often with a sympathetic eye.

The travelers included naturalists, geographers, and ethnographers, but also non-specialists. Works by these less careful observers made up most of the library on West Africa in the late eighteenth century. Most of the authors saw, or at least wrote about, only those aspects of life in Africa that would please their European patrons and audience. Thus Africans were placed far below Europeans on the "Great Chain of

Being"—when they were not viewed simply as another species of wild animal—but gained a special kind of nobility from their close relationship with nature. At the same time, the Romantic movement spurred interest in the perceived primitive simplicity of African life as an antidote to the artificiality of industrial Europe.

The tales of Africa tended to feed off and reinforce one another. Not surprisingly, travelers went looking for and found exactly the things their predecessors described. Henry Smeathman went to the Banana Islands off Sierra Leone in 1771 as an emissary of Sir Joseph Banks, renowned director of the Kew Botanical Garden and the man ultimately responsible for much of the early exploration of West Africa. Looking back on his time there, Smeathman waxed poetic: "I contemplate the years I passed in that terrestrial Elysium, as the happiest of my life. The simple food, which my solitude afforded, was sweetened with rural labor; and my rest was not broken by those corroding cares and perplexing fears, which pride and folly are ever creating in the ambitious emulations of populous communities."

Smeathman was so taken with this part of Africa that upon his return to England he immediately began planning a humanitarian, democratic colony for Sierra Leone. He was not alone. Africa was seen as the perfect setting for a New Jerusalem. A dozen or more Utopian dreamers fixed their sights on Africa, despite the well-documented mortality in previous European settlements. As Curtin points out in his comprehensive study *The Image of Africa,* these planners had something less than a keen grasp of their situation: " . . . the outstanding characteristic [of these projects] is the apparent lack of contact with reality, at least African reality. They were based firmly enough on the European attitudes and theories of the day, but the actual setting was something of a dream world. . . . Two of the expeditions planned for West Africa ended in Australia and Egypt respectively."

Despite some obvious problems with geography, not all of

the efforts were complete failures. In particular, the Sierra Leone Company and the "Province of Freedom"—the eventual result of Smeathman's plans—turned out to be more enlightened and sensitive to African culture than those that would follow. Europeans knew more about Africa in the eighteenth century than they did at any point up to the 1950s. The crude notion of "Darkest Africa," rife with mystery and savages, surfaced in the nineteenth century, despite the ever-growing numbers of scientists of various specialties who went to Africa and collected volumes of data. The popular image of Africa emerged from the tales of explorers and the missionary press, which systematically misrepresented African culture and contributed mightily to the spread of racial bias and cultural arrogance. The stereotypes thus formed were disseminated through a network of public policy journals and pamphlets. More balanced and scholarly opinions remained unread.

Popular descriptions of Africa begin in earnest with the Scottish physician Mungo Park, who forms a kind of bridge between the enlightened travelers of the eighteenth century and the explorers of the nineteenth. Like Henry Smeathman before him, Park traveled for the ubiquitous Joseph Banks, who in 1788 founded the Association for Promoting the Discovery of the Interior Parts of Africa. Sponsorship by the Africa Association, as it was usually called, was no guarantee of success; of the three expeditions prior to Park's two ended with the death of the leader, and the third turned back far short of its original goal.

Park's prospects seemed no better when he set off to chart the course of the fabled Niger River in 1795, since he carried with him a wealth of misinformation from the twelfth-century scholar al-Idrisi and the sixteenth-century Arab traveler Leo Africanus. Those earlier explorers, however, accurately described the two great empires, Ancient Mali and Songhai, that had been founded upon the banks of the Niger. The upper reaches of the river and its tributaries sustained such cities as Timbuctu, Gao, Mopti, and Djenne, renowned for their intellectual, cultural, and commercial activity. The emperors of Mali, particularly Mansa Mūsā in the fourteenth century, exploited the huge gold reserves in the region and became well known throughout the Middle East and Europe. A Majorcan geographer, Abraham Cresques, included a drawing of Mansa Mūsā sitting on his throne holding a gold nugget in his *Catalan Atlas* of 1375, which remained the standard reference for the next one hundred years. By the time Leo Africanus visited Timbuctu, he reported that there was more money to be made from selling books in that city than from the sale of any other commodity.

These were the legends that drew Park and others to the Niger. Although Park failed to reach Timbuctu, or even to trace the Niger beyond Djenne (which actually sits on a tributary nearly 1,500 miles from the river's mouth), he returned to England a hero. His journal, published in 1799 as *Travels in the Interior of Africa,* was a best seller. Park provided the first modern, eyewitness account of the Niger, and his descriptions of large-scale agriculture and commerce sparked European commercial interest in the interior of West Africa for the first time. Yet, as would happen countless times in the next century or so of exploration, the reading public in Europe responded to his descriptions of repeated captures and escapes, of hardship and redemption, rather than to the accurate information.

Park's second expedition, in 1805, was even less successful than the first, but it was the birth of a new kind of exploration. Originally part of an ambitious military scheme to seize 1,000 miles of coastline, Park and a party of soldiers, carpenters, and porters set out from Gambia intent on finding the outlet of the Niger. Forced to begin during the rainy season, most of Park's escort died on the first leg of the journey. Park himself came unglued. Usually a diplomat of some skill, by the time Park and the few survivors were on the river, he was firing on anyone who came near. He sailed past Timbuctu without stopping. Park and the three remaining Europeans were eventually killed in the rapids near Bussa, in northern Nigeria.

The image of Mungo Park sailing blindly down an un-
charted river, refusing any contact and blasting away at all
Africans, serves as a bizarre yet fitting symbol for the era of
exploration and colonization of which he was the harbinger.
As a practical matter, Park's second expedition is also a useful
landmark: it signals the beginning of both government sponsorship of African exploration and a new type of exploration
emphasizing relatively rapid forays deep into the interior, with
an eye toward potential trade and markets. Before Park, the
scientifically oriented enlightened travelers examined small regions in detail. After Park, explorers, often with military training and narrow interests, covered vast areas of the continent
but actually saw and understood little.

More varied and less accurate were the recollections of civil-
ian visitors or residents, who were particularly susceptible to
sensationalism. Typical was J. Smith's *Trade and Travel in the
Gulph of Guinea,* which features the following headings under
the chapter entitled "Human Sacrifice": "Nailing prisoners—
Jack Ketch—Decapitation—Cooking and eating human
flesh—Priests—King Pepple eats King Amacree's heart—Sacrifice human beings to the god of the Bar—Shipwrecks."

Taken together, the varied publications of the 1830s and
1840s formed the basic elements of the myth of wild Africa,
particularly in England but elsewhere in Europe as well, and
even among specialists in African affairs. The image would be
refined by further contact with Africa, but it would not change
substantially for over a century. "In general, the political
classes in Britain were no better informed than ever, but they
were more confident in their information," Curtin notes. "The
errors once confined to a few specialized works had now
become 'common knowledge.' "

About this time, a young Scottish missionary, David Livingstone, stationed in the Cape Colony, became restless and
dreamed of establishing a settlement deep in the interior of the
continent. In 1849 he discovered Lake Ngami (a shallow lake
in the north of what is now Botswana). This and nearly all of

Livingstone's future exploits were trumpeted as major events by his employers, the London Missionary Society, and by the Royal Geographical Society. Such sponsors played a key role in shaping European perceptions of Africa, as they do today. The explorer's tales and accomplishments—enlivened with a bit of hyperbole—were important fund-raising tools. The few well-informed geographers and travelers usually remained silent in the face of such exaggeration, as their own reputations grew when Africa was portrayed in the most extreme terms possible.

Between 1852, when he left the Cape for good and ventured north, and 1856, when he sailed for England from Quelimane, in present-day Mozambique, Livingstone covered nearly 6,000 miles and became the first European to traverse the continent, and the first to see the spectacle he named Victoria Falls. His book describing the journey, *Missionary Travels and Researches in South Africa,* published in 1857, sold 70,000 copies and made him a national hero.

The book was the first to describe the interior of southern Africa. Most Europeans at the time believed the region to be not unlike the Sahara, so Livingstone's descriptions of forests, lakes, and rivers seemed incredible, and his journey the equivalent of a trip to the moon. As the *London Journal* put it: "Europe had always heard that the central regions of Southern Africa were burning solitudes, bleak, and barren, heated by poisonous winds, infested by snakes and only roamed over by a few scattered tribes of untameable barbarians. . . . But Dr. Livingstone found himself in a high country, full of fruit trees, abounding in shade, watered by a perfect network of rivers."

The portrait of Africa that emerges from *Missionary Travels* is vastly different from that of Livingstone's journals, and the differences reveal how powerful the myth of Africa had become by the mid-nineteenth century. Livingstone's description of Victoria Falls—arguably the most striking geological feature of the continent—could hardly be less enthusiastic. He devoted a few brief paragraphs in his journal to the falls, and he underestimated their height and width by about half. Yet this is the description he wrote for publication in *Missionary Travels:* " . . . no one can imagine the beauty of the view from anything witnessed in England. It had never been seen before by European eyes; but scenes so lovely must have been gazed upon by angels in their flight."

Livingstone painted a rosy picture of South-Central Africa because he feared that otherwise all missionary and colonial efforts in the region would be abandoned, and his ambitions crushed. So he glossed over nearly every unpleasant aspect of African exploration. He neglected to mention, for example, dysentery, lack of food, hostile tribes, or the frequent bouts of fever. "We must submit to malaria," he wrote in his journal, "and trust in God for the rest." He was also misleading about the Makololo—a tribe he sought to convert to Christianity. Livingstone's biographer, Tim Jeal, notes that in his private journal Livingstone would write that the Makololo "never visit anywhere but for the purpose of plunder and oppression. They never go anywhere without a club or a spear in hand." And he would tell a friend that "nine weeks hearing their quarrelling, roaring, dancing, singing and murdering, have imparted a greater disgust at heathenism than I ever had before." These attitudes, along with the unpleasant fact that the Makololo often sold members of their subject tribes into slavery, would not reach the general public.

In *Missionary Travels* and his other public pronouncements, Livingstone was unceasingly positive about Africa and Africans: "To one who has observed the hard toil of the poor in old civilized countries, the state in which the inhabitants [of Africa] live is one of glorious ease. . . . Food abounds and very little effort is needed for its cultivation; the soil is so rich that no manure is required." Livingstone succeeded in convincing his sponsors—later to include the British government—to continue funding his expeditions. He also created a lasting though unreal vision of Africa.

While public endorsements of Africa as a paradise and of

Africans as the world's unspoiled children served one purpose, encouraging trade required something else. If Livingstone's depiction of the African way of life was accurate, then Africans should avoid large-scale contact with Europeans, the products of degraded, industrial society. Yet Livingstone persisted in his claim that the Zambezi afforded easy access to the fertile lands of the interior, and that these lands could and should be "civilized" by introducing European culture. That the claim was mistaken—the Zambezi is difficult to enter from the sea and, prior to being dammed in the 1970s, was blocked some 350 miles upstream by the frightening Cahora Bassa rapids—mattered little at this point. Livingstone convinced himself and others that Christianity could not advance in Africa without going hand in hand with British commerce. His vision of Britain as a nation with a unique mission laid the moral foundation for colonial occupation and would lead him to spend the latter part of his life fighting to end the slave trade. That vision would also have far-reaching consequences which Livingstone never imagined.

Livingstone had done an abrupt about-face in his attitude toward African culture in adopting a philosophy which emphasized the positive role of commerce. Jeal points out that while Livingstone retained a deep faith in the capabilities of Africans throughout his life, in the 1850s a growing commitment to commerce as the vehicle for Christianity forced him to abandon his earlier ideas about the values of tribalism. Instead, he began to see great benefits in breaking down traditional tribal societies through European-style commerce. Africa, Livingstone now believed, would only benefit from large-scale European intrusion. Though Livingstone had suffered in workhouses as a child, he nevertheless believed that British inmates of these institutions, with their "glass windows and chimneys," were far better off than African chiefs.

Livingstone was a prophet of imperialism; his theories of trade and the gospel were largely adopted, thirty years after his death, by the British government during the European scramble for African territories. Herein lies another paradox: Livingstone, or at least his image in the public mind, justified colonization in Africa. Yet Livingstone himself recognized that this process was deeply flawed:

> With colonies it is the same as with children—they receive protection for a time and obey from a feeling of weakness and attachment; but beyond the time at which they require a right to think for themselves, the attempt to perpetuate subordination necessarily engenders a hatred which effectually extinguishes the feeble gratitude that a man in any condition is capable of cherishing.

Perhaps the final irony is that in a limited sense Livingstone was correct in assuming that Africans would be better off under European domination than in the grasp of the slave traders. Although Livingstone was one of the first Europeans to travel extensively in Central Africa, the region was hardly free of alien influence. By the late 1860s, Arab slave traders had penetrated deep into Central Africa, bringing bloody wars and destroying local cultures. The myth of Africa as a pristine wilderness, problematic from the outset, was an utter fallacy firmly in place by the mid-nineteenth century.

As with Africa itself, the perceptions of Livingstone and the realities of his character, ideals, and accomplishments did not match. He was a missionary who made one convert—a chief named Sechele who later lapsed—during a lifetime in Africa. He was considered the greatest geographer of his day, yet late in life he believed he had found the source of the Nile when he was in fact on the upper tributaries of the Congo. Livingstone nevertheless became a myth. It was quite impossible for Victorian England to separate the myth of Africa from the myth of Livingstone; the noble, solitary missionary who brought light to the wild and untameable Dark Continent.

Livingstone's status as the leading African explorer began to be challenged in 1856, when a series of expeditions set out to find the source of the Nile, map the geography of the great central lakes, and thus solve the most ancient mystery of Africa's interior. The quest for the Nile's source focused intense European interest on Africa, further solidifying its place in Western consciousness.

The search for the source of the Nile had all the elements of a Romantic opera: an ancient mystery, a quest, and cast of characters from the saintly to the devilish. By far the most intriguing personality of all those searching for the Nile was Sir Richard Francis Burton. Burton was in many ways the opposite of Livingstone; a fiercely proud, impetuous adventurer and swordsman who was also a scholar, a linguist fluent in twenty-nine languages—he introduced the Swahili word *safari*, for "adventure," into English—and a careful student of Arab culture. Burton on occasion disguised himself as an Arab, sometimes even dyeing his skin, and traveled to places usually forbidden to white men. By the time he was thirty-six, Burton had achieved notoriety by becoming the first European to make the pilgrimage to Mecca and by entering the closed city of Harar in Abyssinia.

Burton's narratives of his early adventures, particularly *First Footsteps in East Africa* (1856) and *Lake Regions of Central Africa* (1860), were well received in England, but he made little money from his books, perhaps because of their intimidating length. Burton could be prolix: he wrote thirty-nine books running to some sixty volumes in his lifetime. Yet he was without doubt the most talented writer and the only true scholar among the explorers. He translated numerous works, including the historic *The Book of a Thousand Nights and a Night* and the *Kama Sutra*. Hardly a page in *First Footsteps in East Africa* lacks a lengthy footnote, and many pages have several. But Burton also contributed immensely to the Romantic idealization of the African landscape:

There are few scenes more soft and soothing than a view of Unyanwezi in the balmy evenings of spring. As the large yellow sun nears the horizon, a deep stillness falls upon the earth: even the zephyr seems to lose the power of rustling the lightest leaf. The milky haze of midday disappears from the firmament, the flush of departing day mantles the distant features of scenery with a lovely rose-tint, and the twilight is an orange glow that burns like distant horizontal fires, pushing upwards through an imperceptibly graduated scale of colors—saffron, yellow, tender green, and the lightest azure—into the dark blue of the infinite space above.

Burton believed that lasting fame awaited whoever found the true source of the Nile. By 1869, however, interest in the explorers and in Africa had dissipated. Only David Livingstone kept up the search, largely ignored because his star had fallen following a disastrous attempt to lead an expedition up the Zambezi. Livingstone had been missing for three years and was believed dead, but the short, unemotional obituaries stirred little public interest.

In October 1869, the *New York Herald* sent one of its foreign correspondents, Henry Morton Stanley, on an expedition to locate Livingstone. The *Herald* had built its reputation on sensational and scandalous stories, and the newspaper's editors knew that they could revive worldwide interest in Livingstone by printing an interview with a man everyone assumed was dead.

Stanley began his search for Livingstone from Zanzibar in 1871, traveling west, with nearly two hundred porters carrying 6 tons of gear. About the same time, Livingstone and thirteen African assistants—up from a low of four in 1868—set out to the east for Lake Tanganyika from the town of Bambarre, between the lake and the Congo River. The two met—and Stanley uttered his immortal but inadvertently comic greeting—in the lakeside village of Ujiji on November 3, 1871.

Stanley found that Livingstone—who had been mellowed by age and hardship—was not at all spiteful or iconoclastic, as some had portrayed him. He set out to restore Livingstone's reputation. "His gentleness never forsakes him," Stanley wrote. "His hopefulness never deserts him. No harassing anxieties, distractions of mind, long separations from home and kindred can make him complain. . . . His is the Spartan heroism, the inflexibility of the Roman, the enduring resolution of the Anglo-Saxon—never to relinquish his work though his heart yearns for home."

The canonization of Livingstone began with Stanley's articles and speeches and continued through his worldwide best seller, *How I Found Livingstone,* published just months after he returned from Africa in 1872. The newspapers that had given short shrift to the early reports of Livingstone's death in 1867 now filled pages with stories about him. Africa was newsworthy again. When Livingstone died in 1873, and his body was returned home by three devoted African servants after an extraordinary journey, he was buried in England's most hallowed ground. The papers did not miss the chance to rectify their earlier lack of enthusiasm. Wrote the *Glasgow Herald:*

> Westminster Abbey has opened her doors to men who have played larger and greater parts in the history of mankind; but the feeling amongst many this afternoon was, that seldom has been admitted one more worthy—one more unselfish in his devotion to duty—one whose ruling desire was stronger to benefit his kind and advance the sum of human knowledge and civilization—than the brave, modest, self-sacrificing, African explorer. The virtues which distinguished Livingstone are those which our country has always been ready to acknowledge, which our religion has taught us to revere, and seek to cultivate and conserve.

The creation of the Livingstone myth grew alongside the myth of wild Africa and had a tremendous impact on the relationship between Great Britain and the continent. According to Tim Jeal, Livingstone's death inspired missionaries and helped precipitate British involvement in the scramble for

Africa. Donations to philanthropic and missionary societies increased, and new missions were created on the shores of Lake Nyasa, where Livingstone had long worked, and in Uganda. In 1891, the British claimed the region around Lake Nyasa as the Protectorate of Nyasaland, now independent Malawi. The following year the government annexed Uganda and then, to ensure it had access to the new colony, Great Britain also claimed the land just east of Uganda, which later became Kenya.

Livingstone had another lasting effect on European perceptions of Africa: he inspired Henry Stanley to continue the exploration of Central Africa. Stanley settled the question of the source of the Nile once and for all, which in itself brought him tremendous acclaim.

The immense popularity of Stanley's books further solidified the myth of wild Africa. An awkward writer, Stanley missed few opportunities to indulge in glorious overstatement. In his minutely detailed *Through the Dark Continent* (1878), Stanley wrote:

> To behold the full perfection of African manhood and beauty one must visit the regions of Equatorial Africa, where one can view the people under the cool shade of plantains, and amid the luxuriant plenty which those lands produce. The European traveller, after noting the great length and wondrous greenness of the banana fronds, the vastness of their stalks and the bulk and number of the fruit, the fatness of the soil and its inexhaustible fertility, the perpetual springlike verdure of the vegetation, and the dazzling sunshine, comes to notice that the inhabitants are in fit accord with these scenes, and as perfect of their kind as the bursting ripe mellow bananas hanging above their heads. Their very features seem to proclaim: "We live in a land of butter and wine and fullness, milk and honey, fat meads and valleys."

Stanley also began the practical task of developing the areas the European powers had claimed as colonies. While in the service of Leopold II, King of the Belgians, Stanley established a series of outposts along the Congo in what was then the Congo Free State, providing a foothold that enabled Leopold to claim sovereignty over an area of nearly 1 million square miles—eighty times the size of his home country.

The public perception of Stanley as a great man masked an ugly reality. The colonization of the Congo, which Stanley led, was among the most ruthless in history. Yet few in Europe protested. Only a handful of Europeans not involved in reaping the rewards of colonization ever visited Central Africa. One who made the journey was Joseph Conrad. Once an admirer of the African explorers, Conrad looked at the vast empty spaces on early maps and dreamed of visiting "what was then the white heart of Africa." Upon reaching Stanley Falls on the upper Congo, while in command of a Belgian merchant vessel, Conrad was soon disillusioned. The "great haunting memory" such as the earlier explorers would have left had been plundered by Stanley; all that remained, Conrad said, was "the unholy recollection of a prosaic newspaper 'stunt' and the distasteful knowledge of the vilest scramble for loot that ever disfigured the history of human conscience and geographical exploration." Nine years later, Conrad translated his experiences in Africa into *Heart of Darkness,* an enduring and powerful literary indictment of imperialism.

One image in *Heart of Darkness* conjures up thoughts of conservation at its worst. As Conrad's narrator, Marlowe, sails toward the mouth of the Congo, his ship comes upon a French man-of-war anchored off the coast. "There wasn't even a shed there, and she was shelling the bush," Marlowe says.

> In the empty immensity of earth, sky, and water, there she was, incomprehensible, firing into a continent. Pop, would go one of the six-inch guns; a small flame would dart and vanish, a little white smoke would disappear, a tiny projectile would give a feeble screech—and nothing happened. Nothing could happen. There was a touch of insanity in the proceeding, a sense of

lugubrious drollery in the sight; and it was not dissipated by somebody on board assuring me earnestly there was a camp of natives—he called them enemies!—hidden out of sight some-where.

Conrad nowhere mentions African wildlife, but the image of a ship blindly shelling the bush and some suspected wild natives strikes uncomfortably close to the practice of conserva-tion under colonial rule and afterwards.

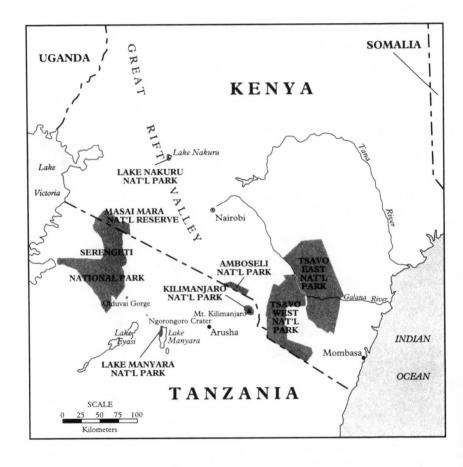

CHAPTER II

▼ ▼ ▼

HUNTERS

"I speak of Africa and golden joys"; the joy of wandering through lonely lands; the joy of hunting the mighty and terrible lords of the wilderness, the cunning, the wary, and the grim.

—Theodore Roosevelt

I*n 1909, just* a few months after leaving the White House, Theodore Roosevelt embarked on one of the most famous African safaris in history. In his immensely popular account of the journey, *African Game Trails* (1910), Roosevelt elevated Henry Stanley's breathless romanticism about Africa to a new level, glossing over the contradictions that plagued Joseph Conrad:

> In these greatest of the world's great hunting-grounds there are mountain peaks whose snows are dazzling under the equatorial sun; swamps where the slime oozes and bubbles and festers in the steaming heat; lakes like seas; skies that burn above deserts where the iron desolation is shrouded from view by the wavering mockery of the mirage; vast grassy plains where palms and thorn-trees fringe the dwindling streams; mighty rivers rushing out of the heart of the continent through the sadness of endless marshes; forests of gorgeous beauty, where death broods in the dark and silent depths.

Roosevelt's safari and his descriptions of it were grounded firmly in the grand tradition of hunters in Africa. These were the men who followed the explorers to the continent. The exploits of the hunters carried the myth of wild Africa into the twentieth century, and reinforced the accepted but mistaken ideas about how Africans hunted and how they felt about wild animals.

Perhaps the most celebrated of all nineteenth-century hunters was the Scotsman Roualeyn Gordon Cumming. Like most of his contemporaries, Cumming lamented the decline of game in the Cape Colony, for which he blamed African hunters. It is unlikely, however, that any individual African killed more than fifty animals annually, and then mostly small antelope. Cumming himself claimed to have shot hundreds upon hundreds of elephants, impala, rhino, and wildebeest (among other animals) in his career. Europeans condemned African hunters, but the tales they told of their own hunts, full of exaggerations and outright lies, captivated the imagination of people back home.

Roualeyn Gordon Cumming embodied all the conflicting motivations that drove many of the big-game hunters. He was simultaneously cruel, voracious, and romantic. Of seeing "an antelope of the most exquisite beauty," he wrote:

> On beholding him I was struck with wonder and delight. My heart beat with excitement. I sprang from my saddle, but before I could fire a shot this gem of beauty bounded into the reeds, and was lost to my sight. At that moment I would have given half what I possessed in the world for a broadside at that lovely antelope, and I at once resolved not to proceed on my expedition until I had captured him, though it should cost me the labour of a month.

Cumming was among the first hunters to capitalize on his African experiences. He published a popular account, *Five Years of a Hunter's Life in the Far Interior of South Africa*, in 1850. That same year he opened an exhibit of his animal trophies in London, and the public came in droves. For an extra fee, people could hear Cumming "the lion-slayer" expound upon his adventures, to a musical accompaniment—performances nightly, with a Saturday matinée.

Like Cumming, Frederick Courteney Selous—who late in life would advise Theodore Roosevelt on how to conduct his safari—was the ideal for young men in Britain. An explorer, naturalist, and big-game hunter, at his death Selous's "bag" was said to number thirty-one lion, at least two hundred buffalo, and scores of elephant. Ironically, one of the largest game reserves in Africa bears Selous's name, as well as his grave. Despite the slaughter, Selous worked in close association with the Royal Geographical Society, particularly with regards to collecting specimens. He also was aware of the growing scarcity of some species. He could hardly have missed it: the only large African mammals to go extinct in recorded history were the quagga (a kind of zebra) and a large antelope called a blaubok, both of which were found in South Africa. The quagga and the blaubok were exterminated by hunters like Selous and the rapid expansion of white ranchers.

Cumming, Selous, and the other members of the Victorian hunting elite, as well as their descendants, including Teddy Roosevelt, had a deep love of wilderness that went beyond the thrill of the chase; hence Cumming could be "struck with wonder and delight" at the sight of a waterbuck. Such hunters loved their quarry, but they did not find killing the thing they loved at all inconsistent. Roosevelt, for one, was as much a conservationist as he was a hunter, and he played a large role in creating national parks as we know them. The all-too-apparent imperialism of white hunters in Africa does not completely explain the complex psychology at work here. Romantic notions of wild animals and wilderness also contributed, forming common ground for hunters, conservationists, and animal lovers.

The writings of Cumming, Selous, and others inevitably attracted more Europeans and Americans who craved sporting adventures, and fed the Western idealization of Africa. The most popular hunter/writers generally wrote the most romantic prose. They also tended to have a rather dim view of the Africans they encountered. The Nile explorer and hunter Sir Samuel White Baker found "the antelope tribe . . . more agreeable than . . . the human inhabitants" of Africa. Hunters often considered Africans just another species, to be noted dutifully in the total animal "bag" for the safari. Another aristocratic hunter named Sir Claude Champion Crespigny killed over one hundred members of one tribe, "including one biggish chief," while Captain Chauncey Hugh Stigand in his book *Hunting the Elephant in Africa* has a chapter devoted to stalking the African.

Cumming, Selous, and the rest set the stage for Theodore Roosevelt. Although Roosevelt was hardly the first sport hunter in Africa, his international stature made him among the most famous before he even left the United States. With the advice of the foremost African hunters of the day, and with the financial backing of Andrew Carnegie, the former President planned an elaborate and costly adventure, during which he would collect specimens for the Smithsonian Institution and the American Museum of Natural History. The safari employed 265 porters—they formed a line over a mile long—to carry the gear, which included hundreds of animal traps, 4 tons of salt for curing skins, balances for weighing kills, and a library of 59 specially bound books featuring such works as *Paradise Lost* and *The Pickwick Papers*. Roosevelt helped defray the costs of the safari by writing articles for *Scribner's* magazine (these were to form the basis of *African Game Trails*), and the Associated Press sponsored its own substantial expedition to shadow Roosevelt and his party. This was a worldwide news event, the greatest safari in history.

Roosevelt's safari was also among the most destructive ever. In ten months of shooting, Roosevelt and his son Kermit bagged more than five hundred animals of over seventy different species. Nine of the animals were white rhino, including four cows and a calf. The white rhino had almost disappeared from southern Africa, and was virtually extinct in East Africa, a fact that the naturalist Roosevelt knew well. All told, Roosevelt, his son, and the other hunters on the expedition shipped to the Smithsonian nearly five thousand mammals, four thousand birds, five hundred fish, and two thousand reptiles.

Roosevelt tried to justify his excessive hunting as necessary for science and to feed the huge safari crew. He convinced few of his readers. Even white Kenyans, many of whom hunted avidly, were aghast. Lord Cranworth, a director of Nairobi's premier safari outfitter, Newland & Tarlton, and a close friend of Roosevelt, deplored what he termed the "slaughter." "Do those nine white rhinoceros ever cause ex-President Roosevelt a pang of conscience or a restless night?" Cranworth asked. "I venture to hope so."

Nevertheless, reports of Roosevelt's safari drew other sportsmen to Kenya, Tanganyika, and Uganda. The rush of hunters gave birth to a new profession: safari guide. The early professionals were men like R. J. Cuninghame, who helped guide Roosevelt's safari, and J. A. Hunter, who at the age of eighteen led the first paid safari to the Serengeti in 1905. The industry boomed, led by hunters such as Baron Bror Blixen, Isak Dinesen's husband, and her lover, Denys Finch Hatton. The golden age of safaris filled the years between the wars, during which time the Serengeti remained a favorite destination for the big-game hunters.

East African safaris in the 1920s embodied excess—dinners served on linen tablecloths accompanied by fine wine while tracking big game through the bush. A Kenyan settler and hunter named Berkeley Cole—another participant in Roosevelt's safari—founded an establishment called the Muthaiga Club in Nairobi just so he could have his drinks properly served while he enjoyed polo, cricket, and croquet. Titled Britons lived on vast estates in a place called Happy Valley as they careened from wealth into decadence and exchanged adulterous glances across the bar at the Muthaiga Club. Yet, at the height of the big-game hunts came the first glimmer of an

uncertain future for Africa's wildlife. In a series of letters to
The Times (London) in 1928 and 1929, Denys Finch Hatton
protested the "orgy of slaughter" taking place on the Serengeti
by hunters in motorized vehicles. Finch Hatton, who preferred
the more stately, restrained foot safari, quotes an American
(who had already shot twenty-one lions from his car) exclaim-
ing, "Let us shoot every living thing we can find today and see
what bag is possible in one day." Referring to such men as
"licensed butchers," Finch Hatton did not record what became of the proposed experiment.

In fact, no such investigation was needed to demonstrate
the effect of unbridled hunting, since southern Africa provided
the object lesson. By the first years of the twentieth century,
the Cape, Natal, the Orange Free State, and the South African
Republic had lost practically their entire wildlife heritage,
driven out by hunters like Cumming and Selous.

The early European travelers in Africa fired blindly into
herds, did not pursue wounded animals, shot females, and
waited by waterholes at night for easy kills. Such practices
gradually fell into disfavor. Subsistence hunting had disappeared in the West with the advance of cities and industrialization, and the hunt became increasingly ritualized. An ever
more elaborate code of hunting conduct was created to fit the
blood sport with the ideals of chivalry and Christian behavior.
The true sportsmen were both unselfish and humane; they
avoided useless slaughter and they gave their quarry a sporting
chance.

This code practically demanded that Europeans denounce
traditional African hunting methods as barbarous and unfair.
The use of poison, for example, was considered an "unmanly"
and "abominable" technique. By the late nineteenth century,
the explorers roundly condemned African hunters. David Liv-
ingston in 1857 described a hunt near his mission station
which involved driving herds into a large pit: "It is a frightful
scene. The men, wild with excitement, spear the lovely animals with mad delight: others of the poor creatures, borne

down by the weight of their dead and dying companions, every now and then make the whole mass heave in their smothering agonies."

Not only were African hunters considered cruel, they were often deemed unnecessary for the African way of life. The onslaught of white hunters, the imposition of game laws, the creation of parks and reserves, and the spread of agriculture gradually reduced the importance of hunting in many African cultures. The key role hunting had played in shaping these cultures, and its continuing relevance in terms of the relationship between Africans and wildlife, was not generally recognized by Europeans. According to Major R. W. G. Hingston, a surgeon and naturalist who had served with the British Army in India, the Middle East, and East Africa, and whose survey of East and southern Africa in 1930 led to the creation of Serengeti National Park, meat was not part of the routine diet of most Africans. Securing meat by hunting, Hingston said, "is the stamp of primitiveness," from which Europeans should lead Africans by teaching them "the meat-securing methods which are practiced by more cultured races."

Hunting was in fact vital to diverse cultures across the continent, as the historian John MacKenzie illustrates in his invaluable study *The Empire of Nature*. The Tswana and Ndebele in southern Africa, the Bisa and Bemba of Central Africa, the ivory-hunting Kamba, Nyamwezi, Shambaa, and Wata, and subsistence hunters like the Ndorobo and Kikuyu of East Africa are just a few examples. Almost all African peoples hunted in one form or another, preying on animals ranging from mice to elephants, in self-defense, for export, and for domestic use. Hunting was not only necessary but preferred: it was exciting and romantic, and provided both recreation and training. Hunting among rural Africans was also elitist, offering rulers a symbolic dominance of the environment, and a means of asserting territorial control. The arrival of Europeans and the subsequent destruction of traditional hunting rights had a profound effect on African culture, causing shifts in diet, economic and social relations, and recreation, and breaking many of the bonds with the natural world.

Even fundamentally agricultural peoples often valued hunting more than tilling the land. In the late 1960s, the anthropologist Stuart Marks studied hunting among the Bisa, who live in Zambia's Luangwa Valley. Marks found that the Bisa farmed an area rich in wildlife, which posed constant threats to their crops. The threat was so great that an old Bisa saying instructed farmers to plant three seeds in each hole: one for the elephants, one for the guinea fowl, and one for the farmer. The Bisa were excellent hunters because they had to protect their crops, and they used the game meat as a supplement to their diet.

Hunting among the Bisa, however, was more than just a practical matter. Only members of special hunting guilds could hunt such animals as elephants, hippo, and ant-bears, while non-guild hunters could kill more common animals like impala and warthogs. The Bisa built hunting shrines, and used a great deal of magic in their hunts. Although the availability of muzzle-loaders led to the breakup of the hunting guilds by eliminating the need for group hunts, and colonial game laws eliminated traditional methods like game pits, hunting remained a central fact of Bisa life.

Not all colonial administrators set out to destroy to the African way of life, but even sympathetic administrators sometimes often failed to understand how and why Africans hunted. In Kenya, for example, colonial game laws were designed in part to eliminate hunting by the Wata, who were among the most skilled bow hunters in Africa. Few of the traditional Wata hunters remain today, but in his book *Ivory Crisis,* the former game warden and ivory trader Ian Parker provides a detailed account of their hunting methods. Drawing the Wata longbows required immense strength, for these weapons were more powerful than the fabled longbows of medieval England. The Wata, however, did not develop the advanced metallurgy necessary to make extremely hard arrowheads, so while an English archer could fire an arrow that would pierce the heaviest armor, a Wata arrow launched with more force could not penetrate elephant bone.

The Wata hunters had no need of such hard arrowheads because they had perfected the art of making poison. Like most hunting tribes, the Wata derived their poison from trees and shrubs of the genus *Acocanthera*. These plants produce a number of chemicals which affect the circulation in a manner similar to the drug digitalis. In minute quantities, digitalis slows and strengthens the heartbeat. In larger doses, this drug and its relatives cause heart failure and death.

The Wata most often used ouabain, another drug derived from *Acocanthera*. They obtained the poison by chopping the shrub into small bits and boiling the wood, bark, roots, and twigs until they were left with a heavy tar. The tar, which hardened considerably when cooled, was then applied to the arrows in thick layers, so that each arrow likely carried over fifty times the dose needed to kill an elephant.

The Wata bowmen would usually stalk to within twenty paces of their prey. From such a short distance they could place the arrow precisely, and they knew where the poison would work most quickly. The elephants died in a few moments, and did not have time to disappear into the bush. In this way the Wata lost few elephants, unlike white hunters. The common assumption that the traditional methods of the Wata and other hunting tribes were either primitive or cruel seems badly misguided—compared to Europeans, the Wata were more effective hunters, made better use of the animals they killed, and caused their prey to suffer less. The view that the Wata were barbaric, however, pervaded colonial Africa, and it was enshrined in many of that era's conservation laws.

Those laws (described in more detail in Chapter III) broke down the African conservation ethic, which begins with the integral role wildlife has always played in African life. Feared wild animals were often imbued with ritual meaning. Many tribes regard particular animals as totems—in some areas of

Zaire leopards are said to be deceased chiefs; certain tribes in Tanzania honor snakes—while at the same time enforcing taboos against killing or eating certain animals. Swahili, in fact, uses the same word, *mwiko*, for "totem" and "taboo."

Beyond religious and spiritual significance, wild animals traditionally served more basic purposes, providing a cheap and readily available source of meat, as well as clothes and a host of household items. The notion of using wildlife to meet human needs, a recent addition to the conservation vocabulary, was second nature to Africans. With the imposition of wildlife laws imported from Europe, the relationship between rural Africans and wildlife gradually unwound. Yet the conservation ethic of rural people remains, and it may be the essential ingredient for preventing the continued destruction of Africa's wildlife.

An appreciation of traditional hunting societies like the Bisa and the Wata provides needed balance to the European perceptions of Africans as wasteful and cruel. It is tempting, in fact, to romanticize Africans as living in complete harmony with their environment, and enforcing cultural sanctions to prevent the overuse of natural resources. But such an attitude—reminiscent of the "noble savage" living in a state of nature—goes too far.

Rural Africans, like any people dependent on their immediate environment for their survival, alter that environment to meet their needs. The anthropologist Robert Harms has studied the Nunu people of Zaire, who live on the southern fringes of the Central African rain forest, by the swampy floodplains of the Zaire River a few hundred miles south of the Equator. The Nunu, Harms says in *Games Against Nature,* sometimes acted in much the same way as people in Western societies. Like colonial settlers in New England, the Nunu claimed ownership of individual parcels of land and turned the products of that land into commodities.

Harms began his investigations expecting to find that the Nunu sought to minimize their impact on nature. He discovered the opposite to be closer to the truth. Once, while he was poling through the swamps in a dugout canoe, Harms asked his companion, an old fisherman named Nsamonie, whether he ever worried about killing off too many fish. Nsamonie laughed at the thought. "The fish come from the river," he said. "The supply is infinite." Conservation would not become an issue until supplies began to run low.

Religious beliefs among rural people can be interpreted as imposing a system of ecological checks and balances. Some of the cultural mechanisms in African societies—hunting taboos and the concept of royal game, for example—seem to regulate the relationship between man and the environment. The Nunu had several institutions that could be taken as environmental regulators. In the swamplands, landowners became "water lords," who controlled not only the dams and ponds but also the drainage areas for each. This reduced the number of landowners to well below the carrying capacity of the ecosystem. Harms points out, however, that the beneficial environmental impact of this system was an unintended byproduct of an institution designed for other purposes: to control a piece of land and the adjacent fishing grounds, and to attract a following. When the needs of the Nunu changed, the landholding pattern changed as well. The impact on the environment, if considered at all, was a distant second.

Still, the Nunu and other indigenous peoples were integral parts of African ecosystems; but Europeans saw them as invaders of paradise. The bias springs in part from the image of Africa as uninhabited wilderness, and nowhere is the process more explicit than on the Serengeti Plain. The Serengeti generally escaped notice until a German explorer and hunter named Oskar Baumann crossed the plains in 1892. Exploring the region required a huge effort; during the dry season travelers from the coast had to cross 70 miles of waterless savanna to reach the tall grass plains, while tsetse, the hard-biting gray-black flies that carry sleeping sickness, and the longstanding refusal of the Maasai to guide hunters and explorers into the Serengeti provided further obstacles.

Oskar Baumann arrived on the Serengeti plains at a time the

Maasai call *enkidaaroto:* "the destruction." Drought and rinderpest (an infectious viral fever) had killed 90 percent of their
cattle, causing famine and creating an ideal environment for
epidemic diseases like smallpox. Wars over the dwindling resources broke out among the Maasai, and their population
plummeted. At the same time, a booming ivory trade fueled
the slaughter of huge numbers of elephant. Baumann thus described an area almost totally uninhabited by humans or their
large animals. This pattern was repeated elsewhere in Africa:
explorers took for granted a landscape relatively free of people
and cattle, assuming it was the natural order of things. In fact,
the human and cattle population of Africa probably bottomed
out between 1898 and 1930, as a result of diseases imported
from Europe.

The descriptions of open, uninhabited land captured the
Western imagination. The relative lack of human inhabitants,
though a historical anomaly, shaped Western perceptions of
Africa to such an astounding degree that even firsthand experience left the idealistic visions unshaken. The Maasai and their
cattle, for example, were crucial elements in the Serengeti ecosystem, but they were merely a footnote to Theodore Roosevelt's safari of 1909, the event that turned the world's attention
to East Africa. That focus has barely wavered over the past
nine decades, and the misperceptions of the role of the Maasai
and other Africans are only now beginning to fade.

CHAPTER III

▼ ▼ ▼

SERENGETI SHALL NOT DIE?

Perhaps one day in the future the new park could be fenced in. Then the animals would have to remain inside it. They would be protected from the settlers near the park and prevented from dying from hunger and thirst when all the timber around their water holes had been felled and all their pastures are over-grazed by native cattle.

—Bernhard Grzimek, 1960

The *Serengeti* Plain turns black with wildebeest come May, when the rains end. A million or more of the bearded animals turn north searching for water and green grass. The great migration of wildebeest, zebra, eland, and gazelle in the Serengeti forms one of earth's most dramatic wildlife spectacles, and one of its enduring natural rhythms.

The migration takes places primarily on the immense grasslands of the 5,600-square-mile Serengeti National Park in Tanzania, an area roughly the size of Connecticut. In places, the grass unfolds in all directions, unbroken save for an occasional acacia tree for 50 miles. Fritz Jeager, a German geographer, surveyed the Serengeti on foot in 1907 and described it simply as " . . . grass, grass, grass, grass, and grass. One looks around and sees only grass and sky."

Jeager's description was accurate, up to a point. The southern portion of the Serengeti is a high, table-flat plateau. The vistas here are so long that everything on the plains seems puny: even a herd of ten thousand wildebeest resembles just so many ants. Elsewhere in the Serengeti the topography changes from almost featureless plain to gently rolling, sparsely wooded hills in the center of the park, to deep gullies and woodland far to the north, across the Tanzania-Kenya border. This northern extension of the Serengeti ecosystem falls within the 540-square-mile Masai Mara National Reserve. Thus, nearly two thirds of the Serengeti ecosystem is protected. Serengeti National Park and Masai Mara National Reserve have emerged as two of Africa's most renowned parks.

Just outside the southeastern boundary of Serengeti National Park lies Ngorongoro Crater, an immense, extinct volcano. Ngorongoro is not actually a crater, which would have steep sides, but a more gently sloping caldera, formed when the molten core of the volcano subsided and the crater sides fell inward. The rim rises 2,000 feet above Ngorongoro's floor. Large herds of wildebeest and zebra, rhinos, lions, and leopards roam the caldera, creating a miniature replica of Serengeti on nearly 50 square miles of woodland and plain.

The Serengeti ecosystem—which does not include Ngorongoro—covers just under 10,000 square miles, nearly enclosed on all sides by natural barriers which discourage large mammals from moving in or out. Lake Eyasi and a rocky, heavily wooded escarpment form the southern boundary. To the east stand a series of rugged, forested hills; the Crater Highlands and the Gol Mountains in Tanzania and the Loita Hills in Kenya. Just to the west of these hills, practically due north of the Masai Mara, are the dry Loita plains, and another cliff, called the Isuria Escarpment, which form the northwestern boundary. To the west lie fertile, long-cultivated farmlands, wooded hills, and Lake Victoria.

The Serengeti is thus an ecological island. This one area—a dot on the African continent—has come to embody the ideals of pristine wilderness and of wildlife conservation. The Serengeti has been the focus of Western fascination since the early part of this century, the heyday of the great white hunters—an image reinforced by Hollywood features like the recent *Out of Africa*, nature documentaries, coffee table picture books, and tour packages. All focus on the Serengeti, and all encourage the illusion that the Serengeti stands as the last bastion of an animal paradise that once spread from the Indian Ocean to the Atlantic. The truth is much more interesting, and understanding both the natural and political history of the Serengeti provides important insights into African conservation as a whole.

The Serengeti, far from being a remnant of a much larger paradise for wild animals, is not much smaller today than it was a million years ago. The Serengeti Plain was shaped by a unique combination of geological and climatic forces. The fortunate coordination of events created an ideal wildlife habitat: perhaps one fifth of Africa's roughly 10 million large mammals live in Serengeti and the surrounding areas. The inhabitants of the Serengeti comprise the migratory herds—including 1.5 million wildebeest, the greatest assemblage of large mammals on earth—as well as less mobile species like Cape buffalo, waterbuck, impala, topi, hartebeest, and a tiny antelope called a dikdik, predators such as lion, leopard, cheetah, hyena, Cape hunting dog, and jackal, along with elephant, rhino, giraffe, baboons, and vervet monkeys, hippopotamus, mongoose, warthogs, hyrax, bat-eared fox, and crocodile. There are some 450 species of birds in Serengeti, making it one of the richest bird habitats in the world, as well as a host of reptiles, including three of the deadliest snakes on earth: the puff adder, the black mamba, and the green mamba.

The Serengeti's large mammals are the visible manifestation of a subtle ecology. Volcanic soils on much of the Serengeti Plain creates an impenetrable hardpan. Thus, although some areas receive nearly 60 inches of rain per year, more than New Orleans and enough to support woodland, only shallow-rooted grasses grow in the thin layer of topsoil. These singular conditions create the short grass plains just outside the southeastern boundary of Serengeti National Park. The soil deepens slightly within the park itself, giving rise to the waist-high vegetation of the long-grass plains. The wildebeest leave Serengeti National Park and go to the short-grass plains in search of calcium, but this region withers at the end of the rainy season, forcing the massive wildebeest herds north and west in search of water and fresh grazing.

The migrating wildebeest dominate the closed ecosystem of the Serengeti by dint of their sheer number—as many now as in the pre-colonial era—and they determine the shape of the plains: little grass remains once the herds move through, and the predators feast on the young and the feeble as the migration moves past. The migration of the wildebeest historically formed an immense triangle. During the wettest time of the year, between December and May, the wildebeest remained on the short-grass plains. As the rains ended, the wildebeest moved toward permanent water in the northwest, in the tallgrass areas. The animals turned more to the north as the dry season progressed, and by October they crossed the Kenyan border and reached the Mara region, where food and water could be found in even the driest years. When the rains began again in late November, the herds headed due south, back to the short-grass plains. Today, with the wildebeest population having grown to roughly 1.5 million, many animals travel due north, while others go east first and then north, and still others follow the triangular route. All told, the migration route covers over 300 miles.

Wildebeest and other species follow Africa's pattern of wet and dry seasons and travel long distances in search of food. Before the arrival of Europeans, Africa hosted a patchwork of such large-scale migrations, among them gazelle, scimitar-horned oryx (perhaps the most endangered antelope in Africa), springboks, zebra, eland, and red hartebeest. A decade ago, only the migrations of wildebeest in the Serengeti and white-eared kobs in southeastern Sudan remained intact. With nearly all the other great migration systems reduced or at an end, the wildebeest have become another unique aspect of the Serengeti.

Serengeti National Park has preserved the wildebeest migration, but it has done great harm to another vitally important part of the Serengeti ecosystem. The Serengeti supported both wildlife and pastoral human societies for over 2,500 years before Europeans felt compelled to protect this supposed wilderness as a national park. The Maasai (the name means "speakers of Maa," the tribe's tonal language) of modern-day Kenya and Tanzania have occupied the pastoral niche in the Serengeti for at least four centuries, and five other distinct ethnic groups also share the Serengeti ecosystem. The predecessors of the modern Maasai migrated from the north, driving out the Galla tribes that had inhabited what is now Kenya and Tanzania; by the mid-nineteenth century, 50,000 Maasai occupied some 75,000 square miles—an area roughly the size of Nebraska.

The Maasai were masters of the art of war, and they used their skills primarily to raid cattle from other tribes. The Maasai believe that God gave them all the cattle on earth, so these raids were more like repossession than stealing to them. Spectacularly arrayed in red paint, wearing towering headdresses of ostrich feathers and lion's manes, and carrying long, heavy spears and buffalo-hide shields, Maasai warriors—the *moran*—could run for days across forbidding country to carry out their raids. The Maasai's hostile reputation spread far beyond the Serengeti; Henry Stanley's parting advice to the Scottish explorer Joseph Thomson as Thomson prepared for a journey from the Kenyan coast toward Lake Victoria was to take a thousand men or "write your will."

Few tribes have attracted as much attention as the Maasai. Anthropologists have written volumes about the Maasai, yet have failed to puncture the image created by more romantically inclined observers. In his book *Through Masai Land* ("Masai" is the former spelling), published in 1885, Joseph Thomson described his first encounter with the tribe: "We soon set our eyes upon the dreaded warriors that had so long been the subject of my waking dreams, and I could not but involuntarily exclaim, 'What splendid fellows!' as I surveyed a band of the most peculiar race of men to be found in Africa."

Isak Dinesen was a fervent admirer of the Maasai, and she did much to spread the cult. "A Maasai warrior is a fine sight," she wrote in *Out of Africa.*

> Those young men have, to the utmost extent, that particular form of intelligence which we call chic; daring, and wildly fantastical as they seem, they are still unswervingly true to their own nature, and to an imminent ideal. Their style is not an assumed manner, nor an imitation of a foreign perfection; it has grown from the inside, and is an expression of the race and its history, and their weapons and finery are as much a part of their being as are a stag's antlers.

Proud and aloof, with a strong sense of their own aristocracy, the Maasai won the admiration of colonial Europeans. Often the Maasai cut striking figures: tall and lean, with fine features, they wear bright red, ocher-dyed togas called *shukas,* finely made ornaments of copper and tin, and many brightly colored beads. They can move lightly and gracefully, and are elegant even standing still, as they lean on their spears one-legged, like herons. Traditionally, both men and women among the Maasai pierce their ears and stretch the lobes to long loops with wooden plugs or, today, empty film canisters left by tourists. Fewer and fewer Maasai, particularly boys, now follow the practice.

Yet something deeper than prideful nature, striking physique, or exotic fashion accounts for the Maasai's lasting place in our imagination. It is the belief that they live in harmony with nature. While true to a degree, this idea leads to the attitude, reinforced by tourist promotions, that the Maasai are part of the landscape, not so unlike the wildebeest and zebra. The Maasai, in truth, like the Nunu in Zaire and indeed indigenous people everywhere, do whatever they must to feed themselves and their families, and that may include taxing the environment beyond its capacity to regenerate itself. The Maasai are just as capable as Westerners of reshaping the natural order of things to fit their needs.

Beneath the cartoon of the noble savage, however, lie some lessons about the ecology of the Serengeti. The region known as Maasailand can support agriculture, wildlife, and livestock in an untidy but effective conglomeration. Even elephants—notorious crop raiders usually seen as the scourge of human settlements—play a vital role; they are the "gardeners" of pastoral systems, reducing bush and small trees and recycling nutrients, thus maintaining the grasslands needed by cattle and other grazers.

A blend of wildlife and livestock appears to be the most biologically productive system, better suited to the semi-arid Maasailand than wildlife or livestock alone. The diversity of species allows for a complex mosaic of grazers and browsers at different levels of vegetation. Some ecologists use the term "grazing succession," meaning that different species feed sequentially on the same pasture. In the Serengeti the succession starts with zebra, then wildebeest, then gazelle. The succession also stimulates the growth of new vegetation. Raising cattle alone, on the other hand, especially in a limited area, quickly reduces the pasture to dust and will ultimately destroy an ecosystem.

Over generations, the Maasai developed a system of communal property and seasonal rotation of grazing lands, with certain pastures used only during droughts, which enabled them to survive dry years, to avoid serious damage to the ecosystem, and to co-exist with abundant wildlife. The Maasai do not hunt, except for young warriors who may kill lions or buffalo to prove their bravery. Colonial administrators, and even some African leaders following independence in the early 1960s, failed to understand how the Maasai fit their ecological niche, and considered the herdsmen and their cattle a serious threat to wildlife, which was increasingly seen as a national and international treasure.

Before colonization, Maasailand extended from northern Kenya to central Tanganyika (which became Tanzania when it merged with Zanzibar in 1964). Near the end of the nineteenth century, the British constructed a rail line from Mombasa, on the coast, to the shores of Lake Victoria, effectively cutting Maasailand in half. In 1904, the colonial government of Kenya compelled the Maasai to vacate the fertile highlands of the Great Rift Valley, and gave them other land as compensation. The colonial administration signed a treaty giving the Maasai rights to these lands indefinitely. "Indefinitely" turned out to be roughly six years, for in 1911, due to an increase in emigration by white settlers, the British evicted the Maasai once again, in the process signing another treaty confining the Maasai to semi-arid land south of the railway line.

The Maasai in Tanganyika did not face eviction from their land until the 1940s, when white settlers arrived to claim the plains between Mt. Meru and Mt. Kilimanjaro, as well as most of the fertile highlands near Ngorongoro. Throughout the 1940s and 1950s, colonial governments sought to appease the Maasai by constructing dams and drilling boreholes where there was no permanent water supply. The water, along with improved veterinary services, led to an increase in the number of cattle, sheep, and goats the Maasai could keep—and the Maasai themselves were growing in number as health care improved and mortality dropped, further increasing stress on their semi-arid rangelands. The administrations failed to connect the resulting environmental problems to the previous reduction in the Maasai's grazing area and the lower mortality rate, and instead blamed the Maasai.

Between the late 1940s and 1970, seven protected areas—Nairobi, Amboseli, and Tsavo national parks, and Masai Mara National Reserve in Kenya, and Serengeti, Tarangire, and Lake Manyara national parks in Tanzania—were established in Maasailand. Today, more than half of the wild animal populations in Kenya and Tanzania are found there. Pastureland outside park borders constitutes an essential part of the savanna ecosystem, but the protected area, particularly in Tanzania, have long been managed as isolated islands of game, where animals would be protected from people like the Maasai.

The roots of that approach to conservation can be found in southern Africa, in the game laws and protected areas established in the Cape to protect the dwindling herds. According to the historian John MacKenzie, the first game legislation was introduced to the Cape by the Dutch East India Company as early as 1657, but the British did not introduce their first major piece of colonial game legislation until 1822. Lord Charles Somerset, the royal governor, lamented the possible destruction of game in the colony, and in an official proclamation he instituted a closed hunting season and a system of licenses for such animals as elephant, hippopotamus, and bontebok (a large dark brown antelope). Landowners, however, could shoot any animal on cultivated land, so as farms grew, wild animals disappeared. It was sixty-four years before the royal government expanded the list of specially protected species, by which time many animals on the list—bontebok, gemsbok, and Burchell's zebra, for example—were on the brink of extinction. The quagga was protected in the Cape Colony after it had already vanished.

Early conservation efforts in Africa culminated in international conventions in 1900 and 1933, called to address the problems of the continent's wildlife. The 1900 conference, attended by all the European powers with African colonies, as well as King Leopold's Congo Free State, produced the Convention for the Preservation of Wild Animals, Birds and Fish in Africa. The convention strengthened the drive toward uniform game regulations based on creating reserves and outlawing traditional methods of African hunting. It divided Africa's animals into five classes, ranging from those to be preserved because of their usefulness or rarity, to those which could be shot at will, because they were harmful or were considered vermin. The last category reflected the influence of the hunters and farmers, as it included big cats, hyenas, wild hunting dogs, otters, baboons, crocodiles, and poisonous snakes—anything that ate game or cattle.

Most parties failed to ratify the 1900 Convention, and it was never enforced. Germany and Great Britain, however, soon enacted legislation based on the provisions of the convention, particularly regarding game reserves. They were prodded by a growing preservationist lobby at home. In 1903, Sudan—which was then jointly administered by Great Britain and Egypt—planned to abandon an excellent game reserve and substitute an inferior area. Edward North Buxton, an aristocrat, hunter, and conservationist with the appropriate title of Verderer of Epping Forest, organized a campaign against the misguided idea and succeeded in quashing it. Subsequently, he brought together colonial officials, hunter-naturalists, and the gentry in a pressure group called the Society for the Preservation of the Fauna of the Empire (SPFE). Since many of its members were famous hunters, however, the British public called it the Penitent Butchers Club.

Buxton and others stressed that game animals should be preserved so that hunting—by Europeans, of course—could continue. A major goal of the narrow-minded and rather arrogant SPFE was to eliminate hunting by Africans, which the Society and many colonial administrators believed threatened to kill all the large game animals. Frederick Selous claimed that of every 1,000 hunted elephants, 997 were killed by Africans. Selous had no evidence for this assertion, but it served the purpose of those who wanted to guarantee the availability of wild animals for the aristocratic hunters. Hunting, in Buxton's view, played a key role in preserving the British Empire because it maintained the morale of officers stationed in remote colonies and attracted the best men.

Despite the incessant lobbying of the SPFE, game laws rarely controlled hunting by either Europeans or Africans. Many of the laws were so intricate—specifying which animals could be hunted, at what time, how, by whom, and what could be done with the skins and trophies—that they could not be readily enforced. In any event, few colonial administrators had the manpower to enforce laws governing white hunters, to say nothing of the vastly more numerous Africans. Once a hunter reached the remote bush, he could basically do as he pleased.

The realization that the laws failed to curb hunting, particularly by Africans, led to increasing pressure for more game reserves and tighter restrictions.

The second international conference convened in London in 1933. The meeting produced the Convention for the Protection of African Flora and Fauna, which essentially restated the guidelines of the 1900 Convention, though it took note of such new inventions as automobiles and airplanes. It also sought to simplify the complex classification of animals, paring down five categories to two: those that required special protection and those that needed only some protection. The convention did away with the notion that vermin—harmful and unattractive animals—could be shot at will, though the practice continued.

The 1933 Convention, like the one thirty-three years earlier, was never ratified by most of the ten nations which signed it. In the long run, MacKenzie argues, ratification turned out to be less significant than the convention's call for permanently setting aside areas for wildlife that had fixed boundaries and were large enough to permit migration. The models were areas like Prince Albert National Park in the Congo, opened in 1925, and Kruger National Park in South Africa, created one year later. Most of the other substantial protected areas in Africa were game reserves that served the needs of hunters by providing protected land on which game stocks could be easily managed. Settlers often opposed reserves because they took up valuable farmland, and the protected status of the game reserves could be removed by the stroke of a governor's pen. National parks, on the other hand, were permanent and were designed for the age of tourism. The age of Africa's national parks truly began with the international agreement of 1933.

Serengeti National Park traces its roots to the report prepared for the SPFE by Major R. W. G. Hingston in 1930. After visiting Northern Rhodesia (now Zambia), Nyasaland (Malawi), Tanganyika (Tanzania), Kenya, and Uganda, Hingston expressed doubts that several species (including white rhino, elephant, and hippopotamus) would survive fifty more years without some action being taken. He proposed nine national parks for the five colonies. Three would protect specific species; the nyala (a medium-sized antelope) in Nyasaland, the bongo (a larger forest antelope) in Kenya, and the gorilla in Uganda. The other six parks Hingston proposed were vast tracts of land based on the plan of Kruger National Park: three areas in Tanganyika—Serengeti, Selous, and Kilimanjaro; one area straddling the Northern Rhodesia-Nyasaland border; one in northern Kenya; and one on the Nile in Uganda. The British government took no action, however, until after the end of World War II. An official proclamation by the British authorities established Serengeti National Park in 1951.

By that time, woodlands covered the northern reaches of the Serengeti, though less than a half century earlier the area had been open, grassy plains, inhabited by people and their animals. What had happened? In a repeat of the *enkidaaroto* of the late nineteenth century, rinderpest and smallpox epidemics had eliminated both animals and humans—some Maasai remained on the plains, but too few to influence the landscape. The bush flourished in the absence of livestock and wildlife to graze the plains and the lack of seasonal fires set by the Maasai to encourage the growth of new grass. Since tsetse favor dense bush over grassland, with the influence of man removed, the ecosystem developed in a way that heavily favored wildlife—all of which are immune to nagana (trypanosomiasis), a disease spread by tsetse—over cattle, which have no such immunity. According to a 1955 report by the Royal National Parks Department, "The tsetse fly stands guard over the area, and even today it is virtually a glimpse into Africa as it was before the white man ever crossed its shores."

The tiny tsetse played a large role in the history of national parks in Africa. When the idea of setting aside game reserves for wildlife was first proposed around the turn of the century, some farmers and scientists objected, fearful that large numbers of wild animals would help spread tsetse. Farmers had good reason to fear tsetse—literally, "the fly that kills cattle." The entomologist John Ford has argued, however, that tsetse had long inhabited the no-man's-land between African settlements, such as the ungrazed areas that separated one Maasai settlement from another in and around the Serengeti Plain. Africans knew of these focal points of infection and avoided them, while Maasai cattle ate young sprouts, preventing them from maturing into tough, thorny scrub, and thus kept the tsetse in check. The hunting practices of tribes other than the Maasai also helped deter the spread of tsetse by regulating wildlife populations that could provide hosts for the flies. Africans, Ford says, had thus established "a mobile ecological equilibrium" with wildlife and their associated diseases.

That equilibrium collapsed when Africans and their cattle began dying in large numbers from diseases brought by Europeans. On the Serengeti and elsewhere, a vicious cycle began: the bush returned because cattle no longer kept the bush down, the flies multiplied, further lowering both human and cattle populations, leading to more habitat for tsetse, and so on.

In the late 1950s, colonial governments began aggressive campaigns against tsetse, using traps and insecticides. The Maasai populations grew and they returned to their pattern of setting fires, thus destroying tsetse-infested bush. Many conservationists lamented the loss of tsetse, called by some "the best game warden in Africa" because of the insect's ability to keep human beings and their livestock out of wildlife areas. That position makes some sense given that the widespread use of insecticide may eventually mean the end of many currently protected areas.

As the tsetse vanished and the number of cattle grew, prominent conservationists and ecologists raised urgent concerns about the health of Serengeti National Park. The SPFE, which by this time had changed its name to the Fauna Preservation Society (FPS), took a lead role, but it was soon to be overshadowed by Professor Bernhard Grzimek, president of the Frankfurt Zoological Society and former director of the Frankfurt Zoo, who would dominate conservation in the Serengeti like no one before or since.

Bernhard Klemens Maria Hoffbauer Pius Grzimek (the surname name is Polish; "Gushimek" comes close to the pronunciation) raised conservation propaganda to a high art. His methods relied on contempt for Africans and provided no lasting solutions, but to his credit in thirty years of working with and for Africa's wildlife, Grzimek probably raised more money for conservation, educated more people about nature, and twisted more arms of more African bureaucrats than any man in history. Until his death in 1987, Grzimek's untiring advocacy for wildlife—to the detriment of humans—made him one of the few white men welcomed by every leader in sub-Saharan Africa, including Uganda's Idi Amin Dada.

Grzimek was widely known in Europe long before he ever saw Africa. He had single-handedly rescued the remnants of the century-old Frankfurt Zoo after World War II, rebuilding it into a world-class operation. Only thirteen animals remained at war's end, and 80 percent of the city was in ruins from Allied bombing. Grzimek—a soldier and one-time member of the Nazi Party—took advantage of the chaos, expanding the zoo's area by one third by putting up street signs, redirecting traffic, and closing roads. He once told Britain's Prince Philip that the best thing that could happen to an old zoo was to be flattened by the Royal Air Force—so long as the animals survived and the rest of the town was also destroyed, so the zoo could expand.

Grzimek and his son Michael visited Africa in 1951 and 1953 on collecting expeditions to the Congo for the Frankfurt Zoo. During their second journey, father and son lived in the forest with the pygmies as they searched for the elusive and exotic okapi, an animal that resembles a cross between a giraffe and a zebra. The elder Grzimek wrote a book based on the trip, and the title he chose, *No Room for Wild Animals,* reveals much about his priorities. Grzimek was convinced that earth's human population was growing much too fast, and that people were crowding out the animals. One of his chapters goes even further; its heading reads "Africa's Wild Animals Are Doomed." Translated into seventeen languages, the book ensured Grizmek's lasting fame. Michael Grzimek, already an accomplished film maker at age eighteen, shot a documentary with the same title and theme as his father's book, and it also garnered international acclaim. The two Grzimeks had staked their claim as the world's leading conservation pitchmen. Their ruinous focus on wildlife rather than broader ecosystems became the model for the conservationists who followed them to Africa.

The Grzimeks' first direct involvement with the Serengeti was as dramatic as their trip to the Congo. They hurled themselves into a controversy that had been brewing since the mid-1940s, when the Maasai began grazing their cattle on the central plain and the floor of Ngorongoro Crater, forced there by a growing human population. Tanganyika's colonial government ordered the herdsmen and their animals out; the Maasai ignored it. In 1956, the Tanganyika legislature decided that since the Maasai would not move, the park boundaries would have to be changed. The legislature essentially offered to turn over the central plain to the Maasai, thus reducing the size of the park from almost 4,500 square miles to under 2,000 square miles.

The move would have been a disaster, and what had been a smoldering debate now became a raging international controversy. Conservationists in Europe sought to remove the Serengeti from British control and turn it over to the United Nations. The FPS commissioned an ecologist to study the area and make recommendations. Bernhard Grzimek, however, had had enough of the government's dithering. He offered the governor of Tanganyika the proceeds from Michael's film to buy the Serengeti and return it to the animals.

The British authorities politely declined the offer, but invited the Grzimeks to survey the wildlife on the plains. In 1958, the two scientists pioneered the use of light aircraft in wildlife research when they followed the wildebeest migration in a single-engine Dornier painted with zebra stripes; but they got the facts of the migration quite wrong. They somehow overlooked the huge herds in the northern Serengeti, and thus missed the crucial dry-season grazing areas. Despite this oversight, the Grzimeks concluded that the new boundaries for the park proposed by the legislature were too small and would destroy the migration. The colonial authorities, however, decided not to wait for the results of the Grzimeks' survey. The FPS had recommended that the northern plains should be added to Serengeti National Park, that the floor of Ngorongoro Crater should be declared a nature sanctuary, and that to compensate the Maasai for their lost land, a conservation area should be established in the highlands around the rim of the crater. The government adopted all of these ideas, and in the process created the Ngorongoro Conservation Area (NCA), where natural resources would be shared, in theory, by the Maasai and the wild herbivores.

Shortly after the decision was announced in early 1959, Michael Grzimek, having just finished shooting another documentary, died when the Dornier collided with a griffon-vulture and crashed near the Loliondo Mountains, north of Ngorongoro. His father returned to Frankfurt, completed the film, and wrote another book. Again, film and book had the same title: *Serengeti Shall Not Die.* The book was translated into twenty-three languages, and the film won an Oscar for Best Documentary. *Serengeti Shall Not Die* is the manifesto of preservationism, but it also was another of Grzimek's propaganda tools, filled with misleading, often falsified data. Bernhard Grzimek here completes the thought he began in *No Room for Wild Animals,* that Africa is dying and that what little remains must be saved from mankind.

Grzimek was vehemently opposed to granting grazing rights to the Maasai, as proposed in the Ngorongoro Conservation Area. The idea of striking a balance between wildlife and human needs was a creative and constructive approach, but Grzimek refused to see the importance of local people for conservation. Tanganyika was fertile ground for such an innovative idea. Tanganyikan politics lacked the factionalism seen in Kenya, primarily because the country's first president, Julius K. Nyerere, succeeded in creating a national pride that in some respects superseded tribal loyalties. Nyerere also understood the economic and spiritual role wildlife could play in a modern Africa state.

In 1959, Tanganyika seemed poised to take the crucial step of allowing local people to share their land with wild animals in and around a protected area. Bernhard Grzimek, however, was horrified at the thought of people wandering around in "his" national park, so he fought the NCA as he fought all the battles over wildlife conservation, with any weapon at his disposal; "First by soft line, then by hard line, next by bribery, and if necessary by outright blackmail," according to one journalist in Nairobi quoted by Harold T.P. Hayes in his book *The Last Place on Earth*. Grzimek once described himself as "a showman of pity." Indeed, his campaigns to save wild animals were based on manipulating the emotions and expectations of both the general public in Europe and politicians in Africa.

Grzimek worked furiously and successfully behind the scenes to undermine the principles of the NCA. Once a unique effort to sustain both wildlife and pastoralists, the NCA is today just another park or reserve, and a poorly managed one at that. The goals set for the NCA in 1959, however, were much higher, and they have never been realized. The harmonious co-existence of people, livestock, and wild animals has not been achieved, and the rights and needs of the local Maasai community are often ignored.

At the outset, the NCA accommodated—in addition to wildlife—animal husbandry, agriculture, and the development of such services as roads, wells, granaries, schools, and health clinics. These gave the area multiple-land-use status, and the resident Maasai were the beneficiaries. The Maasai could graze their cattle on the short-grass plains at the base of Ngorongoro and in a central woodland area. The crater itself, along with a smaller crater nearby called Empakai and the highland forests, was reserved for wildlife. But the areas available for grazing could support only so many cattle, and as the herds grew, parts of the range showed clear signs of deterioration. The Maasai increasingly brought their herds into the craters, leading to conflict with conservation authorities and to direct competition with wildlife.

In 1975, the Tanzanian government banned all agriculture throughout Ngorongoro, to prevent farmers from encroaching on wildlife habitat. To meet the demand for agricultural products, however, especially maize flour, the Maasai often resorted to illegal cultivation. The Maasai are poor farmers, and in any event have too little land legally available, so they are forced to sell some of their cattle for grain, and thus become, by their traditional standards, yet more impoverished. Even this option often disappears because of problems transporting grain into the NCA along Tanzania's roads. Potholes large enough to swallow a truck give the roads the appearance of having been recently bombed.

The present inhabitants of Ngorongoro cannot maintain themselves much longer. Conservationists and the Ngorongoro Maasai are trapped in a Catch-22: if agricultural practices are not allowed, the Maasai will have to trade more cattle for grain, and soon they will not have enough livestock to buy the cereals they need to survive. If agriculture is allowed, the area will lose much of its unique scenic value and soil erosion could threaten the entire watershed. The combination of agriculture and pastoralism creates unbearable pressures on the ecosystem. A better system would be to allow the Maasai more room for their cattle, while at the same time improving the roads into the area so that the Maasai could buy grain at lower prices. Restoring the NCA as a true multiple-use area may be in the best interests of all involved, but such a course would buck a long tradition of preservationist management in Tanzania.

The tendency to ignore the needs of people who live on the border of national parks betrays a bewildering lack of common sense. The absurdity of such an attitude could not be more evident than on the Serengeti Plain. Many Maasai live in areas that remain critical to the ecological and environmental stability of the protected areas, and the wet-season domain of the Serengeti herds lies almost entirely within Maasai rangelands, which the Maasai have traditionally managed as communal property.

Yet, Kenya has moved toward more private ownership of land, even though privatization is incompatible with pastoralism. Pastoralists survive on semi-arid lands because they are opportunists, making use of the best resources available. Private ownership destroys this system.

The social and ecological problems of East Africa cannot all be traced to the national parks, but the existence of those parks reflects a willful ignorance of the history of the region. Fossils found at Olduvai Gorge—which lies between Ngorongoro Crater and the park boundary—reveal that the same species of wildebeest grazed the ancient plains, migrated in a similar pattern, and shared the land with our human ancestors. The proximity of Olduvai to Serengeti is wonderfully ironic: the site of Mary and Louis Leakey's greatest discovery, the man-ape *Australopithecus*, side by side with Serengeti National Park, the modern symbol of wild Africa, while their son, Dr. Richard E. Leakey, works nearby to keep man out.

As an extension of the idea of keeping discrete areas for people, livestock, and wildlife, Richard Leakey proposed building huge fences. Leakey took over Kenya's wildlife conservation programs in April 1989, at the request of Kenyan President Daniel T. Arap Moi, and is now director of the Kenya Wildlife Service (KWS). Given enough time, money, and political clout, the hugely energetic Leakey might fence most of the national parks in East Africa. Putting one large fence around Masai Mara and Serengeti, and another around

Tsavo National Park in southeastern Kenya, which had been badly hit by poachers, was one of Leakey's first ideas. The idea of a fenced park plays on a Western ideal of wild Africa by making the mistaken claim that a fence is a barrier against both man and nature, creating in effect a time capsule; the land inside the fence shall endure, untainted by man, regardless of what happens beyond.

Before coming to KWS, Leakey held the title of chairman of the East African Wildlife Society, but otherwise had no practical knowledge of wildlife. His most important qualifications were his personal integrity, international reputation, the support of the president, and overwhelming self-assurance. The last should not be underestimated. Corruption in the wildlife department had been maintained under both colonial and independent rule by intimidating any potential reformers. But trying to intimidate Leakey only stiffens his resolve, as his political foes have learned, and he has cleaned house aggressively. Part of Leakey's mystique is his casual disregard—his bodyguards notwithstanding—for the death threats he regularly receives.

The fence around the Serengeti, Leakey argued when he was first appointed, would still allow for the wildebeest migration. More importantly, the plan served as Leakey's calling card to the world. It was an empty gesture: Leakey works in Kenya and most of the Serengeti is in Tanzania, and in any event he is too intelligent to believe that the fences were practical or necessary. While he probably never planned to go through with the fences because they were too expensive—the cost of fences for Masai Mara and Tsavo alone would probably have been upward of $50 million—and because of the risk of embarrassment should they fail, Leakey is also too savvy a politician to pass up an opportunity to garner the instant worldwide attention he knew would come from an ambitious yet outrageous idea.

Leakey is still widely associated with the plan to enclose the Serengeti, though he has quietly overcome his infatuation with

Gargantuan fences. He now admits that fences and migratory species do not mix. Smaller fencing projects, however, are under way throughout the country. One limiting factor is the cost of both materials and maintenance, but another is technology. Electric fences generally keep elephants at bay, but practically no man-made barrier can outlast a determined elephant. Elephants have been known to drop trees on electric fences, or to use their tusks to get under the wires.

In some cases the fences protect crops and livestock from damage by elephants, buffalo, hippo, and other wildlife. "There are areas, quite large areas, where the issue is not migration, it's forage," Leakey says. "It's forage because sugarcane tastes nicer than acacia. That has to stop if these animals are going to survive, and when you have got big plantations and encroaching settlement next to a park, a long, fenced boundary makes good sense." Leakey's most recent fencing initiatives have walkways and gates that allow people inside protected areas to gather wood and other natural resources, and this scaled-down version of the fencing effort Leakey first proposed may indeed be useful in certain areas. The fences, however, are more than just wire and wood. They are powerful symbols of the traditional method of conservation in Africa.

Lake Nakuru National Park, just 80 miles northwest of Nairobi, has been completely fenced in. The lake is small and rather unremarkable, except between October and April when it hosts vast flocks of flamingoes. Driving toward the park from the city, however, provides one of the most striking sights anywhere in Africa: a twelve-strand electric fence surrounding the entire park, lake and all. Though the fencing project at Lake Nakuru began before Leakey took up his current position, it nevertheless speaks volumes about the direction of conservation in Kenya under his leadership.

Talk of building fences may win applause on the lecture circuit, but the fences themselves cannot last. Fencing in large parks—even if the fences allow people to move in and out— creates open-air zoos, troublesome elephants notwithstanding.

All they lack are the concrete walkways, iron bars, and helpful displays. A fenced park in Africa is a symbol of failure, of an inability to reconcile the needs of man and animals. These fences can also be seen as the logical extension of conservation as it has long been practiced in Africa, with its lack of understanding of the need for a living, fully integrated ecosystem that includes human beings.

Fences seek to preserve a pristine wilderness that never existed while they endanger cultures that long ago adapted to living with wild animals. The single-minded desire to save wildlife, particularly elephants and rhinos, regardless of the harm that effort might cause the local people, led conservationists to idealize national parks as the ultimate good. Yet creating a park means removing whoever happens to live on the newly protected land, and keeping them out. Fences simply add an exclamation point.

If the trend toward fences and private ownership of ever smaller parcels of land continues, the Maasai may become a landless tribe facing a bleak economic and social future. The dislocation of the Maasai is already evident. The road from Nairobi to Arusha, Tanzania, runs through the heart of Maasailand, but few herdsmen can be seen. Here and there Maasai lean on their spears, their *shukas* dulled with road dust. Grimy cement buildings with hand-painted "hotel" signs and wooden stands selling Coca-Cola mark the settlements along the route, where dozens of old Maasai men gather in twos and threes, glaring at the white tourists in minivans on their way to the national parks.

CHAPTER IV

▼ ▼ ▼

SAVE THE
ELEPHANTS!

*An iron band of ruthless destroyers is drawing
around it; and it may be safely predicted that in
twenty years, the noble African elephant will be a
rare animal.*

—the explorer Joseph Thomson, in 1881

T*he tourists who* flock to the Serengeti and the other
spectacular parks in East Africa often come with one
animal in mind: the elephant. No other species carries as much
symbolic or emotional force. Fascination with elephants is
hardly a new phenomenon—man has by turns worshipped,
idealized, contemplated, or slaughtered elephants, but rarely
ignored them. The Greeks fashioned chryselephantine (ivory
and gold) sculptures over 3,500 years ago, and China's ivory
carving tradition is at least as old. Ganesh, the Hindu god of
wisdom, has an elephant's head; Solomon's throne was made
of ivory, as were the benches in the Roman Senate. Yet today,
to an unprecedented degree, the efforts to save the elephant
dominate nearly all discussions of conservation in Africa.

In the late 1980s, the elephant emerged as conservation's
central figure, the embodiment of everything worth saving in
Africa. A concerted campaign to stop the ivory trade and save
the elephant began in the United States and Europe, bringing
together traditional conservation organizations and the animal
rights movement. In light of the elephant's clear intelligence,

strong family structure, and its key role in the ecosystem, this seemed entirely appropriate. With heated debates over the ivory trade keeping the elephant on the front pages, elephant mania spread. But the focus on elephants, like the debate about fencing the Serengeti, only strengthened the deepseated misperceptions about Africa and what conservation there requires.

The campaign to save the elephant was not really about a species but about one population of animals: those elephants living in East Africa. The campaign fed off the popular predisposition for collapsing the entire continent into a few countries near the Indian Ocean. Played out in the international arena with only the passing participation of Africans—with the notable exception of Richard Leakey—it hammered home the message that Africans were incapable of protecting their wildlife. These destructive messages may be the most lasting residue of the elephant campaign. Millions of dollars poured in as conservation organizations exploited ghastly pictures of elephants with their faces cut off. This horror show worked because elephants are the prototype for the mischievous term "charismatic megafauna," used by some in conservation to refer to the few animals that have reached star status. Few of the dollars thus raised have reached Africans actually working in elephant conservation, because the issue was stopping the ivory trade, not hands-on programs on the continent.

In the end, the fight over the ivory ban turned on public relations. International conservation groups provided expertise in mustering public support that those opposing the ban could never hope to match. Richard Leakey, a genius at winning converts to his point of view, also fought on the side of the ivory ban. At Leakey's urging, Kenyan President Moi put the torch to a 12-ton pile of confiscated tusks worth an estimated $3 million. It was a public relations coup of immense proportions, but many people, in Kenya and elsewhere, felt Moi would have been better off selling the ivory and using the money to upgrade the management of the parks. Image, however, was all in this latest incarnation of the elephant debate, and Leakey knew well the power of international conservation to dictate events in Africa.

While elephant mania is a new phenomenon, elephants have long been a lightning rod for conservation. Practically every generation hears it will be the last to see elephants in the wild. Fear of imminent extinction goes back to the Romans, who actually had good reason to be worried; elephants once roamed among Roman garrisons in the Sahara—Hannibal's elephants probably came from this population—but the northern subspecies eventually disappeared. Pliny may have first sounded the alarm over the plight of the elephant, and it was picked up again almost as soon as Europe reestablished extensive contact with Africa in the nineteenth century.

Joseph Thomson, who explored Maasailand in the 1880s, had a particularly bleak view. Thomson exaggerated the threat the ivory trade posed to elephants, but not by much. The slaughter of elephants by white hunters, particularly in southern Africa, was staggering. A well-outfitted hunter could shoot upward of two hundred elephants in a single safari, and several thousand if he made a career of it. Some hunters killed so many elephants that ivory overflowed their wagons and had to be abandoned in the bush. The elephants, however, did not die out; they simply retreated to less accessible lands.

Game legislation in the nineteenth and early twentieth centuries emphasized restricting elephant hunting and creating breeding reserves for elephants. The men who fashioned such policies were not wildlife specialists but colonial administrators concerned primarily with efficient government. These pragmatic men focused on ivory, without doubt the most important commodity Africa could supply Europeans—so important, in fact, that human slavery was often simply an adjunct to the ivory trade. Transporting ivory from the interior to the coast required huge amounts of manpower to haul tusks weighing upward of 100 pounds apiece, and selling the ivory bearers at the end of the trip was an added profit. African

chiefs used ivory to bargain with European settlers, and missionaries used it to finance their far-flung outposts. Ivory sales
financed one of Central Africa's largest trading houses, Man-
dala Ltd. of the African Lakes Corporation in Malawi; ivory
remained an essential part of the economies of Kenya and
Uganda until the start of World War I, and of the Central
African Republic into the 1970s.

The ivory trade has always fueled concern for the future of
the elephant and led to new calls for strict wildlife legislation.
According to John MacKenzie, in the late 1880s, a commissioner for the British Central African Protectorate (now
Malawi), Alfred Sharpe, believed the best way to control elephant hunting was to shut down the market for ivory. He
thought this course impossible, however, and instead supported a ban on the export of tusks weighing less than 15
pounds. Over the next century, colonial and then independent
African governments tested practically every variation on that
theme in an attempt to save elephants while preserving the
ivory trade, but never enforced any of them.

The dream of stamping out all elephant hunting by removing the commercial stimulus was never far from the minds of
conservationists. The ivory trade grew year by year and prices
rose; by 1979, it had reached $60 per kilo. Then came an
incredible ivory boom: in just ten years, the price increased
fivefold. A growing demand for ivory in Japan, reflecting the
general strengthening of Japan's economy, drove much of the
increase. Middlemen, mostly based in Hong Kong, paid Africans only 10 to 30 percent of the price for raw ivory; even so,
the money—a fortune in most of rural Africa—provided a tremendous incentive to hunt elephants.

The sense of crisis deepened with each new piece of evidence of the impact such hunting was having on elephant
herds, particularly in East Africa. A study of elephant population trends and the effects of the ivory trade, conducted by an
independent panel of experts called the Ivory Trade Review
Group, reported that the elephant population had fallen from

1.3 million in 1979 to 625,000 in 1989. Half of the continent's elephants were being killed every eight to ten years, and the losses in East Africa reached 17 percent per year. At the same time, the amount of ivory leaving Africa each year rose from 200 metric tons in the 1950s to about 900 metric tons throughout most of the 1980s. As the big male elephants—those with the largest tusks—were killed, the tusks being exported became smaller and smaller, meaning that increasing numbers of younger elephants had to be killed to supply the same amount of ivory.

The Ivory Trade Review Group released its study in June 1989, less than five months before the biennial meeting of the Convention on International Trade in Endangered Species of Wild Flora and Fauna (CITES), the international governing body for the trade in wildlife products. The release of the long, complex, and rather dry report was perhaps the key event leading CITES to impose a global ban on the trade of ivory, even though the report itself did not endorse the idea. (Several members of the group, angered over the way their findings were misused, have now written a book arguing that the ban will not work.) Before the findings were known, many conservation groups supported a solution known as "split-listing." Under CITES, the species facing the greatest threat of extinction are placed on a list called Appendix I, and all the countries that are parties to the convention agree to ban commercial trade of species on the list. Slightly less precarious species are listed on Appendix II, which allows for limited and controlled trade. In 1975, the year the treaty came into effect, the African elephant was placed on Appendix II of CITES by a vote of the convention (wild populations of the Asian elephant have been listed on Appendix I since 1975).

For years the debate raged over whether to move the African elephant to Appendix I. Until the spring of 1989, most people favored moving the East, West, and Central African populations to Appendix I while leaving the southern African elephants on Appendix II, primarily in recognition of successful elephant management in Zimbabwe and South Africa: at the turn of the century, Zimbabwe (then Rhodesia) contained fewer than two thousand elephants; today, there are more than fifty thousand.

Split-listing was a reasonable position, though some ivory trade experts were concerned about how an effective monitoring system could be established, with ivory from one part of Africa being legal while that from another would be illegal. The debate, however, never even approached that issue. The continentwide census figures released just before the CITES Convention galvanized public belief in Europe and the United States that elephants were headed for extinction, and the sheer force of public outrage prevented any reasoned debate on the merits of a ban on ivory. The governments of Kenya, Tanzania, and Somalia, along with a number of international conservation organizations, as well as the major ivory-consuming countries, under intense political pressure from the United States and Europe threw their support behind the total ban on the ivory trade.

The ivory ban caused heated confrontations among African nations and among Western conservationists. The countries of southern Africa, particularly Zimbabwe, Botswana, and South Africa, argued that they had well-managed elephant populations, and that they depended on the revenue generated by the government-run sale of ivory and, in South Africa, elephant skin—which may actually bring in more money than ivory—from legally hunted or culled animals to run their game parks. Kenya, Tanzania, and other East African nations, with the support of most international conservation and animal rights organizations, countered that without a ban, poaching would destroy their elephant populations in short order.

The refusal to recognize regional differences in Africa resulted in part from the popular perception of Africa as a single entity, where a simple solution would work. Some people in the conservation community understood well the subtleties of the ivory trade, but the general public's overwhelming, emo-

tional response to the perceived crisis—a response fueled by
lurid advertising campaigns—made anything less than total
support for the ivory ban a practical impossibility for any conservation organization dependent on member contributions.

During the CITES conference, held in Lausanne, Switzerland, the conservation groups, who were observers, met every
afternoon following the regular session. At one of these meetings (which often grew heated) a poll was taken: how many of
those in attendance, excluding people representing groups
based in Africa, had ever been to the continent? One hand
went up.

The majority of people lobbying African governments had
no understanding of the day-to-day realities of African conservation or African life. Yet groups like Friends of Animals and
Greenpeace can, with the power of the purse, exert tremendous influence. Other groups, such as the African Wildlife
Foundation, the Environmental Investigation Agency, and the
French organization Amnistie pour les Eléphants, went so far
as to write proposals for upgrading the elephant to Appendix I
for sovereign nations, among them Tanzania, Somalia, Kenya,
and Senegal, to submit to the conference. This raises a question that goes to the heart of conservation in Africa: to what
extent should privileged conservationists, who know relatively
little about Africa, determine how many elephants live in
Kenya, or Zaire, or Zimbabwe?

Elephants bring together diverse interests—conservationists, animal rights activists, ivory traders, sport hunters—all of
whom have large amounts of money to spend on the people
and projects that fit one set of criteria or another. Trying to
please all of these groups often places well-meaning Africans
in precarious positions. At the CITES meeting, for example,
Costa Mlay, the newly appointed head of Tanzania's Department of Wildlife, served as a spokesman for East Africa's elephants, inspiring the delegates to provide the utmost protection, saying that every country had to sacrifice to save this
noble species. Then, on the last day of the meeting, Mlay stood

up and asked the convention to provide a hunting quota for elephants in Tanzania, so the government could sell sport-hunting licenses. "The roof came down on him but good," according to one observer. Mlay had no choice but to make the effort; sport hunting for elephants is a million-dollar industry in Tanzania. The convention stood firm, however, repeating to Mlay his own calls for sacrifice. Tanzania was not given a hunting quota.

Tanzania joined the ivory ban, but five southern African countries—Botswana, Malawi, South Africa, Zambia, and Zimbabwe—fought the arm-twisting and voted against it, saying they would continue to sell ivory. (Congo and Gabon also voted against the ban, but have chosen not to continue to sell ivory.) So far, however, they have found few takers. The ban appears to have succeeded in closing the legal international ivory market, a point even the skeptics of the ban have conceded. An official of Zimbabwe's Department of National Parks and Wildlife Management was unable to find any buyers for ivory during a trip to Asia in late 1990 to gauge the condition of the market. Japan would like to reopen the trade, all else being equal, but that country has become so sensitive to world opinion and its status as an environmental outlaw that it will not act unilaterally to break the ban. China and South Korea, other potential markets for ivory, apparently have no qualms over public opinion but lack the financial resources needed to make so much as a ripple on world trade.

Despite the apparent early success of the ban, many conservationists in southern Africa and elsewhere remain convinced that a continentwide approach to elephant conservation is doomed. No one has the resources to police all of sub-Saharan Africa for ivory poachers and traders. The lure of ivory remains, and eventually new markets will spring up and the easy money will drive up poaching. In the long term, the ivory ban will likely collapse. Already reports from the tropical forests of Africa indicate that hunting of elephants for ivory has continued without a break despite the ban, and authorities in Brussels confiscated over 200 pounds of ivory from Gabon on its way to South Korea. If it could be fully enforced, the ban might serve a useful purpose in the short term by allowing those elephant populations under severe stress to recover, and by reducing international demand for ivory. Even the countries most enthusiastic about selling ivory agree that Africa cannot continue to export 700 tons of ivory each year. A reasonable export is perhaps 10 percent of that figure, so closing most of the world's ivory markets will be essential.

The rationale for the global ivory ban rests on the dubious assumption that halting the ivory trade will save elephants. Emphasizing the trade, rather than elephants, is a mistake. If people continue to kill elephants, for whatever reason, then the population will decrease. The solution is to protect elephants first, and worry about international trade later. Studies of the effectiveness of the ban seem to indicate no causal relationship between poaching and the trade ban, but a close relationship between investment in park management and a reduction in elephant deaths.

The apparent success of the ivory trade ban in closing most international markets does not equal effective elephant conservation. Achieving the goal of lowering ivory prices, in fact, can have unforeseen consequences: the price of ivory in Cameroon has fallen to the point that ivory, long used for ceremonial purposes, is once again within the means of tribal leaders near that country's Korup National Park. As a result, poachers are killing elephants in Korup for the local market. The killing of elephants has increased here and elsewhere in Africa. This is undoubtedly smaller than the international market, but Cameroon's experience highlights the unpredictability of the trade.

Details of the ivory trade, however, were less important during the debate over the trade ban than the public attraction to elephants and the condemnation of poachers. Richard Leakey's greatest ally in the fight over the ivory ban is the persistent belief among many people outside of Africa that all of the continent's elephants live in Kenya, or at least face the same threats as Kenya's. Political conflict between Kenya and Somalia drives ivory poaching in Kenya's parks. The Somali poachers carry automatic weapons because they are supplied to local people by the army, or because the poachers themselves are soldiers. In late 1988, World Wildlife Fund obtained a letter from Somalia's recently deposed president, Mohammed Siyad Barre, to one of his army commanders authorizing Somali soldiers "to bring into the country elephant tusks from Kenya and Ethiopia." The letter goes on: "I further instruct you to reward them along the lines laid down in the relevant regulations." The government of Somalia would thus buy tusks from Kenya and Ethiopia, with the clear understanding that the tusks were coming from poached elephants. As a result of this letter, along with other evidence that Somalia was trading in poached ivory, the United States imposed a moratorium on all ivory from Somalia in January 1989, nine months before the worldwide ban went into effect.

Kenya's militaristic approach to poaching may be appropriate in this context. The man in charge of the campaign, Abdi Omar Bashir, embodies Kenya's war on poachers. The forty-four-year-old Bashir—whose somewhat disingenuous title is Deputy Director for Security—has an advantage over his colleagues in the newly created Kenya Wildlife Service (KWS). Unlike practically anyone else in KWS, and perhaps unlike anyone in Africa, Bashir need not be troubled by the ambiguities of wildlife conservation in a developing country. His orders are simply to protect the tourists and the animals from poachers. Bashir's office resembles the headquarters of an army on the move: a radio crackling with reports from lieutenants in the field, the walls covered with detailed maps wrapped in plastic, so battle plans can be drawn and redrawn. He looks quite at home striding about the room, pointer in hand, describing the routes poachers use, and how he will shut them off.

"Nearly all the poachers—99.9 percent—are Somalis," Bashir says. He taps the map with his pointer. "They cross the

Tana River, pick up local people here, and enter Tsavo. Some go down that way"—Bashir points to the northwest—"toward Meru National Park." Tsavo was heavily poached until quite recently, Bashir explains, partly because of its location between two rivers. "The area is inaccessible when the rivers are high—we could not get in with our vehicles, but the poachers were already there." Now Bashir has gotten a step ahead of the poachers. During the 1990 dry season he put men in the park, with enough supplies to last out the rains. In an area once patrolled by five men, Bashir now has about one hundred highly trained operatives.

In the colonial era, game scouts and wardens were the scions of the wealthy landowners. Their main interest therefore lay with protecting the land from rural villagers, who then became (in the eyes of the park authorities) poachers. Now Bashir is recruiting people who grew up with wildlife to protect it. "We have tried to recruit people who were as hard as the poachers themselves from the northern areas. The boys when they join in are already trained, through the environment. They are not people who say, 'Where is my ration today, where are my boots?' They can walk barefoot if necessary."

Bashir, who came from a police paramilitary unit, sees himself fighting a war for Kenya's economic survival. Poachers can make Kenya unsafe for tourists, and without tourism Kenya would lose its largest source of hard currency—U.S. dollars, German marks, English pounds—needed to repay foreign debt or purchase goods from abroad. But winning the war does not by itself guarantee the survival of the mass tourism industry in Kenya. Tourism rises and falls on the shifting attitudes of a relatively few well-off residents of Europe, North America, and Japan. Thus far, Kenya has exploited the myth of wild Africa by making it accessible. The challenge facing Leakey, and and the rest of KWS is to keep that myth alive.

The dependence on tourism may eventually come back to haunt Kenya, because maintaining the country's image abroad may close off options now used elsewhere on the continent.

Leakey, for example, would like to bring back safari hunting, which Kenya banned in 1977, because it has been shown to be an effective way to earn money for conservation. Courting hunters, however, could severely damage Kenya's reputation as the most reliable guardian of wildlife in Africa. Leakey is being squeezed: if he allows sport hunting, he brings in money but risks eroding his base of tourist support; if he keeps hunters out, he must rely on tourists to flock to Kenya's parks in ever greater numbers. He may still find himself in a difficult situation, as even the current numbers of tourists are beginning to damage some of the parks.

The same balancing of image on the one hand and hard cash on the other certainly played into Kenya's decision to support the ivory ban. Elsewhere, however, the constellation of factors that drives ivory poaching shifts, and new challenges arise. Namibia, Mozambique, and Sudan confront poachers armed with weapons obtained during civil war, many of whom use the money gained from ivory to support rebel causes. Conservation obviously cannot flourish in this atmosphere. Botswana, on the other hand, suffers from too many elephants—they are destroying woodland ecosystems that provide habitat for dozens of other animal species—as the government stopped safari hunting of elephants in 1978, and poaching remains limited despite a rather ineffective parks department. The rich forests of Gabon shelter healthy elephant populations, possibly Africa's largest, but no one yet knows how many, or how best to ensure their survival, if indeed any action is needed.

Abdi Omar Bashir's campaign against ivory poachers works in Kenya, but not necessarily anywhere else in Africa. Regional subtleties, however, tended to get lost amid the shouting over the ivory ban. What stood out during the debate was the preoccupation with shutting down the trade on the one hand and on the other the desire to know precisely how many elephants (and other animals as well) live in each of Africa's parks. This fascination with the animal census, reflected in the reaction to the study by the Ivory Trade Review Group, in itself betrays a certain misunderstanding, because more elephants live outside than inside the protected areas. Nevertheless, animal census figures provide a tangible measure of the success of anti-poaching campaigns, and they create their own authority.

The Grzimeks conducted the first aerial survey of the Serengeti, and they allowed no room for debate: there were 99,481 wildebeest, 57,199 zebra, 194,654 Thomson's and Grant's gazelle, 5,172 topi, 2,452 eland, 1,717 impala, 1,813 black buffalo, 1,285 kongoni, 837 giraffe, 284 waterbuck, 178 stork, 115 oryx, 60 elephant, 57 roan antelope, 55 rhinoceros, and 1,621 ostrich. The Grzimeks allowed that they might have missed a few, but only a few. They can perhaps be excused for the laughable certainty of these figures; they were the first people to conduct aerial surveys and thus were probably unaware that the process is fraught with errors. Yet, claiming to have counted from the air exactly 194,654 four-foot-high gazelle, or 55 rhino—which have a remarkable ability to melt into the bush, becoming practically invisible from a few feet away—today seems either arrogant or fraudulent.

Census figures nevertheless seem to be magnets for money. A surefire way to excite donors is to trot out today's survey, which demonstrates the latest grave development, while surveys showing more animals than expected are generally suppressed. The animal census has thus become an indispensable tool of park management. In the late 1970s, there was suddenly a great surge of interest in how many elephants remained in Africa, and whether the population was increasing or decreasing. Elephants, however, inhabit such a vast area that making an accurate count is economically and technically impossible. Any estimate of the number of elephants in Africa is no more than a guess.

In 1979, the International Union for Conservation of Nature and Natural Resources (IUCN), a conservation group based in Switzerland, in collaboration with WWF and the New York Zoological Society, completed a continentwide survey of

African elephants. That survey established the minimum figure of 1.3 million elephants, which would be the basis of such hostility ten years later. This figure reflected the educated guesses of countless observers with widely varying skills, yet it immediately took on the qualities of fact and permanence in the press and even in scientific circles that remain to this day. The census has been updated periodically, but the newest figures are little better than the original guesses.

The key person in the IUCN survey was the noted elephant researcher Iain Douglas-Hamilton. Douglas-Hamilton's interest in census taking is relatively recent, as he began his career studying elephant behavior, albeit almost by accident. In 1963, while still an undergraduate zoology student at Oxford, he worked briefly as an assistant to John Owen, director of Tanganyika's national parks, and studied wildebeest. Douglas-Hamilton resolved at that point to pursue a doctorate in zoology, and he returned to Owen two years later with a proposal to study the Serengeti lions for his doctoral research. Owen turned the young scientist down, because George Schaller—already widely known for his work on the mountain gorillas in Zaire—was about to begin a project on the lions. Owen told Douglas-Hamilton that while the Serengeti was not a possibility, Tanganyika's Parks Department needed some research done on the elephants in Lake Manyara National Park, southeast of Ngorongoro Crater. Douglas-Hamilton and his Kenyan-born wife, Oria (a relative of the creator of Babar, famed elephant of children's books), would spend the next decade studying Lake Manyara's elephants.

Douglas-Hamilton recognized that to carry out his research he would have to get close enough to each of the over five hundred elephants in the park to be able to identify them on sight, closer to wild elephants than anyone had been before. The best way to distinguish one elephant from another is by looking at the pattern of cuts and tears in the ears, and by the tusks. For Douglas-Hamilton, compiling a photographic record of these characteristics often meant confronting head-on an elephant in full charge, with ears flared wide. His habit of approaching elephants on foot soon gave Douglas-Hamilton a reputation for recklessness which was supported by other evidence of his unconcern for personal safety; he contracted bilharzia, broke his back in an untimely encounter with a rhino, crashed his airplane, and had his Land Rover dismantled by an angry bull elephant. His recklessness also got him into a situation where he had to shoot one of the elephants he was studying.

Although Douglas-Hamilton's reputation at times overshadowed his work, his willingness to take on research that more prudent researchers avoided allowed him to make some important contributions to our knowledge about elephants. He was among the first to use the techniques of individual recognition in wildlife research, and he was the first to analyze in depth the family groups that are the basic unit of elephant social organization. Now, however, Douglas-Hamilton seems content to be known as the world's leading elephant-counter, his poor eyesight notwithstanding. The title may turn out to be less flattering than Douglas-Hamilton would like.

Douglas-Hamilton designed the questionnaires used in IUCN's 1979 survey and subsequent surveys as well. Those questionnaires and regular requests for updated information were circulated to game scouts, wardens, and other people working in the bush who, it was assumed, could estimate the elephant population of a given area. In Niger, for example, the survey was sent to the staff at Parc National du W du Niger (it is located at a spot where the Niger River folds into a distinctive "W" shape). There were few funds or staff available to conduct an East Africa-style elephant census, complete with airplanes and computers; the government had other priorities after suffering through the country's worst drought in recorded history. Nevertheless, the park staff filled out the survey with its best guesses as to how many elephants there were and their range, despite the fact that the staff didn't even know where the elephants went during the rainy season. When the continental elephant survey was issued—with great fanfare—there in black and white was the estimate of 700 elephants for Parc National du W du Niger and 1,500 for all of Niger, with no discussion of how much guesswork went into the figures.

The 1979 survey claimed to be a scientific study of thirty-five countries, but in nineteen of those there was only one source of information, so there was no chance of cross-checking data. In fourteen countries the single informant could give only "rough estimates" of elephant numbers. In other words, they guessed. One individual came up with the elephant counts for five countries.

The survey estimated a total of 16,000–17,000 elephants in West Africa; in 1989, the population was set at 19,000. Is this "increase" due to successful conservation? Not likely. It simply illustrates how difficult it is to count animals—even huge ones like elephants. At the same time, according to the surveys, more than half of Niger's elephants supposedly died between 1979 and 1989. This "failure" also seems fanciful, but the crisis mentality over declining elephant populations persists. The gloomy figures are credited, the rosy ones scorned, because bad news raises more money than good.

The fascination with numbers of elephants knows practically no bounds. In Malawi's Kasungu National Park, researchers set out to make an aerial count. The standard procedure involves dividing the area to be covered into long transects, which vary in width from area to area depending on terrain, the species of interest, the number of flights to be made, and so on. The researchers then hang long parallel struts on either side of the plane. The plane flies at an altitude calculated so that when the two animal-counters who sit behind the pilot look out the windows, the amount of land between the struts corresponds to a predetermined transect width. The plane flies up and down the transects, and the number of elephants counted within them serves as a sample for extrapolating the population of a much larger area through a rather complex statistical analysis.

In Malawi, the researchers were using the aerial figures as a check on an estimate derived from the volume of elephant dung in a given area, in an effort to come up with an accurate system for counting elephant without the expense of an airplane. This "dropping count method"—based on a formula incorporating the number of times an elephant defecates in twenty-four hours, the decomposition rate of elephant dung on the ground, and the number of droppings found—requires time and manpower, the commodities readily available in Africa, but little money.

The aerial censuses estimated approximately 2,500 elephants in Kasungu, a park of broad-leafed woodland on the Zambian border, just 70 miles northwest of Lilongwe, Malawi's capital. With this data, and estimates from other areas containing elephants, estimates for Malawi as a whole came to between 4,000 and 4,500 elephants, based on both dropping and elephant counts. This was the figure submitted to the continental survey. It turned out, however, that one of the census takers in the airplane was consistently counting elephants outside of the strip, skewing the Kasungu National Park figures upward by some 1,500 elephants. By the time the scientists recognized the error, the figure of 4,000 to 4,500 elephants had already been published and thus had become established as holy writ.

When the new elephant population figures for the continent were released—including a corrected figure of 2,300 for Malawi—people suddenly panicked about the devastating loss of nearly 50 percent of Malawi's elephants. Numerous articles appeared, including one in *Time* magazine, speculating on the cause of the decline, and proposing solutions to the increase in poaching. The description of the census corrections was reported in the scientific literature in 1987 but was never widely publicized, so people around the world leapt to the defense of elephants that never existed.

Conservation organizations and international aid agencies often use the elephant census figures to determine where to spend their money. The figures thus become a means of keeping score, determining which countries are losing and which winning. When the numbers do not mean anything real, the meaningfulness of the process collapses.

Census figures can also be manipulated when they don't say what people may want to hear. Botswana and Zimbabwe maintain that their elephant populations are increasing and must be culled to protect the habitat. A number of conservation groups—most with an animals rights agenda and no experience working in Africa—have called into question the data presented by the two countries, suggesting to the press and others that they have been faked. The elephants' doom is money in these groups' pockets. Successes do not seem to have the same result.

Most of these organizations focus their attention on East Africa, where the decline in elephant numbers is best documented. Few doubts have been raised about the accuracy of the information for the region. The open plains and wooded grasslands—unlike the forests of West and Central Africa—are suited for aerial elephant counts. The science of elephant counting theoretically supports improved protection and management. The real question is what to do with the information.

The census became part of a broader theory of elephant ecology and management which held that each part of the elephants' range could only support a certain precise number of animals, and that when the population exceeded that predetermined figure, it had to be reduced, usually through the technique called "culling." An elephant cull is a horrifying spectacle. Rangers spot the elephants by helicopter, then move in with automatic weapons and slaughter an entire herd in minutes, amid the screams of panicked elephants.

The culling process, in theory, is brutally rational: killing the herd preserves the age structure of the local elephant population as a whole (in any event the younger elephants would be so traumatized by what they had seen that they probably would not survive), and too many elephants living in one place quickly decimate their environment, leading to massive starvation. Nevertheless, elephant culls are so disturbing that Cynthia Moss, who has spent her career studying the elephants in Kenya's Amboseli National Park, has come to the rather extreme view that it would be better to have no elephants than to subject some to culling.

Such passion obscures the hard choices that must be made in elephant conservation. Tsavo National Park in southeastern Kenya provides the classic example of what happens when there are too many elephants on too little land. The park, designated primarily to protect Kenya's largest elephant herd in 1948, covers 8,000 square miles, divided into Tsavo East and Tsavo West by the Nairobi-Mombasa Road. By the early 1970s, the elephant population had grown so vast—both as a result of natural increase and because elephants were forced into the park by increasing human settlements on surrounding land—that the once extensive woodlands were being destroyed. Observers likened the carnage to the battlefields of World War I. When a severe drought hit the region in 1971, perhaps as many as fifteen thousand elephants in and around the park died of starvation. Ivory could be gathered like maize, and villagers from near and far—also hard-hit by the drought—rushed in to collect the bounty. When no more dead elephants were to be found, they took up poaching, and the elephants, deprived of the sheltering forests, were easy targets on the open plains.

In Tsavo it may well have been kinder to kill some elephants, thus saving the woodlands and improving the chances for the rest of the elephant population, but no culls were conducted. Even here, however, the situation was not clear cut; elephants play a major role in the cycle of forest regeneration, and a steep reduction in the elephant population may have altered this process. Elsewhere, the problems become yet more complicated. Culling based on elephant censuses is particularly problematic. In Zimbabwe, scientists decided in 1975 that the population of the Sengwa Wildlife Research Area, south of

Lake Kariba, thought to be over five hundred, was far too high, and should be brought down to one hundred or fewer individuals through a massive culling operation. The park authorities shot four hundred elephants, and conducted a census on the last day of the operation. To their dismay, they counted precisely as many elephants as they had on Day 1. Wild debate broke out. Some argued that elephants were moving onto the area as fast as they were being shot, others that some unlucky elephants from neighboring areas had wandered into the culling area; still others faulted the original census figures.

The scientists directing the culling operation then took a rather unorthodox approach: rather than deciding how many elephants to remove, they fixed the number that should remain. This meant putting radio tags on herds totaling three hundred elephants, and shooting the rest, some four hundred animals. Thus, from a population which in 1975 was believed to be roughly five hundred elephants, park authorities culled eight hundred and three hundred still remained. "That was not one of our better efforts," Rowan Martin, one of the leaders of the operation, says now, in one of the great understatements of conservation.

The sickening films of elephant culls turn up repeatedly in nature programs, usually to make a point about cruelty and waste of life. Viewing such films, one almost agrees with Cynthia Moss—better no elephants at all than to subject any elephant to this. The images convey powerful but simplistic messages: killing elephants is wrong at all times and in all places, and the people who carry out such acts deserve the same condemnation. The ethical component of that statement is highly debatable, and the characterization of those involved in culling as cruel brutes is patently false. The rangers sent out to shoot elephants in a culling operation find the task more awful than anyone who has not lived and worked near elephants can imagine. Few, if any, people who have ever witnessed or participated in a cull found it less than agonizing. Many refuse even to discuss the experience.

Our emotional attachment to elephants deepens our instinctual outrage over culling—the response would be quite different if someone decided to start culling bushpigs. That attachment has grown as continued research has filled in the gaps in our understanding of elephant behavior. Conservationists clearly need to learn the subtleties of elephant behavior in order to find the most effective means of elephant conservation, but too often research and management never meet.

The elephants throughout East Africa now rank among the most intensively studied animals on earth. The region has so many elephant biologists that between them they probably know most of the elephants by name. Yet the years of research also reveal the magnitude of the fundamental problem: in a continent struggling to feed a booming human population, an adult elephant must eat 300 pounds of food per day. In a dry climate, that means elephants need a range of up to 1,000 square miles.

Few of the elephant researchers have demonstrated any interest in the more practical aspects of elephant conservation. Some, like Cynthia Moss, have brought their important scientific achievements to the general public, greatly increasing the awareness and understanding of elephants and their role in the African ecosystem. But as Moss admits, "I always thought [studying elephants] was a marvelously selfish thing to do."

Moss carried on and deepened the behavioral research begun by Iain Douglas-Hamilton, as Douglas-Hamilton moved away from science and into international conservation politics. Moss, an American who received her field training from Douglas-Hamilton, spent more than fourteen years studying the elephants in Amboseli, and her work provides a clear picture of the close bonds formed within elephant families.

Elephants live complex social lives. Females stay with their immediate families, which average nine or ten animals in Amboseli, while males leave the group when they reach maturity to lead generally solitary lives. The family group consists of an older female—the matriarch—along with her older daughters and their offspring, both male and female. This group usually acts together, eating, drinking, traveling, and resting at the same time, under the guidance of the matriarch. The natural bonds between these closely related elephants are reinforced by physical contact—rubbing, touching with trunks, playing among the younger ones—and by vocalizations, some of which are deep rumblings below the range that a human ear can detect.

Elephants form tight bonds with other family units, which may or may not be closely related. The strength of the bonds, Moss says, can be judged by what she calls the "greeting ceremony." Tremendous screaming and trumpeting marks the meeting of two closely bonded families that have been apart for some time. The elephants click tusks together, flap their ears wildly, and intertwine their trunks. At these moments, Moss is convinced, elephants are experiencing joy.

Like Douglas-Hamilton before her, Moss has now turned her passion for elephants from scientific research to conservation. The transition is not an easy one. Only one member of the close-knit community of elephant researchers (called by some the "Prima Bwanas"), Joyce Poole, has tried to tie together the disparate strands of research, conservation, and management. Poole studied the sexual behavior of male elephants in Kenya's Amboseli National Park for fourteen years. She spent much of that time with Cynthia Moss, Poole's work on male elephants providing the counterpoint to Moss's focus on females. Poole conducted important research in Amboseli: once or twice a year, adult male African elephants enter a physiological and psychological state known as musth. Long recognized in Asian elephants (*musth* is a Hindi word) and described in 1952 by the African safari hunter and game ranger John A. Hunter, musth plays an important role in mating. Male elephants over the age of thirty-five spend most of their time alone or in peaceful co-existence with other adult males. This harmony comes to an abrupt end when an elephant enters musth. The musth bull goes in search of females, his temporal glands start to swell, he begins dribbling urine, the testosterone level in his blood rises sharply, and he becomes extremely aggressive toward other males, and humans as well. Indeed, everything about the animal changes; Poole can detect an elephant in musth from half a mile away simply by the way he walks.

Elephants rarely fight. Males will often engage in friendly tests of strength, but these bouts do not escalate to real violence. Musth bulls, however, wage battles that can result in broken tusks or even death, with one bull throwing the other to the ground and goring it with his tusk. These fights may last for eight hours or more.

Musth confers great sexual advantages. While a non-musth bull can mate, he will always give way to a musth bull, so if a musth bull finds a female in estrus, he will usually be able to mate with her. Musth bulls also do an excellent job of advertising their presence to other elephants by their secretions and behavior. They announce that they are healthy, horny, and ready to fight.

After years of observing the same relatively small population of elephants, and following individual bulls over the two or three months that they are in musth, Poole now believes that musth enables a bull to put all of his reproductive energies into a short period of time. A musth bull spends that time pursuing females and chasing off or fighting other bulls. Poole found that the bulls lost weight throughout the musth period, and by the end were quite thin. The bulls obviously could not afford to expend so much energy year-round, so musth has apparently evolved as an alternative strategy. The time of year a bull comes into musth depends on his position in the dominance hierarchy: to survive and mate, a bull cannot be in musth at the same time as another bull dominant to him. The older, dominant bulls tend to be in musth at the best times for finding females in estrus.

Poole continued her work on the sexual behavior of male

elephants until Richard Leakey hired her in June 1990 to direct the elephant conservation program at the Kenya Wildlife Service. She now must confront the whole range of conservation dilemmas: if and where (not to mention how) to build elephant-proof fences, if and when to shoot crop-raiding elephants, identifying the top priorities among elephant populations scattered throughout Kenya's twenty-eight parks and reserves and the remaining elephants outside these protected areas. Understanding the sex drive of a bull elephant was a good deal simpler.

Poole bristles a bit at being defined as a "manager," preferring the term "conservationist." Semantics aside, Poole now directs one of the most important, and certainly the most visible, elephant conservation efforts in Africa. She sees her options from the perspective of an animal behaviorist, which means she is somewhat at odds with her new colleagues in other African wildlife departments. Like most wildlife officials in the region, Poole supports the ivory ban, but she will use her own criteria for determining whether the ban has achieved its objective.

"Everyone gets hung up on the numbers," Poole says. "The point is that the drop in the elephant population due to poaching was so fast that you hardly had any adult males in some areas, the matriarchs were gone, the family structure was destroyed. You were destroying a species. To me, an elephant is more than an animal that is gray, thick-skinned, with a trunk, tusks, and big ears. It is the whole social makeup of that animal. So what if you had a million elephants, if all you had were orphans running around?

"For a population like Tsavo, if one is not just concerned about numbers but the structure of the population, then it is going to take decades before you are back to a normal population," Poole contends. "If that is your criterion, then the ivory trade should not be opened for an extremely long time. But that's not most people's criterion. For most people, it's just numbers."

The emphasis on population structure seems like a rational

alternative to census mania. It may not be quite so simple, however; elephant populations may be much more resilient than Poole suggests, even when family units have been destroyed and the age structure badly skewed. In 1919, for example, Major P. J. Pretorius—a descendant of the man for whom the South African capital is named—set about exterminating the elephants around the town of Addo, some 450 miles east of Cape Town, because growing human settlements were pushing up against a nearby protected area, and the animals were raiding crops. In eleven months, Pretorius shot one hundred twenty elephants, and by year's end only about sixteen remained in the park. The remaining few took cover in the inaccessible areas of the park, in a dense low evergreen thicket. The hunt was called off.

In 1931, only twelve elephants—two young males and ten females—remained. The area was officially protected, and renamed Addo Elephant National Park. The elephants still raided crops, however, and they continued to be shot. Elephant reproduction kept just ahead of the hunters' guns, and by 1953 the population had grown to seventeen. The next year, park authorities constructed a fence of railway ties and cables around 5,400 acres of the park. The park has gradually been expanded, and now encompasses nearly 20,000 acres. As human population pressures increased in the region, the elephants thrived within the fenced sanctuary; in 1964 there were 35 elephants, in 1976 the number had reached 77, and by 1991 173 elephants lived in Addo.

Without intending to, the park authorities had set up a controlled experiment: what happens to a remnant elephant population freed from the pressures of poaching and human settlements? The results are striking: in thirty-four years, a small population of young elephants grew almost ninefold, and still retained a high degree of genetic variation. Today, due to the limited size of the park and pressure on their habitat, there are so many elephants in Addo that they may have to be culled in the next five to ten years.

Addo National Park is an extreme example of both elephant

demographics and park management. When faced with a conflict between humans clearing more land for farming and animals searching for pasture, the government's first response was to kill all the elephants. When that failed, they put up a fence, and now they may have to return to killing the elephants.

Our knowledge of elephants has advanced immeasurably since Major Pretorius began his assault on Addo. Joyce Poole and other scientists soon may be able to design innovative conservation programs based on their deep understanding of elephant behavior. That would be a major accomplishment, as it would place science, not emotion, at the center of the debate about elephant conservation. In a larger sense, using scientific research to solve the problems facing wildlife management is beginning to move conservation away from the simplistic assumptions about Africa. For too long, scientists came to Africa, collected their data, and went home, leaving our misperceptions undisturbed. After nearly a century of conservation in Africa, scientists and wildlife managers are just beginning to explore their common ground.

CHAPTER V

▼ ▼ ▼

THE SCIENTISTS TAKE OVER

In those days there was little question of research being geared for park management, and a determined smash-and-grab raid for PhD's was started by youngsters who regarded the Serengeti and its animals as a vast natural laboratory to be looted at will.

—Myles Turner

Joyce Poole *brings* scientific training to the practical tasks of conservation. Few people have taken that route. That so many scientists came to Africa to study wildlife and only a handful remained to help conserve it reflects the scientists' professional training and interests, but also the historical animosity between scientists and park managers. No one symbolizes that conflict better than Myles Turner, a warden in Serengeti National Park from 1956 to 1972. Turner knew the land, people, and animals better than anyone save for the Maasai. By the mid-1960s, however, Turner began to bridle at an annoying trend: the Serengeti had become a popular topic among researchers, and the opinions of a game warden and former hunter no longer carried much weight. "Scientists are in charge of the animals these days," Turner told the writer Peter Matthiessen in 1969. "We just keep things going for them. But now and then we catch them out—there are still a few things they don't know."

That statement is still true. Scientists working in the Serengeti and elsewhere often labor under the same myths that plague other aspects of conservation. Scientific research has usually occurred in a cultural vacuum, with little interaction with Africans. Biological and ecological examination of the minutiae of an African ecosystem not only misses the cultural forest in pursuit of exceptional trees, but scientists sometimes appear to be studying wildlife into extinction.

The battle lines between science and park management could not be drawn more clearly than they were in the Serengeti: some of the world's finest young researchers flocked there, only to be met at the gate by Myles Turner, a man who had lived in Africa since the age of five and who had little patience for neophytes pursuing their doctoral diplomas. In Turner's eyes, science contributed nothing to the conservation of wild animals. He felt the scientists came to Africa merely in search of professional advancement.

The Tanganyika Game Department offered little practical support when Turner arrived in 1956 to take over the post of warden for the Western Serengeti. He and his wife moved into a thirty-year-old mud house, with supplies consisting of a little cash, some cement and timber, two aging vehicles, and a half dozen decrepit rifles. A staff of ten served the entire park.

And Turner stepped right into the middle of the political storm over the park's boundaries. The colonial government, under intense pressure from abroad, had enlarged the park and created the Ngorongoro Conservation Area, as recommended by the Fauna Preservation Society. To Myles Turner fell the task of establishing the park's new borders. Turner took a disciplined, no-nonsense approach to his job, and with few supplies or supporters and an immense park to patrol, it is no wonder that he had little use for anything that did not contribute in a practical way to the management of the Serengeti. Turner nevertheless got along quite well with Bernhard Grzimek, who as much as anyone was responsible for opening the Serengeti to scientific study.

Turner had been at his post for two years when he was informed that two German zoologists would be arriving in the Serengeti by plane, so he began to clear an airstrip. He had completed about half the job—the rest of the strip being downed trees and thorn bush—when he heard the drone of an engine coming in over the trees. Turner looked up to see a single-engine plane painted with zebra stripes, Michael Grzimek at the controls. "They'll never land here," Turner thought at the time. But land they did, using every inch of the cleared strip. Michael Grzimek was a skilled but reckless pilot, and his daring may have contributed to the crash that killed him in January 1959. His death did more to further the cause of science in the Serengeti than anything he achieved while alive. The park's board of trustees made a public appeal for a memorial, and created the Michael Grzimek Memorial Laboratory. The laboratory in turn became the centerpiece of the most ambitious scientific effort in Africa, the Serengeti Research Project (SRP), which began operations in 1961.

For Turner, a few scientists like the Grizmeks or George Schaller, who conducted his pioneering research on the Serengeti lions during Turner's tenure, did not unduly clutter the Serengeti's open spaces. Science and park management were on an equal footing until 1966, when the Serengeti Research Institute (the renamed SRP) opened its new building, with $600,000 worth of facilities and housing for up to twenty scientists. The balance between science and management had shifted dramatically.

Researchers poured over the plains, and Turner's distaste for science hardened into contempt. What galled Turner most was the number of animals that researchers killed "for study." Though Turner himself repeatedly turned down the scientists' requests for shooting licenses, his superiors at park headquarters often overruled him. Serengeti in particular attracted many scientists whose research plans called for shooting wildlife in protected areas, which was prohibited in Kenya and Uganda but not in Tanganyika. As a result, between 1964 and 1971 researchers killed thousands of animals in the interests of science. Hundreds of orphaned calves were abandoned to die of starvation or to be taken by predators or poachers.

Considering that Turner and his rangers were obligated to

arrest local people for shooting animals in the Serengeti, Turner found it ironic that he was also frequently enlisted to pull the trigger for research killing. In 1969, he announced to the parks director, John Owen, that he would no longer take part in such hunts. Not long after, Turner brought in the international media and conservationists—including Martha Gelhorn, a well-known journalist and Ernest Hemingway's third wife—and several of their reports roundly condemned the killing of animals for research in the Serengeti. The practice is now rare.

The killing gnawed at Turner, particularly because he was most often asked to shoot buffalo, his favorite species. Toward the end of his life Turner worked in the Masai Mara, and one day he was out on a long hike with Holly Dublin, a young ecologist from Seattle who had come to Kenya in 1981 to conduct research for her doctoral dissertation. "He used to walk along carrying this huge gun and puffing on a cigarette," Dublin recalls. "I was walking a couple steps behind him when he turned to me and said, 'All right, I would like to know.' I said, 'What's that, Myles?' And he said, 'Did shooting all those buffalo ever achieve anything?'"

It probably did not. Wildlife researchers in Africa historically ignored the disruptions their studies can cause the animals, and rarely considered how the results of the research could be translated into more effective management of parks or of wild populations in general. Many scientists sincerely believe that they are working for conservation, and scientists and park managers must share the responsibility for the failure of science and management to find common ground. In Africa—East Africa in particular—boxloads of scientific papers have not contributed to conservation in a meaningful way. In his memoirs, *My Serengeti Years,* Turner put the matter bluntly:

> Out of the many hundreds of thousands of dollars spent on research in East Africa during the "fashionable" decade of the

1960s, little if anything has been achieved to my knowledge. Far better if the money had been spent on anti-poaching and education. How much was spent on research in East Africa during those heady years? I have heard the figure of $10,000,-000 quoted by a man in a position to know. He may be right. One thing is sure: it was a great confidence trick, and virtually nothing has ever come out of it to help the hard pressed animals of East Africa.

Turner might have added that the people of East Africa also saw no benefits from the wealth of scientific data coming out of the Serengeti. Yet Turner overstated his case. Certainly the bulk of the research carried out in the Serengeti and elsewhere in Africa consisted of more than a con game. The research contributed valuable information about the diet, social structures, reproduction, and diseases of many of Africa's animals. Few people, perhaps not even Turner himself, would argue that the research should never have been done, or that scientific investigations in the Serengeti caused great harm, except in the extreme case of killing the animals. Turner's quarrel with researchers stemmed from his accurate observation that the knowledge they gained provided no tangible benefits to wildlife or people. Yet the common perception is that field research is the equivalent of, or at least a vitally important part of, successful conservation.

What has emerged from the onslaught of science in the Serengeti? The black rhino that once thrived in the region is on the brink of extinction, *if* there are any left. The buffalo population in the northern Serengeti, once the stronghold of the ecosystem, has been drastically reduced by illegal hunters, while hunting and increased agriculture on the park borders has forced the elephant population to leave for the Masai Mara in Kenya. All this has been exhaustively documented through scientific research, but with little direct support for the work that could conceivably provide some relief. Only recently has the human factor been taken into account in the Serengeti (see

Chapter VIII). Despite millions of dollars for science, little work has been done with the rural communities around the park, and management activities continue to suffer from a lack of funding.

The perceived role of science in African conservation springs in part from a deep faith in the scientific method. Science and technology are the most powerful tools that the West has at its disposal. The inhabitants of the primeval African wilderness cannot protect it, many people outside of Africa believe, so it follows that the West must take on this task, and must send in its finest troops, the scientific foot soldiers.

Myles Turner's encounters with the first wave of scientists in Africa produced an overwhelmingly negative reaction. But Turner's experience may not be entirely applicable elsewhere in Africa, particularly in southern Africa, where science and management have been more closely linked, and in the tropical forests of equatorial Africa. In the forests, scientists contribute vitally important information about biological diversity that the untrained eye cannot see. The layman thinks of a tropical rain forest as a uniform green carpet, while the botanist counts one hundred unique species of tree at a glance, and the entomologist revels in an entire zoo of beetles. Here science points out those particularly significant areas that should be protected but otherwise might be overlooked.

The current efforts to restore degraded tropical forests in Africa and elsewhere illustrate how conservation and science can support each other. Forest restoration is a numbingly difficult project. A tropical forest depends on an intricate web of relationships among plants, insects, birds, mammals, fish, and humankind. Putting the pieces of the puzzle together again requires a deep understanding of these relationships that only years of scientific study can bring. The restoration projects—the most sophisticated of which are in Latin America—marry science to conservation, and they may provide invaluable information about how best to manage the resources of the world's tropical forests.

What fascinates us about the rain forests is what we cannot see: animals hidden in dense jungle, and, even more subtle, the vital processes that create such staggering diversity. Science opens this world that would otherwise be closed. The effort to attract wide public support for rain forest conservation to a large degree depends on science, as the forests lack the charismatic megafauna so easily found on the plains. Unlike the rain forest, the African plains need little explanation. No place on earth offers a better opportunity to observe the behavior of large mammals than the Serengeti. The power of open spaces to captivate the human imagination both created the myth of wild Africa and attracted the scientists. Science and myth manage to co-exist quite comfortably in our image of Africa. Rather than modifying our perceptions to more accurately reflect African reality, as portrayed by research, we have adopted the myth that scientific research in its own right could save the wilderness.

A more mundane consideration also contributed to the onslaught of scientists in the Serengeti. The plains sit between 3,000 and 5,000 feet above sea level, guaranteeing a comfortable climate nearly year round. Most scientists, reasonably enough, include personal comfort in their calculations about where to conduct their research, and therefore prefer the pleasant prospect of several years or more in the Serengeti over, say, Gabon, where tropical forests at sea level mean month upon dreary month of rain, heat, humidity, and numerous tropical parasites, among other discomforts. Scientists know a great deal about certain unique areas in Africa, like the Serengeti, but hardly anything at all about the vast remaining areas, which may be uncomfortable but no less important.

The bibliography of professional literature on the Serengeti lists over five hundred publications, not including the countless popular articles, books, and films. With such a mass of scholarship, one would expect a breadth of approaches and techniques. Unfortunately, the Serengeti specialists are a rather select group. Most received their training at either

Texas A&M University or Oxford. In their heyday these two institutions cornered the market on research in the Serengeti and Tanzania for their home countries. The United States and the United Kingdom, along with (West) Germany, produced most of the researchers working in East Africa.

The limited number of institutions sending researchers to Tanzania led to a problem familiar to wildlife biologists: in effect, the scientists came from a limited "gene pool," and they were vulnerable to changing environmental conditions. A peculiar sort of environmental catastrophe struck in 1967, in the form of academic pettiness at Oxford. Until that year, students of both ethology (the study of animal behavior) and ecology at the university pursued doctoral research in East Africa. Due to a political dispute between several professors, however, the ecology students were told to either switch departments and start studying animal behavior, or leave the university. Few chose to leave, and thus the study of the Serengeti for many years focused narrowly on animal behavior, using techniques pioneered in large part by a single Oxford professor, Niko Tinbergen. Tinbergen, who shared the Nobel Prize for Physiology or Medicine in 1973 with Konrad Lorenz and Karl von Frisch for their work on revitalizing the study of animal behavior, emphasized the detailed analysis of the ways in which an animal responds to various stimuli in its environment. His method relied on a broad, observational approach to the behavior of a single species, rather than to the interactions between numerous different species and the larger ecosystem.

The most visible result of research in the Serengeti was a comprehensive textbook edited by Sinclair and Norton-Griffiths entitled *Serengeti: Dynamics of an Ecosystem*. First published in 1979 (a sequel is in the works), it has become the bible for scientists interested in the Serengeti. It is indeed an impressive piece of work, filled with contributions from prominent researchers. A thorough reading of its thirteen chapters— "Grassland and Herbivore Dynamics," "Feeding Strategy and the Pattern of Resource Partitioning in Ungulates," "A Simulation of Grazing, Browsing, and Fire on the Vegetation Dynamics of the Serengeti," for example—provides more detailed information about the Serengeti's wild populations than is available for practically any other group of animals on earth.

The editors, Anthony Sinclair (a student of Tinbergen's at Oxford) and Michael Norton-Griffiths, suggest the book has a purpose beyond compiling the current scientific knowledge. Scientists working in the Serengeti, they claim, intended "to obtain sufficient understanding of how the ecosystem worked, so they could advise on the proper conservation of the area." *Serengeti: Dynamics of an Ecosystem* would further this process by providing "the information and rationale for a sound, long-term management plan for the Serengeti ecosystem." Sinclair and Norton-Griffiths also feel compelled to defend the amount of money spent on research in the Serengeti by stating that their book provides "a synthesis of results which can be used as the basis for management proposals."

Save for a paragraph or two, however, *Serengeti: Dynamics of an Ecosystem* contains no recommendations about how the results of the various studies could be used for conservation. Norton-Griffiths directed the Serengeti Ecological Monitoring Programme from 1969 until 1977, while Sinclair is a noted ecologist on the faculty of the University of British Columbia with long experience in Africa, so they were certainly in a position to know what should or should not be done in the region. Yet their book says only a few words about how to manage the Serengeti.

Perhaps they did not know what to say. The 1960s and 1970s saw an explosion of research into wild populations, in Africa and elsewhere, but also a widening gulf between new fields such as community ecology and the traditional disciplines of forestry, fisheries, and the like. In the past ten years, finally, both sides have begun searching for ways to bridge the gap. Scientists are shaping a new discipline that takes account of conservation concerns, while wildlife managers are looking for ways to put research to work.

In the early 1980s, attempts to reconcile conservationists who practiced applied science with their more academic brethren crystallized into a new field called "conservation biology." Conservation biology traces its birth to the publication of a book by that name in 1980, edited by Michael E. Soulé and B.A. Wilcox. In a second book with the same title published six years later, Soulé, who is on the faculty of the School of Natural Resources at the University of Michigan, attempted to sketch the outlines of the new field.

"The idea of conservation biology," wrote Soulé, "seems to convey several things at once, including scholarship, a common purpose, and the potential for making a significant personal contribution to the world." Soulé went on to quote Victor Hugo: "There is one thing stronger than all the armies in the world: and that is an idea whose time has come."

The time for conservation biology has arrived, but the discipline is still experiencing growing pains. Soulé pointed to two potential problems, elitism and isolation, and both have yet to be solved. Conservation biology remains of interest primarily to members of university departments in Europe and North America, and it is just beginning to find its way into the day-to-day activities of conservation. "If conservation biology becomes isolated in the mental world of academia, it will be of little use," wrote Soulé. "Its prescriptions will not be informed by the real-world problems of managers, by the actual circumstances of the people who are most involved and affected. . . ."

Soulé was right to be worried about the isolation of conservation biology from actual conservation management. Part of the problem stems from a lack of training. Only a few universities have taken the first steps toward degree programs in conservation biology, which would necessarily include training (to the extent possible) in how to function within the government bureaucracies and other institutions of the developing world. To compound the problem, few wildlife managers have had extensive scientific training, so a state of mutual ignorance persists. With limited resources for conservation biology, little money is available to speed the transfer of information from the academy to the field, or, perhaps more appropriately, in the other direction.

Traditional, rigorous scientific training does not guarantee effective conservation; indeed, the caution such training encourages may hinder the urgent action that is sometimes required. Scientists usually enjoy the luxury of entertaining any number of alternative hypotheses before deciding which best explains a given situation. A successful field program, however, demands action. As Soulé puts it, "in conservation, dithering and endangering are often linked."

Scientists also covet the ability to see nature in all its complexity. This vision can be paralyzing, leading merely to repeated calls for more research. Many of the studies in *Serengeti: Dynamics of an Ecosystem*, for example, conclude with just such a recommendation. Those calls were answered, but still nothing changed. Michael Norton-Griffith's Serengeti Ecological Monitoring Programme (SEMP), dormant after the closing of the Kenya-Tanzania border in 1977, was revived in 1985. In 1988, Anthony Sinclair and Bakari Mbano, a Tanzanian biologist, evaluated SEMP. The result, a nineteen-page report, recommends that the status quo remain undisturbed, with expatriates in control until Tanzanians receive further training and can take over the job. That recommendation rings hollow in light of the years of research in the Serengeti which have made no contribution to training local people.

The review by Sinclair and Mbano is the only evaluation of the scientific activities conducted off and on by SEMP over the past twenty years. In their report they concluded that while aerial surveys of animal populations had been successful, the attempts to train Tanzanians in any sort of ecological monitoring had been an utter failure. In other words, the one effort that could have made a practical contribution to conservation of the Serengeti had produced nothing. The project purchased thousands of dollars worth of high-tech computers and sophisticated software, which the Tanzanians, due to lack of training, were unable to use. In any event, it would have been impossible to maintain that equipment out in the bush, where it would have been most useful.

All the detailed results of SEMP's research—data on rainfall, hunting, predation, vegetation maps made with the help of satellites, etc.—are aimed at an audience outside of Africa, predominantly other scientists and funding organizations. Chock full of census maps and figures, and also of repeated statements about the relevance of monitoring to conservation, the reports never even hint at how the data should be incorporated into either short- or long-term decisions about managing the parks.

When the border between Kenya and Tanzania was closed in 1977, and SEMP in Tanzania shut its doors, the Kenyan government continued to monitor the wildlife populations in the Mara through an organization called the Kenya Rangelands Ecological Monitoring Unit, or KREMU (it has now got a more up-to-date name, the Department of Resource Surveys and Remote Sensing). In the late 1970s, KREMU's pilots conducted monthly aerial surveys, while ground ecologists studied habitat types, productivity, and conditions. Holly Dublin, a former student of Sinclair, made use of this and other data in the Masai Mara Ecological Monitoring Project, which she still directs.

Dublin thus has seen the relationship between conservation and research from both sides, and believes that scientists and managers share the blame for the hostility that has prevented them from working together. Wiry, energetic, with a sharp tongue and a temper to match, Dublin combines research skills with a management-oriented style, an approach that even won over Myles Turner. Yet Dublin was often frustrated by what she saw as the failure of park managers to take advantage of research designed for their use. "The bottom line in the Mara is that management is not interested in what we are finding out, even when they ask us to get the money to do the studies."

Dublin is among those conservationists seeking to narrow the chasm between pure research and its practical application from the management side. Sometimes she succeeds. The Ecological Monitoring Project provides park authorities with baseline data on everything from the size of the elephant population to long-term changes in vegetation. Several years ago, the warden of Masai Mara shut off one whole section of the park because it was being overrun by tourist minibuses, and he asked Dublin and her staff to monitor the area. After about six months, the monitoring team reported to the park authorities that the closed area still had not recovered from the damage caused by the heavy traffic. Dublin told the warden that, based on their findings, the area should remain closed for another six to twelve months. The warden went along with the researchers' recommendations. "Some things do fit together," Dublin says about the incident.

Such a success—due in large part to Dublin's willingness to stand her ground—may be the exception that proves the rule. Much of the research in the Serengeti ecosystem is self-serving. In fact, Dublin feels the situation may be worse now than it was in Turner's day. "We know there is a horrendous poaching problem in Serengeti National Park, we know that it needs to be brought to the public," she says. "We've got researchers who have lived in that park for ten years, and they are still fighting our results. To me it is one of the most nauseating parts of conservation. People worry about their jobs. Who wouldn't want to work in the Serengeti? People think, what if somebody says, 'My God, you mean they have been poaching there for twelve and a half years and you didn't say anything?' "

Dublin's cynical, shoot-from-the-hip manner does not always win friends, and sometimes a touch of paranoia creeps into her voice. Paranoia is something of an occupational hazard for people who have worked in Africa for a long time. Myles Turner was paranoid about the scientists; scientists in turn are paranoid about someone proving them wrong or, even more frightening, replacing them. Paranoia also drives conservation groups to guard what they see as their turf, and defines many of their so-called successes.

The most far-reaching effort to ground science firmly in the day-to-day realities of wildlife management stems from the work of Richard Bell. Bell, a bear of a man who has worked in Africa for over thirty years and now makes his home in Zambia, has long sought to change the role of scientific research in conservation. One of the few graduate students in ecology at Oxford in the mid-1960s who chose to pursue his degree elsewhere rather than switch specialties—he moved to the University of Manchester, and thence to the Serengeti to study the feeding patterns of grazing animals on the plains— Bell has continued to follow his instincts and his active imagination. Everything about wildlife and ecology in Africa intrigues him: archeology, geology, soils, vegetation, history, even running a wildlife department, a most unusual interest in someone who began his career as a scientist in the Serengeti.

Bell argues that ecological monitoring of the kind Dublin conducted in the Masai Mara could theoretically play an important role in conservation, but only if it is knitted together with a management approach specifically designed to respond to the data produced by the scientists. In practice, Bell says, "Wildlife management always has and will continue to proceed without the benefit of formal research. Wildlife research is expensive in time, money, equipment, and trained manpower. We have limited resources. Is research really necessary?"

Bell answers yes, but only under a new definition of the proper role of research within conservation: to improve the understanding of complex ecological, economic, and social systems in order to allow conservation agencies to achieve their objectives more effectively. "If one accepts this definition, it is hard to sustain the argument that research is unnecessary unless you believe that conservation agencies either have no objectives or are operating at maximum efficiency," says

Bell. "Neither scenario seems terribly likely."

Research, in Bell's view, must become part of management. Yet focusing research efforts solely on those areas likely to be of interest to management—biological inventories, for example—necessarily means ignoring other potentially valuable approaches. "We can't tell in advance what research will turn up. So managing science is akin to gambling, a blend of caution and inspired rashness; it is best to study the form, hedge one's bets, and play the occasional wild card, preferably at someone else's expense."

Bell calls his form of gambling "adaptive management." The idea is simple: it essentially formalizes trial and error. Conservation and wildlife management require a mastery of diverse disciplines—ecology, sociology, economics, and so on. The relationship of conservation to these disciplines, however, is exceedingly complex and poorly understood. Therefore, conservationists and wildlife managers operate in situations where the outcome of their actions is uncertain. As Bell puts it, "Whenever we do something in conservation, we are never certain that the result will be as we expect, and we can be confident that there will be at least some unexpected side effects."

Wildlife managers must adapt to these uncertainties, looking on everything they do as a trial, with the appropriate recording of procedures and monitoring of results. This leads to a disconcerting result: management transformed into a type of research. For the past fifty years or so, wildlife managers—the Myles Turners of the world—had as much affinity for researchers as they did for hyenas. For Bell, however, the collision of opposites produces a vigorous hybrid of manager and researcher. Realizing Bell's vision will require a complete rethinking of the professions of wildlife management and of science.

Bell has already taken that leap for himself, and he is now a partisan of a radical style of conservation that seeks to break down the myths that have until recently dictated events. "The goals of conservation in Africa are not based on logical choices, and they are not, for the most part, open to logical discussion," Bell argues. "Some actions receive widespread acceptance; others do not, based simply on value judgments made by conservationists, few of whom are African. Take the leopard, for example. Leopard abound in much of sub-Saharan Africa, and in fact pose a threat to life and property. But it is still listed as an endangered species, because it is attractive to Westerners. I am not saying that we should stop protecting leopards; far from it. But we have to examine the values that dictate conservation, and realize that our values and those of Africans can conflict so dramatically that our goals become unworkable." The conflict of values in a sense begets conservation. "If everyone was a conservationist," Bell notes dryly, "there would be no need for conservation."

Bell has avoided the paranoia that so often strikes his colleagues, though of them all Bell has perhaps the most reason to be watchful. Bell has the honor of being the only person to be fired from the Serengeti Research Institute, and his habit of speaking his mind—often rather bluntly—has given him a somewhat unsavory reputation among many of his co-workers. Bell is one of the few true philosophers in conservation. Though he generally shuns contact with the international conservation community, preferring to leave the back-slapping and fund raising to others, Bell's ideas are widely known, and a frequent cause of arguments. "I think he is a catalyst," Holly Dublin says. "I don't necessarily agree with him on everything, but I always walk away thinking, and in science that is a major contribution. A lot of people never prove anything or institute anything or implement anything, but they do make other people try to prove them wrong."

Bell enjoys saying things people do not like to hear, partly because he believes it is important to discuss what he considers the often unpleasant truth, and partly out of sheer mischievousness. "We can't conserve everything," Bell declared one day not long ago, as he sat in his small office in Chipata,

Zambia. "Instead, what we need is a strategy of the attainable. But to get there we have to acknowledge that certain types of wildlife are harmful to people and should be controlled, or are insignificant and need not be managed. We also need to abandon the idea that big parks are always better than small ones. If we want the parks to survive, the best thing might be to make them small."

Not a drop of romanticism about Africa and conservation is to be found in Richard Bell's sweeping philosophy. Such notions, he believes, will be the end of wildlife. The only hope is that wild animals will become a valuable enough commodity that Africans will gain a tangible economic benefit from having them around. The notion of allowing people to use wildlife lies at the heart of Bell's approach to conservation. This hard-nosed attitude tends to alienate many conservation groups, which disturbs Bell not at all. The mere mention of animal rights organizations within Bell's hearing can lead to lengthy tirades about soft-headed people who should stay the hell out of Africa.

Bell maintains a healthy optimism about the future of conservation in Africa. "The conservation literature makes it sound like the situation here is desperate, but I don't really think that is the case. Nearly four percent of sub-Saharan Africa is allocated to national parks or reserves, as much as any other continent. Some of the poorest nations have set aside ten percent or more of their land, and the amount of protected land in other countries is increasing steadily. Africans are prepared to pay a high price—damaged crops, lost opportunity, and direct expenditure—for conservation of their wildlife. There will be more losses, of land and even of species, but the situation in Africa compares favorably with any place on earth."

Ecology, ethology, conservation biology, and the related specialties fall on one side of a great rift in the debate over the future of Africa's wildlife. On the other side lies economics, another uncertain science. Just as Myles Turner and his generation of wildlife managers often butted heads with scientific researchers, so today many conservationists often find their way blocked by economists with drastically different visions of how Africa's resources should be used.

The words "ecology" and "economics" derive from the same Greek root: *oikos,* meaning "house." Yet ecologists and their allies rarely see eye to eye with economists. "To the ecologist it seems self-evident that the 'economic' philosophy is shortsighted, aesthetically repugnant, and in the long term self-destructive," Bell says. "To the economist, the 'ecological' approach seems unworldly, unrealistic, and unnecessarily restrictive."

In Africa, the conflict has become one of ideologies rather than science. Bell points out that conservationists have lost credibility in both more developed and less developed areas of Africa because they often make value judgments, frequently based on a simplistic vision of Africa, about the choices facing rural Africans, rather than arguing from well-substantiated theories. Bell argues that "ecologists must examine their own positions in order to realize that people acting from economic motives are not, as they often seem to believe, stupid, if not actually wicked."

Western economists argue that wildlife will disappear unless it can pay for itself by tourism, by using abundant supplies of game meat, or by selling such valuable products as skins or ivory. While providing economic benefits to local people certainly must be a part of a broad-based approach to wildlife conservation, it cannot be the only goal. Richard Bell, responding to the oft-heard phrase about Africa's "priceless" natural heritage, said, "No, we have to define the price and pay it." Paying the price requires some sacrifice, and giving up the idea that all conservation areas will be moneymakers. If economics becomes the cornerstone of conservation, and economic conditions change in such a way that the money ceases to flow from tourism, or animal production schemes, or whatever, and a financially more rewarding use for the land comes along, then conservation ceases.

Many Africans consider saving their natural heritage a matter of national pride, a far more lasting motivation than economics. In Tanzania, for example, that pride runs so deep that it resembles a religious faith. Tanzania has set aside nearly 15 percent of its land in protected areas for wildlife—by comparison, the continental United States has set aside less than 4 percent of its land. The ethical commitment to wildlife has a down side: it may put the country in a terrible bind if the time comes when some of that land is needed for uses other than wildlife. Given Tanzania's poverty, that time may not be far off.

Tanzanians are hardly alone among Africans in their deep attachment to their natural heritage. The "wildlife must pay" philosophy seems dangerously misguided in light of the great pride most rural people take in their country's wildlife and wild places. These feelings, however, will not take precedence over other more fundamental needs, such as food, shelter, basic hygiene, and health care. The challenge is to fulfill these legitimate needs while reconciling and integrating conservation and economic development.

That is the basic premise of an approach to conservation called "sustainable development." The term itself has become a kind of mantra, though it communicates little and in fact seems to mean vastly different things to different people. "Sustainable development" entered the vocabulary in the early 1980s as an economic term highlighting the need to understand the future implications of current economic policies and practices. It referred to a development strategy that managed all assets—natural, human, financial, and physical—and could be applied equally well to the developed and the developing world.

Sustainable development moved from development jargon into the mainstream with the 1987 publication of the report of the U.N.'s World Commission on Environment and Development, chaired by Prime Minister Gro Harlem Brundtland of Norway. The Brundtland Commission, as it is usually called, was charged with developing no less than a "global agenda for change." The commission came close to achieving its lofty goal, judging by the speed with which the conservation community adopted its ideas.

Simply put, the Brundtland Commission saw sustainable development as a process in which the exploitation of all kinds of resources takes place with an awareness of future as well as present needs. The commission was the most significant manifestation of the growing closeness between conservation and development. Indeed, the back cover of *Our Common Future* announces that the report "serves notice that the time has come for a marriage of economy and ecology." Conservationists began to recognize that the only way they could protect the environment was to become much more intimately involved with pragmatic financial ventures such as animal husbandry and agroforestry—areas usually considered to be deep within enemy territory.

In terms of Africa's wildlife, the ethic of sustainable development—the search is on for a more meaningful phrase—means that conservation organizations which once focused solely on animals now must fit people into their equations. It is an ethic derived from inexact sciences like economics and sociology, and its implementation relies on other ill-defined fields like conservation biology. None of these specialties provides guidelines, only blurred ideas on the general direction conservation should take.

What is painfully clear, however, is that the most direct threat to wild animals and their habitats is the driving imperative of both rich and poor to over-exploit otherwise renewable resources. Much of the earth's remaining biological wealth is in rural areas of the tropics where poor families struggle to draw their livelihood from the land. The inhabitants of these areas, far from centers of economic activity, often lack the political power or financial resources to improve the quality of their lives. More disturbing, the degradation of entire ecosystems—whether it be Maasai rangelands, coral reefs that shelter marine life to feed a fishing community, or tropical forests that provide villagers with essential fuelwood, protein from bush-meat, building materials, and medicines—threatens the sur-vival of the poor themselves.

World Wildlife Fund was one of the conservation organiza-tions that recognized the need to incorporate people into pro-jects which once involved only animals. In 1985, WWF cre-ated the Wildlands and Human Needs Program, the goal of which was to improve the quality of life of rural people through practical field projects that integrate the management of natural resources with grass-roots economic development. It is a far-reaching effort to join community development with the protection of natural resources.

Africa presents perhaps the greatest challenges for such a program, because Africa has both tremendous human poverty and an immense wildlife resource. Efforts like the Wildlands and Human Needs Program must overcome the conflicts in-herent in bringing together two fields, conservation and devel-opment, long separated by temperament and training. Less than a decade ago, the notion that a conservation organization would be involved in so-called "quality of life" issues—better health care, increased child survival, greater opportunities for women, and assurance of resource ownership—would have been inconceivable. Today, conservationists see that these are the preconditions for stabilizing the population, which is nec-essary to diminish competition over deteriorating resources.

Richard Bell has spent the last five years at the head of one of the most ambitious conservation and development pro-grams in Africa, the Luangwa Integrated Resource Develop-ment Project (LIRDP). The project's title says a great deal: its principal aim is to improve the standard of living of villagers in Game Management Areas, the buffer zones that abut Zambia's national parks. The project thus seeks to take a huge step toward the integration of conservation and development. LIRDP coordinates government activities in regions like the Luangwa Valley, internationally known for its wildlife, and elsewhere in Zambia. It brings together a variety of approaches to conservation and economic development, including road building, agricultural research, women's programs, marketing and cooperatives, small enterprises like crafts and furniture, forestry, fisheries, water development, wildlife management, sport hunting, natural resources research, and tourism.

Few people other than Bell have the experience or energy to run such a sprawling effort. Even with Bell at the helm, LIRDP has become a maze of regulations and committees, the latter spending most of their time discussing what the other committees have done. Though unwieldy and inefficient, the committees are an attempt to get over obstacles to returning control over resources to rural people, while at the same time promoting participation at all levels of government and society. Control over wildlife is gradually being transferred to one subcommittee which consists solely of local representatives such as chiefs and elders.

The structure of LIRDP cuts across numerous government ministries, many of which have never worked together before, and probably would rather never work together again. In African bureaucracies, ministries often become isolated fiefdoms, jealously guarding their influence against what they see as competing interests. The Zambian ministries cooperated in LIRDP because Kenneth Kaunda, president of Zambia until 1991, demanded it. LIRDP survived because of the intense personal support of Kaunda, along with the drive and skills of Bell and his co-director, Fidelis Lungu. Now that Kaunda has been replaced by a democratically elected president, the future of LIRDP is unclear.

Since it began operation in 1983, with a large grant from the Norwegian Aid Agency (NORAD), LIRDP has had some notable successes. In April 1991, LIRDP was authorized to work across Zambia, and it is now one of the most far-reaching experiments of regional decentralization of resource management in Africa.

The success or failure of such an initiative will not be apparent for years to come, if ever. Such a multi-sectoral approach

The people who live near
these spectacular falls call
them mosi-oa-tunya:
"smoke that thunders."
In 1855, David Livingstone,
the first Westerner to see the
falls, named them for his
sovereign, Queen Victoria.
(Jonathan Adams)

The Ikoma entrance to Tanzania's Serengeti National Park, on the park's
western edge. (Jonathan Adams)

The growth of tourist camps means increased contact between people and elephants. (Erica McShane-Caluzi)

Ivory confiscated from poachers in Malawi. (Erica McShane-Caluzi)

Despite the international ban on the ivory trade, some ivory markets remain open. This young man looks for a buyer; the smaller tusks are probably from elephants no more than a few years old.
(Erica McShane-Caluzi)

Salaries for park rangers have fallen in much of Africa. Rangers like this one in Zimbabwe's Mana Pools National Park may be in the field for weeks at a time with few supplies. (Jonathan Adams)

Lions lie in riverine thicket and forest along the Tapoa River, Niger, in 1981. (Tom McShane)

The same stretch of river ten years later. Elephants have destroyed most of the vegetation along the riverbank. (Erica McShane-Caluzi)

Elephants have stripped the bark from the rubber trees on this plantation in Gabon. As a result the tree will die, causing a major loss of revenue to this commercial enterprise.
(Erica McShane-Caluzi)

Students at the college of African Wildlife Management, Mweka, Tanzania. Left to right: Charles Kara (Sudan), Andrew Bwanali (Malawi), Chandida Monyadzwe (Botswana), Manirabaruta Theomeste (Burundi), A.G. Rutazaa, Instructor (Tanzania).
(Naomi Rutenberg)

A pair of black rhinoceros, a mother and calf, in Serengeti National Park. Many rhinos have been killed for their horns, and only a few still live in the park.

(Jonathan Adams)

The annual meeting of the Nyaminyami Rural District Council. Before addressing the meeting, each speaker raises a fist and recites, in the Shona language: "Pamberi ne muka. Pamberi ne budiriro. Pasi ne vateyi." "Forward with wildlife. Forward with development. Down with poachers." (Jonathan Adams)

Nyaminyami District, in Northern Zimbabwe, is one of the poorest in the country, with little rain and infertile soil. The region, however, supports significant wildlife populations, and Nyaminyami was one of the first districts to become involved with the CAMPFIRE program. (Jonathan Adams)

Not everyone can afford electric fences. Villagers near the Lopé Reserve in Gabon contructed this fence out of wire, sheets, and tin cans to keep elephants and buffalo out of cultivated fields.
(Erica McShane-Caluzi)

A Lichtenstein's hartebeest in Kasungu National Park, Malawi. The only member of the genus Sigmocreus, *Lichtenstein's hartebeest is native to the miombo woodlands of east and southern Africa.* (Erica McShane-Caluzi)

This electric fence along the boundary of Kasungu National Park in Malawi keeps elephants out of tobacco and maize fields bordering the protected area.
(Erica McShane-Caluzi)

Wildlife scouts in Malawi destroy a meat drying rack used by illegal hunters. Henry Kachoyo is at right. (Erica McShane-Caluzi)

Henry Kachoyo (standing at left) and his family. (Erica McShane-Caluzi)

Beisa oryx in Awash National Park, Ethiopia. This is a rich volcanic region of high productivity but low rainfall. The oryx and other species face heavy hunting pressure. (Erica McShane-Caluzi)

A waterbuck in Manovo-Gounda-St. Floris National Park, Central African Republic, not far from where Gilbert Bangandombi-Kotali was shot. (Erica McShane-Caluzi)

A typical farm perches on the Chikwawa Escarpment in Malawi.
(Erica McShane-Caluzi)

These men and their children were arrested for hunting illegally in Nyika National Park, Malawi. (Erica McShane-Caluzi)

Tom McShane (center, with backpack) and park rangers on patrol in the Vwaza Marsh Game Reserve, Malawi. Two of the rangers in the picture have since died from sleeping sickness, two were killed by villagers during an anti-poaching operation, and one died of AIDS. (Erica McShane-Caluzi)

Joshua Nyirenda (center) and some of the rangers who caught him hunting in the Vwaza Marsh Game Reserve. (Erica McShane-Caluzi)

Joshua's 1856 Tower musket. The beads are a protective talisman.
(Erica McShane-Caluzi)

Logging in the Lopé Faunal Reserve, Gabon. Logging certainly disturbs wildlife, but while the larger animals, such as elephant and gorilla, move out of the area during logging, they do not hesitate to return once the loggers leave. (Erica McShane-Caluzi)

Tsetse target. The flies are attracted to the dark central panel and then are poisoned by insecticide on the netting. Such targets are among the greatest threats to wildlife in Africa, as eliminating tsetse opens land for livestock and cultivation. (Erica McShane-Caluzi)

Lioness and young cubs, Serengeti National Park. On the order of 2,000 lions remain in the park. (Jonathan Adams)

Wildebeest on the move in Kenya's Masai Mara Game Reserve. The annual migration of over 1 million wildebeest is one of Africa's greatest natural spectacles. (Jonathan Adams)

to resource management is extremely complicated—many critics say too complicated. It does, however, illustrate the constituencies involved in addressing resource use issues, and the complexities of trying to involve every interested party.

Efforts like LIRDP—known collectively by the unwieldy title of Integrated Conservation and Development Projects, or ICDPs—are innovative, experimental, and far from perfect. Development professionals working for the World Bank, various arms of the United Nations such as the United Nations Development Program, the Food and Agriculture Organization, and governmental aid agencies, have long struggled to implement grand schemes for pulling rural people in Africa out of poverty. Few of the projects can claim great success, and some have been catastrophes. So it is not surprising that projects attempting to make people's lives better and leave their environment intact have had some trouble getting off the ground.

Conservation and development projects have given rise to a new phenomenon that might be called "making doughnuts." The projects generally take place on the periphery of parks and protected areas, and they attract the support of aid agencies like the United States Agency for International Development (USAID), ODA (the British equivalent), the European Development Fund, the World Bank, and others. Such agencies focus, naturally, on what they do best: agricultural and rural development. The projects they support draw more people to the area but tend to overlook the park itself, which was the justification for the projects in the first place, and which often provides the raw materials—wood, water, and food—such projects need. Near Parc National du W du Niger, for example, USAID has instituted a multi-faceted conservation and development project that includes tree planting, agroforestry, and small-scale business development, and so on, but next to nothing for park management. Not surprisingly, there is money for research. The park warden, a Nigerien, has been left wondering about the priorities of this supposed conservation effort. In the past, conservation dollars went into science rather than park management. Now rural development is all the rage, and still there is nothing for park management. Everyone likes parks, but no one wants to pay for them.

Why proceed down the road toward integrating conservation and development? Because there is no other choice. Protecting parks with armed men and fences may play a role in some areas, but standing alone these efforts cannot succeed. Innovative approaches to resolving the conflicts between people and parks will become increasingly important parts of strategies for saving wildlife in Africa and elsewhere, because such programs make up some of the process by which rural people will solve their own problems.

The gradual integration of conservation and development provides the most telling example of people looking beyond the myth of wild Africa and addressing the real needs of all the continent's inhabitants. No one can say for certain how this process will play out, but it will most certainly fail if Africans are not included at every level. The most persistent illusion in the Western vision of Africa is that Africans can be and should be ignored. Overcoming that perception requires both reexamining Western values, and, through education and training, providing Africans with the tools they need to take on the responsibilities that ultimately only they can meet.

CHAPTER VI

▼ ▼ ▼

CONSERVATION POLLUTION

*In Africa, wildlife is always regarded as something
we should kill and eat. Stopping people from utiliz-
ing wildlife the way they used to do is something
they don't really understand.*

—Chandida Monyadzwe

N *ot long ago, Sedia* Modise was building a rhino fence.
Several aspects of this project were peculiar: first, the
fence was located no more than five miles from the center of
Gaborone, the capital of Botswana; second, few if any rhinos
remained there. The project begins to make sense once you
realize that Modise works for Botswana's Department of
Wildlife and National Parks, and that the fence will keep
rhinos in, not out.

Modise runs the Gaborone Game Reserve, a splendid
1,000-acre park containing kudu, ostrich, zebra, reedbuck,
hyrax, and baboons, among other animals. The reserve also
houses a rare white rhino, sent here from South Africa, which
has one of the last breeding populations on the continent. Modise's fence rings a rhino sanctuary. Modise built the fence
almost single-handedly, with occasional assistance from the
members of a wildlife club at the local university and a Peace
Corps volunteer. The Gaborone Game Reserve functions on
few resources, chief among them being Modise's personal
commitment to conservation. An educator by temperament,

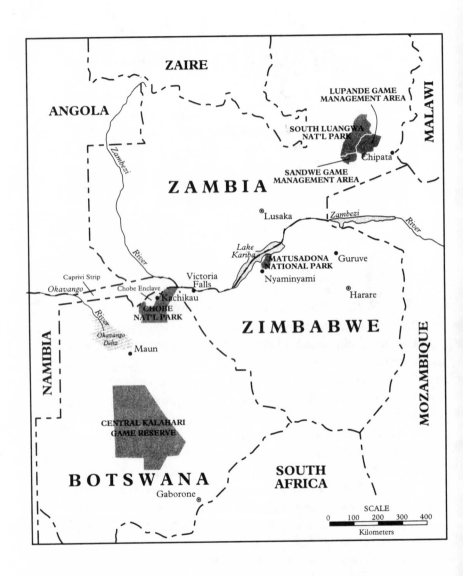

the burly and forthright Modise has shaped the reserve to meet the needs of Gaborone's children and students, few of whom would otherwise have the opportunity to see or learn about wildlife. The park's scanty buildings contain interactive educational materials and dioramas, and a nearby rockface features copies of the famous prehistoric rock paintings found far to the north in the Tsodilo Hills, along with paint for children to create their own.

Modise builds fences and runs the game park practically as a hobby, as the park is not included among his many administrative duties in the Wildlife Department. His hectic schedule leaves little time for reflection, yet he maintains a sunny disposition. Given a choice, he would spend all day with the children. "We are involving youth in conservation," he says. "The message that wildlife is important is beginning to reach the next generation."

While Modise tends to Africa's future, to the north, in Tanzania, a man named H. I. Sariko worries about the present. Now an instructor, until recently Sariko had one of the most dangerous jobs in conservation: he was commander of an anti-poaching unit in Tanzania's vast system of parks and reserves. Sariko and his men pursued poachers who were often better armed, so they had to be expert at bushcraft, tracking, ballistics, police work, and the law.

With training in law and wildlife conservation, Sariko, a stocky man with a ready smile, could move easily between the bush and the courtroom. Tanzania, however, like many African countries, does not have the resources fully to patrol all of its protected areas, so anti-poaching specialists like Sariko rarely have time to see cases through from arrest to trial, and instead turn their prisoners over to the police before court proceedings begin. Unlike the wardens and rangers, the local police are unfamiliar with the laws concerning wildlife. Much to the frustration of Sariko and his comrades, many of the people they arrest are never punished.

Sariko's work illustrates just a few of the many skills required of an African conservationist. A Tanzanian colleague, A. G. Rutazaa, seeks to pass on some of this essential information to the people who will be running Africa's parks and reserves into the next century. After working in several national parks, Rutazaa has turned to teaching.

Rutazaa, Sariko, and Modise—a teacher, a cop, and an administrator—would seem at a glance to have little in common. Yet all three could be described in general terms as park wardens. Their diverse responsibilities reveal the difficulties of training people for conservation. And, too often, that training takes place outside of Africa.

Sariko and Rutazaa, for example, came from Tanzania to study at the Smithsonian Institution's Zoological Research Center in Front Royal, Virginia. They ended up studying polecats, weasel-like animals which live in North America. Other African students conducted radio telemetry studies of black bears, another species limited to North America, in Virginia's Shenandoah National Park. The practical benefits of this well-intentioned, but mostly irrelevant, training is not at all clear. No doubt, polecat research and radio telemetry are valuable endeavors, and for some of the several dozen students from around the world who enroll here each summer—all of whom have already embarked on careers in conservation—the training may make the difference between success and failure. When Sariko and Rutazaa returned home, however, not only would they fail to find any polecats, they would find few of the technological or professional resources available to them in Virginia.

Gradually, Africans have taken over the responsibility of actually carrying out conservation programs in Africa, but they rarely have a role in designing such efforts. Most often they simply carry out the plans of the generally white, European and American specialists, or, at best, Western-trained Africans. Right now, training African conservationists at Western institutions such as the Smithsonian Institution, the University of Massachusetts, or Colorado State may be inevitable, as few African universities have appropriate facilities, and such training seems the obvious route for moving Africans into decision-making positions in conservation.

The training African conservationists receive abroad, particularly the emphasis on scientific research, simply perpetuates Western conservation values and methods. This leads to an odd situation in which Africans inherit and pass on a conservation ethic created in large part by the great white hunters. The impact of this intellectual process can be seen in parks, where Western attitudes shape efforts to undermine such fundamental activities as subsistence hunting.

The opportunities for professional training in Africa have begun to grow recently, but for many years only one remarkable institution, the College for African Wildlife Management, in Mweka, Tanzania, produced the skilled people needed to run most of Africa's parks. Rutazaa, Sariko, and Modise all trained at the college; in fact, Sariko and Modise graduated in the same class.

The College for African Wildlife Management—usually called Mweka—has been training people from across the continent and from as far away as Cuba and Sri Lanka in wildlife conservation and management since 1963. In that time, over sixteen hundred students from thirty-one countries (including twelve non-African countries) have come to Mweka's 52-acre campus, a jumble of buildings originally constructed as a school for the Greek sisal-farming community and then used as a nurses' training center. Today, over one hundred students are enrolled, the majority from Tanzania, Kenya, and Uganda, though there are large contingents from Botswana and Zambia as well.

Mweka traces its roots to a meeting in 1961 called the Symposium on the Conservation of Nature and Natural Resources in Modern African States, held in Arusha, Tanganyika. At the meeting, Julius Nyerere issued what became known as the Arusha Declaration on Wildlife Protection:

> The survival of our wildlife is a matter of grave concern to all of us in Africa. These wild creatures amid the wild places they

inhabit are not only important as a source of wonder and inspiration but are an integral part of our natural resources and of our future livelihood and well-being.

In accepting the trusteeship of our wildlife we solemnly declare that we will do everything in our power to make sure that our children's grandchildren will be able to enjoy this rich and precious inheritance.

The conservation of wildlife and wild places calls for specialist knowledge, trained manpower and money, and we look to other nations to cooperate in this important task—the success or failure of which not only affects the continent of Africa but the rest of the world as well.

The Arusha Declaration highlighted the need for professional training in conservation. The responsibility for founding an institution to provide such training fell to a British Army officer, Major Bruce Kinloch, who was then Tanganyika's chief game warden.

Kinloch and Dr. Hugh Lamprey, Tanganyika's senior ecologist, who was to become Mweka's first principal, searched much of East Africa for a suitable site for the school. They settled on Mweka because they had no money and the government of Tanganyika was willing to give them the derelict and abandoned buildings for free. With initial grants from USAID, the Frankfurt Zoological Society (FZS), the African Wildlife Leadership Foundation, the British government, and others, Mweka took in its first class of twenty-five students.

Dr. Lamprey and his small staff had to start from scratch. "We produced a syllabus for training wardens," he recalls. "Its scope was a wide one, because we saw that it would be necessary to provide technical training in about ten to fifteen major subjects, among which were basic biology and the natural history of the wildlife species of Africa. More practically, students had to learn the methods and techniques in wildlife management, how to manage a force of rangers and scouts, how to manage national parks and game reserves, the building and maintenance of facilities like roads, park headquarters, park gates, the maintenance of park vehicle fleets, bulldozers and generators, police work, the law, the wildlife laws of the countries concerned, the process of making arrests, how to conduct a case in court, how to survey, how to map, how to undertake wildlife census work. Wardens have to be unusually versatile and resourceful."

In addition to versatility and resourcefulness, the other qualities wardens must have are commitment and a thick skin. Conservation remains something less than an honorable profession for many Africans, especially those who see animals as competitors for land and food. Andrew Bwanali, a soft-spoken student from Malawi, has felt the scorn of his elders. "When I was coming here, I went to visit my home and tell them I was leaving. People asked me, what are you going to learn there? I told them I would learn about animals. They thought it was funny, someone coming all the way from Malawi to Tanzania just to learn about wildlife."

Rutazaa, who now teaches ornithology and mammalogy at Mweka, also has difficulty explaining his chosen career to friends and family. "When I go home, and people ask me what am I doing, I hate to explain it to them," he says. "They can't understand, except when I tell them I am a hunter. I can't tell them I am conserving animals, because they say, why? why? why?"

Similar questions have no doubt plagued Mweka's graduates from that first class in 1963 onward. The training provided at Mweka has evolved since then, but the basic purpose remains the same: to provide a professional training for park wardens and game scouts. The college does not grant a degree, but rather a certificate or a diploma—roughly equivalent to secondary school students in the British system. The certificate course takes two years, and enables a student to become an assistant game warden. The top students can earn the diploma—and with it the qualifications to head a park or reserve in many countries—after another year's study at Mweka.

Most of the students come from jobs in wildlife conservation rather than directly out of high school, and almost without
exception the student's home government or a private organization, such as Catholic Relief Services or the African Wildlife
Foundation, foots the bill for the $5,000 annual tuition. The
fees collected from students do not cover all of the college's
expenses, so it is run as a government/private hybrid, with a
substantial subsidy from the Tanzanian government along
with grants from a number of conservation organizations and
aid agencies. An international board of governors, consisting
of wildlife officials from Tanzania, Kenya, Uganda, Ethiopia,
and Zambia, and representatives from WWF, the African
Wildlife Foundation, and FZS, has the overall authority for
administration.

For many years, Mweka and a school at Garoua, Cameroon, which teaches in French (Mweka's classes are in English), were the sole institutions training Africans for careers in
conservation, and Mweka had by far the greatest scope and
experience. "There are no other institutions in the whole of
Africa which provide what you might call technical training,
and [Mweka] fills a most essential niche," says Lamprey, who
is now retired and lives in London. "Without Mweka College,
many of the wildlife departments and national park organizations in Africa would not have adequate staff."

Mweka provides the counterpoint to non-African training
programs, but even Mweka has felt the influence of Western
attitudes about conservation. The college stumbled economically and philosophically in the mid-1980s. Funding from both
the government of Tanzania and outside sources fell, as did
enrollment, in part because similar schools were opened in
other African countries, such as the Naivasha Wildlife and
Fisheries Institute, at Lake Naivasha in Kenya. In a more disturbing trend, the school tried to emulate foreign universities
and seemed to be drifting away from its primary goal of training wardens in professional skills that would make them better
wildlife managers. The quality of the instruction at Mweka

dropped: students at the time called the material they were being taught "rubbish." The majority of Mweka's students still returned to their posts in Africa's national parks and reserves after completing their studies, but the college was in danger of becoming a mini-university or a preparatory school. Mweka's administrators, for example, changed the way students earned credit toward a degree to a system that would allow them to gain exemptions from the first two years if they were accepted at an American university. The risk was that Mweka would turn first-rate wardens into second-rate scientists.

Most of the basic science courses taught at Mweka and other institutions are unnecessary, for such training is irrelevant to the major duties of a park warden or game scout. Even in-depth study—beyond a working understanding—of clearly pertinent fields such as botany, zoology, and ecology may not be necessary. What is badly needed, instead, is a greater emphasis on teaching wildlife managers to deal with people.

John Boshe, who now heads WWF's office in Dar-Es-Salaam, taught at Mweka for seven years, and served for a time as vice-principal. He believes that wildlife training in Africa has become more sophisticated but has moved in entirely the wrong direction. He surveyed four wildlife training institutes—Mweka, Garoua, the Nigeria Wildlife Institute, and Egerton College in Kenya—and discovered that their curricula consisted primarily of basic and applied sciences, with a dash of the humanities thrown in. Boshe points out that the problems facing most managers of national parks and reserves are today much more sociological than biological. Wardens of modern parks desperately need training in administration, economics, law, public relations, psychology, and sociology. Boshe recommends dedicating close to half of the training curriculum to these areas, whereas now they take up only a fifth or less.

Mweka's current class of students, perhaps more than any previous generation, understands the delicate task of balancing the needs of wildlife with those of people. Two recent developments illustrate the changing attitudes. The first is the evolving role of the game warden. When Mweka was created, wardens, acting in the tradition of Africa's colonial administrators, were primarily concerned with controlling wildlife populations and protecting people and crops. "Control" in this context usually meant killing. "In the earlier days, in the days before the crisis over elephants and rhinos, the wildlife departments had a lot to do in controlling excess numbers of elephants and buffaloes," Hugh Lamprey says. "So it was necessary to teach students how to hunt, to be good shots, to know when and where to shoot elephants to protect crops, and so on."

Now the tide has turned and the emphasis is on protecting wildlife from man rather than the other way around. The requirement that each student kill one elephant and one buffalo in order to graduate has been abolished, though they still study ballistics, marksmanship, and the other elements of the hunt.

Wilfred A. Foya, Mweka's senior faculty member, points out that when he arrived at the college in 1977, shooting so-called "dangerous game"—lion, leopard, elephant, buffalo, and hippopotamus—was still an essential part of the training. "Rangers were judged by how effective they were at shooting," he says. "Our students would be in the field for ten days, just tracking and killing. That is just not a viable exercise any more."

The other significant change in Mweka's approach to training conservationists is a new course, instituted in 1989, entitled "Man and Wildlife." As the name implies, the course explores the relationship between rural people and wildlife, and how these people can come to recognize that conserving wildlife has direct benefits for their own lives.

The students and administrators now seem to have taken that approach to heart. For Chandida Monyadzwe, a thoughtful and articulate woman who conducted conservation education programs in Botswana before coming to Mweka, developing more effective means of using wildlife resources will be the key to successful conservation. "Now people want more land for themselves because they don't see the value of wildlife, they only want the land to use it for their cattle and their farms," she says. "With better utilization schemes, people will see the value of wildlife and will really manage it properly. When you go around and try to teach people about wildlife now, you know they listen to you, but as soon as you leave they say, 'What is the use of teaching us when we don't benefit?' Using wildlife will help conservation, because just preaching that word—conservation, conservation, again conservation— won't help."

Monyadzwe and the other women at Mweka are pioneers among African conservationists. The first woman graduated from the college in 1987, and the 1989 class of nine women— "ladies," Monyadzwe says—was the largest ever. Most of the women students are from Botswana and Tanzania, where there are fewer barriers for professional women than in those African countries, for example, where Muslim traditions predominate. In other countries, such as Sudan, the Wildlife Department is considered a paramilitary unit, and the rigorous training generally does not attract women. Among the Mweka students, however, some of the gender distinctions break down, particularly during the training field trips. "On safari we are all men," Monyadzwe says with a grin.

Much of the training at Mweka takes place in the classroom, and lectures feature lively exchanges between instructors and students. Yet the heart of the operation is not the large lecture hall, festooned with mounted skulls, but the garage, where a staff of twenty-five labors to keep the school's fleet of vehicles in operation—no small task considering the sorry state of most roads in the region. Without such round-the-clock support, Mweka would be unable to accomplish the Herculean task it performs six times each year: taking the entire school, including students, instructors, cooks, carpenters, and engineers, on safari.

The longest safari of the year is a month-long exercise in

woodland ecology for first-year students and law enforcement for those in their second year. The safari furthers conservation in Tanzania while also training Mweka's students. In 1989, for example, the first-year students conducted a survey of the local peoples in the Uzungwa Mountains, an environmentally crucial area where the government recently established a park to protect one of the last mountain forests in East Africa. The second-year students formed anti-poaching patrols in the Selous Game Reserve, providing vital support to the management of the area.

Sariko serves as one of the instructors for the anti-poaching safari. He sees poaching as a product of ignorance. "The level of conservation awareness is very low," he said. "Now we have an acute poaching problem, because people do not realize they are harming the country by hunting wildlife in the national parks and reserves. The only thing that is keeping our wildlife populations healthy is the vigilance of the government, not the awareness of the local people."

This lack of awareness was made clear one evening in the small city of Moshi, at the foot of Mt. Kilimanjaro, as a valiant but hopelessly outmanned team of Mweka volleyball players went down to defeat at the hands of a team from the local sports club. Several hundred fans took up the cause of the underdog, chanting, *"Simba! Simba!"*—Swahili for "lion," Mweka's symbol. The fans, however, knew little of what the college did, or who the students were. "The people in the United States know more about Mweka than do the people of Moshi, who live just a few miles away," said Sariko.

The citizens of Moshi may have been ignorant of Mweka, and uninformed about the Western conservation ethic and its attendant institutions, but that does not mean they were unaware of conservation entirely. The Western ethic grew in large part as a response to industrialization, a process only now beginning to take place in most of Africa, so it is likely to remain incomprehensible to most Africans at a basic level for some time to come.

Lasting conservation efforts will more probably grow out of the efforts of those professionals trained at Mweka, and through local values and skills, than from the wholesale application of foreign ideals. This demands a deeper appreciation of how Africans, particularly traditional African hunters, interact with their environment. These misunderstood hunters, so long condemned as the scourge of wildlife, bear but little resemblance to the poachers created by conservation propaganda.

▼ ▼ ▼

CHAPTER VII

MILES AND MILES
OF BLOODY AFRICA

*How can you tell me I don't belong in a place where
I've lived my whole life?*

—Joshua Nyirenda

The small herd of elephants roaming Malawi's Vwaza
Marsh Game Reserve turned and headed north, perhaps smelling water nearby. A few hundred yards back, some
game scouts patrolling the reserve on foot watched as the elephants crossed an opening and then disappeared again into the
trees. Suddenly, the scouts heard a gunshot somewhere off in
the distance: sound can carry up to three miles in the woodlands of southern Africa. Following such a noise over rough
terrain like the Vwaza Marsh takes a great deal of skill and
experience, but for the scouts this was familiar territory. Although remote, the Vwaza Marsh Game Reserve, a rich wildlife area in northwest Malawi, near the border with Zambia, is
well patrolled.

Malawi's scouts are among the best trained in Africa, and
their training paid off here; coming through the bush the
scouts were surprised to find not just a dead elephant, an unfortunately common experience, but someone with a gun sitting on the elephant as well. The man was arrested, his weapon
and the ivory were confiscated, and he was convicted and sen-

tenced to two years hard labor or a $200 fine—a substantial amount of money in rural Malawi.

The man the scouts captured was more than sixty years old, and his name was Joshua Nyirenda. He was of small stature, and by the time of his arrest he was a tired old man with a mantle of gray hair. Even faced with a jail term, however, there was still life in his eyes, and the sense that after almost forty years of living off the land in and around Vwaza Marsh Game Reserve, he knew something that the game scouts and the conservationists didn't. This wasn't a protected area, this was home.

The nature of the combatants in the war against poaching has been vastly misrepresented. Few poachers are efficient killing machines armed with automatic weapons, and not all scouts are poorly equipped and poorly trained. Poachers and scouts are more alike than they are different. Both are simply Africans trying to make the best of exceptionally difficult circumstances.

No one, not even Joshua Nyirenda, knows where the name "Vwaza" came from, though it has been suggested that it is the sound of pulling your foot out of the mud—and there is no shortage of mud in this area. Vwaza forms part of a vast expanse of woodland that covers the southern third of Africa, stretching 2,000 miles from Tanzania in the east to Angola in the west, and 1,000 miles from the equatorial rain forests in the north to the arid savannas in the south. This carpet of tall trees and sparse grass is known by its Bantu name, *miombo,* after the species of *Brachystegia* and *Julbernardia* trees—similar in appearance to the oaks of the American West—which dominate the landscape. The miombo woodland is possibly the greatest dry forest on earth.

The miombo woodlands are not well known for their extensive herds of wildlife, nor are they renowned for beautiful landscapes. The woodlands are a flat, monotonous stretch of trees, green and lush during the approximately six-month wet season, but dry and lifeless (most often burnt black) during the dry season. Spotting wildlife in these woodlands can be a challenge: while traveling through miombo in what is now Zimbabwe in 1882, Frederick Selous complained: "There appeared to be no game whatsoever in this part of the country . . . in the course of the day we saw a wart hog and a small herd of zebra." Even animals as large as elephants and buffalo are often obscured behind a wall of vegetation in miombo forests. Perhaps the most common sight is an antelope charging off into the bush, its tail flashing. The back half of an antelope does not make for famous national parks or long stays by tourists. Even those people who have worked for long periods in Africa have little love for miombo—mention the word to a group of African conservationists and they will most likely roll their eyes and groan.

Driving through these woodlands demands nothing so much as the ability to endure numbing boredom; roads stretch on for hundreds of miles without even a curve. Occasionally a small village appears, a few square huts crowded next to the road as if the villagers were grasping for any diversion to break the monotony. Against this unchanging landscape, every mundane thing that happens in these villages seems magnified: the children scream louder, the goats and sheep bleat more insistently. If it wasn't for the fear of crashing into the livestock, or of breaking an axle in a pothole, nothing would keep a driver awake while crossing the miombo. It was the miombo that led an anonymous British official to coin the phrase "miles and miles of bloody Africa," and there is no better way to describe it.

The Vwaza region in most ways is typical of the miombo zone. A few hills break up the horizon, but in general its broad, flat terrain covered with forest stretches into the distance. Vwaza, however, has one feature that sets it apart from the surrounding uniformity: water. An extensive area of wetlands bisects Vwaza and provides water throughout the year. Animals for many miles depend on the water in the Vwaza Marsh during the long six-month dry season.

Natural forces and governmental decisions by both colonial and African administrators have for the most part kept man out of Vwaza. The combination of tsetse infestation, competition and crop damage from elephant, buffalo, and hippo, and poor soils mean that much of the region is untouched bush.

Vwaza falls within the great tsetse fly belt that stretches from the Luangwa Valley of Zambia northward into Malawi. Unlike the tsetse elsewhere in Africa, the species found in miombo—*Glossina morsitans*—does not require dense riverine thickets to survive. This species has spread throughout the miombo zone, and limits the number of people and livestock the area can support. Nagana, the cattle disease spread by tsetse, effectively removes any thoughts of rearing livestock, and sleeping sickness is endemic: 5 to 10 percent of the population living in the Vwaza region today tests positive for the disease, the highest prevalence in Africa. Tsetse can be so thick at times that they will cover the bed of a pickup truck traveling through the forest.

With a relatively healthy wildlife population and few people, Vwaza was an obvious choice for classification as a protected area. Colonial administrators first expressed interest in the region in 1956 when they reserved the Vwaza Marsh for themselves as a controlled hunting area. Boundary changes were made over time until 1975, when the government declared the area a game reserve and removed—with small compensation—the last of the small number of people living there.

The Vwaza Marsh Game Reserve now has three game scout camps and twenty scouts to patrol the 380 square miles of protected area. People living around the reserve, some of whom were removed from within, still consider the land theirs—land on which they can eke out a meager living. These are the people we routinely condemn as poachers, though they hardly fit the role we have created for them as the scourges of Africa's wildlife.

Joshua Nyirenda was born in northern Malawi sometime in the early part of this century. His family tended a small farm in an area rich with game. His father was the community hunter responsible for providing meat to his family and close relatives as a supplement to their own crops. The hunting skills and traditions passed from father to son; Joshua went on hunting trips with his father and learned how to trap small game with snares made of vegetable fiber, and how to operate a homemade rifle with hand-cast bullets. Eventually Joshua replaced his father as the primary provider for the family, and began passing the knowledge he had gathered about hunting in the Vwaza Marsh on to his own son.

Joshua, his family, and his neighbors lived in a remote, sparsely populated area on the southern boundary of the Vwaza Reserve. The few widely spaced villages contain mud-and-stick houses surrounded by maize and sweet potato fields. Joshua's extended family in this patriarchal society consisted of his brothers and his sons, and their families. When Joshua said he was hunting with his son, he might have been referring to anyone from a son to a cousin to a nephew to a grandchild. Joshua had the ultimate responsibility of providing for them all.

The importance of children in this society cannot be underestimated. One of the goals of the patriarch was to have as many children as possible, preferably boys as they carry on the family name, wealth, and lineage. "You must have as many children as you can rear; they help you with the work in the fields, they help around the house, they hunt with you, and they bring you joy," Joshua said. They also care for you as you get old. The point of work was to be able to share with your family and your children, and hunting in the reserve provided some of the means of meeting their needs. When he was caught, Joshua was waiting for his son and other members of the community to return to help carry the elephant meat back to the village.

The hunting methods Joshua used to bring down that elephant resemble those his great-grandfather might have used, as hunting in this part of Africa has hardly changed with time.

Joshua's weapon when he was arrested was an 1844 Tower Musket, a relic of Arab ivory and slaving trips that is now in a museum. His entire hunting party could have stepped out of the 1840s: three men, one musket, one homemade muzzle-loader, no tent, no shoes, and little more than rags for clothing. They had tracked an elephant for days, covering more than 15 miles over rough country before getting a shot at it.

Hunting with old or homemade firearms is a dangerous business. Guns misfire or explode, and Joshua bore the scars of an African hunter: one look at his face was enough to prove that his type of hunting was not for amateurs. Joshua had a gun explode on him twice. He smiled when asked about his injuries. "The first time was with a gun I had made," he explained. "We were hunting and found *nyama* [game], I pulled the trigger and nothing happened—then bang, the back of the gun shot me." At this Joshua crinkled his eyes as though he found it funny. His face was such a patchwork of scars and holes that it was hard to believe he had survived.

Despite his injuries, Joshua remained a formidable man in the bush. His small but well-muscled frame carried him for miles. He knew when and where to burn the underbrush to stimulate a flush of green grass that would draw animals into the open for hunting, and he knew what areas held water throughout the dry season. His knowledge of the Vwaza Marsh and its animals was as detailed and specific as that of someone who has grown up in a small town and knows everybody by name.

Even a hunter as skilled as Joshua, however, could find the miombo a daunting place. In the miombo, unlike the savanna of East Africa, plants dominate over animals. Broad-leaved trees 20 feet high, their crowns touching, are the hallmark of the habitat. The grass can grow to twice the height of a man, but at times it is just ankle-deep scrub. During the dry season, villagers burn off the grass to facilitate movement of their meager cattle and livestock, to stimulate new grass as food for their animals, and to clear the underbrush so they can hunt more readily. These fires—if started when the land is bone dry—burn in immense conflagrations that scorch the trees and leave the land black, dry, and desolate until the next rains, which may not come for four months.

The plants have evolved to fill their ecological niches so perfectly that the animals rarely get ahead. Miombo plants are rich in secondary chemicals, tanins, and poisons which can be called up when animals attack. When an animal begins to eat a plant, the plant responds by mobilizing its chemical defense system, producing acidic or foul-smelling oils that drive the feeding animal away. These chemicals remain in the animal's body for hours, so that in effect plants can limit how much and how often the animals eat.

With the plants full of chemical weapons, the animals do not stand much of a chance. Even so, several unique animals have evolved in the miombo woodland. Among those that Joshua Nyirenda hunted were two antelope species: Liechtenstein's hartebeest and sable antelope. Both have developed the ability to squeeze out their existence from the sparse grasses that grow under the woodland canopy, but there the similarity ends. Liechtenstein's hartebeest looks like an afterthought, a mixture of animal leftovers. The face is long and narrow, with close-set eyes, giving the creature a rather stupid appearance. The hartebeest's horns form a peculiar double curvature like the letter Z, and the animal always looks as though it is standing on a hill, since the front end is much higher than the back.

Even the name "hartebeest" does not fit. It was originally given the designation due to its apparent likeness to other animals that inhabit the savanna regions of the continent. It is now thought that this hartebeest is quite different—an archaic form possibly more closely related to the wildebeest, another animal that resembles something put together from spare parts. As a result, Liechtenstein's hartebeest recently has been reclassified in its own genus, *Sigmocerus*.

The sable antelope, on the other hand, ranks as one of the most graceful and beautiful animals in Africa. A large creature, named for its glossy black color, the sable antelope has long horns running parallel to each other in a graceful and pronounced curve sweeping backward, and a well-developed mane of long, stiff hairs that extends from the top of the neck to the shoulder. The sable antelope thus resembles a noble form of horse.

Both sable antelope and hartebeest are found throughout the miombo woodlands, though usually scattered in small herds. The low population density, and the need for a relatively large area of woodland to support each individual antelope, means that these animals are particularly sensitive to changes in their habitat. As man continues to expand his influence, the antelope have retreated into the most remote areas, often within national parks and protected areas.

The habitats for hartebeest and sable antelope were not so remote that they fell outside of Joshua Nyirenda's traditional hunting grounds. Joshua's arrest for killing the elephant was just a passing inconvenience. His extended family paid his fine and he returned home to resume his role as head of the household. A year or so later, another group of game scouts on patrol following up tips from the village and the sound of gunfire found Joshua and his son sitting at a waterhole waiting for animals to come and drink. Since his musket was now a museum piece, Joshua had constructed a muzzle-loading gun from a length of pipe, some carved wood, and a few small pieces of scrap metal. Despite this untrustworthy weapon, Joshua had killed two Liechtenstein's hartebeest, a warthog, a tiny antelope called a duiker, and a bushpig, when he was arrested for the second time. He displayed the same smile, the same acceptance of his fate as on the first occasion. Both times he said, "This is my home."

Joshua and his son were convicted of hunting in the game reserve. Since this was their second conviction, they were given stiffer sentences of $500 fines or five years hard labor. The family could not afford to pay both fines, so Joshua went to prison while his son returned home to help clear the fields

and begin planting the next year's crops. Though both Joshua
and his son were skilled hunters, an important and respected
position in their world, agriculture remained the focus of their
lives. Joshua's age got him out early, and he continued hunting. But this time Malawi's Department of National Parks and
Wildlife decided to change their attitude and to use his knowledge of the region to better understand the reserve and the
needs of the people around it. So for the first time Joshua
began to share his deep understanding of Vwaza with the department. For half a century Joshua Nyirenda was a hunter—
some would consider him a poacher—and a provider to his
family, but toward the end of his life he formalized something
he had always been, a conservationist.

Joshua was educating conservationists who were obsessed
with capturing men like himself, and he undoubtedly enjoyed
the irony of the situation. Anti-poaching efforts now absorb
the majority of the resources available for park management,
and dominate popular perceptions about conservation. Such
work is widely portrayed as a war—an image that people in
and out of Africa perpetuate to raise money. Yet recent research indicates that anti-poaching patrols are less effective at
controlling poaching than more basic, and considerably less
expensive, investigative techniques.

The war on poachers will always fall just a little short of its
goals, for no matter how well equipped the game scouts may
be, with high-tech tents and camping equipment, radios, heli-
copters, and airplanes, it will never be enough. More often
then not, these items, sophisticated but ill-suited to the rigors
of the African bush, become excuses for not getting the job
done. An all too common complaint made by scouts to their
commander is: "Sir, we can't go on patrol today, the radio is
buggered." If current trends continue, the war on poaching
may soon resemble the war in Vietnam: a massive, well-armed
force struggles in vain against a poor but unyielding foe.

Conservationists are gradually recognizing the futility of
waging constant war on poachers. The wisest approach may

be to make a virtue out of necessity by using the hunting skills of local people. Richard Bell, for example, who worked in Malawi for years before moving to Zambia and co-directing the Luangwa Integrated Resource Development Project (LIRDP), advocates incorporating poaching into conservation. The suggestion, like others Bell has made, is anathema to many conservationists, but it makes sense to capitalize on knowledge and techniques of the local hunters. Bell's plan would encourage poaching for high cash value products—particularly ivory—at the expense of subsistence poaching. Under the plan, the conservation authority would buy the ivory, trophies, skins, and whatever meat is not used locally, and then resell it. Revenue as well as most of the meat thus would go directly to local communities; and the conservation authority would earn money to support its programs, and would be in a better position to control illegal hunting and generally to control the marketplace.

Such a plan obviously depends on the existence of a legal market for ivory. Bell would not only encourage the ivory trade, he would actually reduce the number of game scouts on patrol. Again, this is an idea guaranteed to send a shudder through most Western supporters of conservation. The image of the noble game scout has been repeated so often in the popular media that his effectiveness is taken for granted. The only problem, most people assume, is a lack of funds to send more scouts into the bush, so the idea of cutting the number of scouts seems like surrender.

Bell, however, has the numbers to support his contrary position. Two research efforts, first in Kasungu National Park and later in the area administered by LIRDP, revealed that the best way to stop illegal killing of large mammals, most notably elephants and rhinos, is to employ investigative methods, much like the police, in villages. Most hunting of animals with firearms is practiced by a few village professionals, and it is relatively easy to keep an eye on these people and monitor their movements once they are identified. Following Joshua Nyirenda's arrest, for example, the park authorities monitored his movements to and from the village, leading to his second arrest. The park warden knew when Joshua had entered the game reserve, and had a rough idea of where he had gone, so the anti-poaching patrol had a relatively easy job in catching him.

In the LIRDP area in Zambia, investigations led to nearly four times as many arrests as did patrols, and captured more than five times as many firearms. Given that scouts in the area spent less than one day per month investigating reports of poaching, compared to nearly seven days on patrol, the efficiency of investigations over patrols becomes even clearer. "In terms of arrests, one man-day spent investigating is worth twenty-eight days on patrol," Bell says. "And in terms of capturing firearms, one day spent investigating equals forty-four days on patrol."

The cost of carrying out investigations in the villages is much lower and shows better results than equipping a large number of anti-poaching patrols and expecting them to carry out the work themselves. While the patrols in the field still have a role to play, the myth that surrounds the end results of such actions dies slowly and at great expense. Unlike cops on the beat, anti-poaching patrols are not a deterrent by themselves.

Anti-poaching patrols certainly never deterred Joshua Nyirenda. Joshua saw numerous changes over the years in the miombo where he hunted, in animal populations and their distribution, and in the status of the land and those charged with its protection. In the widely accepted story of conservation in Africa, park scouts and poachers are sworn enemies, at opposite ends of the spectrum in terms of their relationship with wildlife. Yet scouts and poachers often live quite similar lives, blurring the line between those who protect wildlife and those who make use of it.

A scout named Henry Kachoyo was among those who heard Joshua's gunshots both times he was arrested. Like most of Malawi's wildlife scouts, Kachoyo was well trained. Scouts in Malawi (unlike those in other parts of Africa), are expected to be able to read and write, and usually must have finished, at least, primary school. They frequently undergo a period of apprenticeship as porters for the more experienced scouts, thereby weeding out those who might have an affinity for life in the bush from those who don't. The scouts are trained in police techniques, the law, and firearm use and safety, and are expected to spend up to twenty-four days a month in the field away from home, usually camping. Rangers, who lead scout groups, are expected to have a secondary school education, and most of them have been trained at one of Africa's wildlife colleges. This background and training makes Malawi's game scouts an effective force, experienced in working in the field and reporting back to their superiors on what they have seen and done.

Henry Kachoyo had been a member of Malawi's Department of National Parks and Wildlife for many years before being transferred to the northern part of the country to work in the department's research unit. The government provided him with a uniform, boots, housing, a World War II vintage .303 rifle for protection, and training. Like Joshua Nyirenda, Henry Kachoyo's main concern was providing for his family. Unlike Joshua, he could not hunt or even collect plant material, since both are illegal in Malawi's protected areas. Henry and his family relied on the government for food and for transport to collect it, something that was not always available. This meant that Henry and his family often resorted to hunting and gathering, just like Joshua. Only instead of being out in the bush, Henry was required to hunt and gather in the local markets, often among people who resented his position and his role in their society. Sometimes food was not available at all, and sometimes the merchants made it available at a higher price.

Working for the government, the department staff usually live far from their friends and extended family, and thus lack the extensive support system to help plant crops, prepare food, and care for the sick. Families such as Henry's may not have the labor to cultivate enough land to feed themselves, and indeed may not cultivate any land at all. What crops they can grow are often damaged by animals. Oddly enough, this description sounds more like the stereotype of how a poacher lives—on the fringes of civilization, with limited contact with family, tribe, or nation.

Occasionally the bad feelings between game scouts and the local people turn especially nasty. One year shortly before Christmas, the scouts of Vwaza Marsh Game Reserve arrested a villager for hunting in the reserve. In the process of bringing him to park headquarters, he escaped back to his village. Since the scouts know most of the people in the area, they knew where to find him. Crossing the large river which forms the southern boundary of the reserve, the scouts found themselves far outnumbered by an angry mob of villagers. Giving up any hope of trying to retake the man they had arrested, the scouts attempted to retreat. In the heat of the confrontation, someone began throwing stones, and the villagers attacked. Two of the scouts were badly injured and drowned trying to cross the river back into the reserve. When the park authorities found the bodies, they discovered that both had received skull fractures. "Why did it happen? Those were people we buy our food from," one scout who survived said after the incident. Another scout repeated the lament of police everywhere: "We were just doing our job."

Unfortunately, the job of a game scout sometimes means violent conflict between people who share the same history, culture, and values. Both Henry Kachoyo and Joshua Nyirenda grew up in small villages surrounded by family and friends. The difference for Henry was that he finished primary school and ended up not as a farmer in the village but as a game scout hired by the government to patrol Kasungu National Park, not far from his home. Henry had a bottomless curiosity about his natural surroundings, and through his work with a young Zimbabwean researcher he became the department expert in miombo flora. He surrounded himself with books in a constant effort to increase his knowledge. At the time he was posted to the Vwaza Marsh, he was in his mid-forties, a father of nine children. Just starting to turn gray, Henry could march for days in the bush without tiring. When offered a drink of water, he would smile and say, "I'll have a smoke, it kills the thirst," and would light up a cigarette.

Henry Kachoyo's commitment to his work knew no bounds, whether it was research expeditions or anti-poaching patrols. While Joshua Nyirenda's face would light up at the sight of an animal, Henry's would light up at the sight of a plant, practically any plant. At some point during most collecting trips, Henry would come up over a hill, his face breaking into a wide grin and his eyes growing wide, as if he'd just spotted an especially rare and beautiful species. Everyone else on the trail behind him would hurry up to see as well, only to find Henry looking at a rather nondescript tree and saying, "I've never seen that tree in the reserve, we must collect a sample for the office."

While Henry Kachoyo was committed to his work, he was also committed to his family. He never ceased in his efforts to educate his children; it is no mean feat to send nine children to school where school fees and books must be paid on a salary of approximately $175 a month, and of course they must be fed as well. Though his formal schooling was limited, Henry's great desire to learn whatever he could showed him the value of education. His knowledge of plants put him in a position to work around educated people, and his pride was his collection of books. "These are my teachers, and my children's teachers," he would say. He never stopped pushing his children or his colleagues.

By the time Henry Kachoyo was posted to northern Malawi he was the department's botanist, the man who knew the country's vegetation and who could teach it to the younger generation of staff coming up through the system. He was in demand everywhere. Following his work in the Vwaza, he was posted to three other parks and reserves to help with vegetation work before finally going back to Kasungu National Park to be near his home and prepare for retirement. He was even asked to stay on for an extra year or two to train people to follow in his footsteps. There is a small core of Malawians in the Vwaza who are now botanists because of Henry Kachoyo.

The growing expertise of Malawi's park managers is beginning to change conservation in the Vwaza. For the first time, conservation authorities are seeking out the villagers and asking for their opinions. In the village of Filimon Kumwenda, not far from where Joshua Nyirenda lived, the department is no longer just a police force but is becoming a force for development. With support from the German government and WWF, villages are going into the beekeeping and honey production business. Beekeeping is a traditional occupation in Malawi, but it had fallen off over the past 10 years as the human population grew and the forest receded. To revive the practice, Wildlife Department staff trained in beekeeping are working with villagers to help them establish hives in the reserve by forming beekeeping clubs. Before this effort began, the villagers were not allowed into the Vwaza Game Reserve to collect honey. However, they went in despite the law and ended up burning down trees to get at the hives. With improved extraction and marketing techniques, the villagers can now use the reserve without harming the ecosystem, and in return they have promised the Wildlife Department that they will not hunt or collect firewood within the reserve's boundaries.

Now that villagers have a stake in the Vwaza, interesting benefits are turning up. Not long ago an elephant was found dead in the reserve, shot by a local hunter. Village members of the Filimon Kumwenda Beekeeping Club provided the information that led to the arrest of the culprit. This success depended on a combination of goodwill toward the park authorities generated by working with the local community and intelligence work in the villages. As a honey cooperative member said: "We found an elephant that had been killed in our reserve. We asked questions in the nearby villages and found out who did it and where the gun was. We told this to the wildlife scouts so they could catch this man. If these people continue to do this, we will not have the reserve for our bees." The gun and ivory were recovered, and the hunter was arrested. It is their new benefits and involvement in decision making that have brought these Malawians onto the side of conservation.

Joshua Nyirenda did not live to see the advances made by the beekeeping project. He finally ran out of steam and died in his seventies, a ripe old age for someone living in the bush. No doubt today his son, with the same appreciation for the land and what it can provide, is still trying to avoid anti-poaching patrols as he hunts the same land as his father and Joshua's father before him. His family continues to carve out whatever living the land can provide.

Henry Kachoyo retired from the Department of National Parks and Wildlife and returned to his plot of land and the home he had been preparing for some time. He moved back to the land, to a life little different from that of Joshua's family. After his retirement, Henry began suffering from pain in his eyes and headaches. The pain worsened, and suddenly Henry died at fifty-two, leaving a wife, nine children, and one grandchild. Henry died of sleeping sickness, a disease he had contracted from working in remote areas like the Vwaza. And what of his family? A letter from his daughter Joyce sums it up:

I hope you are doing fine with the weather of U.S.A. moreover from this side, not so bad but cool and warm have accumulated us here.

Actually, the aim of writing this kind of letter to you is to identify ourselves from problems which have occurred here due to the death of our father. Since in his absence I and Oliver Kachoyo left school due to the shortage of fees and clothes. This has been so because, support so that we should educate ourselves in order to help our younger brothers couldn't be found, and you already know the situation of our mother that she is growing older and older and no assistance can be obtained from her, and nine children have been left by our father. This gives our mother a great problem because everyone in our family is walking naked and it gives shame to those who are seeing us. We have no where we could arise our problem.

Finally, I say goodbye and have a nice stay in the U.S.A. together with your family and comrades.

In the end, Henry Kachoyo's family is just like Joshua Nyirenda's, maybe worse off. Both these men loved the bush, both possessed intimate knowledge of the Vwaza, and both had a deep respect for its wildlife. The two men followed different paths, Henry choosing to finish his schooling and pursue a career in government service, but neither strayed far from village life. In the village, Henry and Joshua could have been the best of friends. This story has no heroes and no villains. Ultimately, both Henry and Joshua were just trying to survive.

CHAPTER VIII

STRIKING
A BALANCE

*I am not one to dwell in the past. I want to look to
the future. I think the future of conservation lies in
getting the cooperation, understanding, and participation of the local people. If we do not, then we will
surely fail. I believe we have begun this process soon
enough.*

—Costa Mlay

F*or people living* along Tanzania's southern coast, survival depends on acquiring more cattle. The villagers in
the region do not have enough cattle to make ends meet, but
the people in central Tanzania have a surplus. The fastest and
cheapest way to get the cows from one place to the other would
be a huge cattle drive, straight across the plains and the forests.
The government of Tanzania has proposed just such a drive,
with twenty thousand cattle per year moving the 300 miles to
the coast.

The proposed cattle drive is on hold, but it could be revived
at any time, leaving Costa Mlay, head of the Wildlife Division
of Tanzania's Ministry of Natural Resources and Tourism, in
an awkward position. Mlay and other Africans playing leadership roles in conservation have the difficult task of balancing
the needs of their own governments with the desires of Western conservationists. Like Henry Kachoyo, Costa Mlay must
reconcile the divergent values of people who have been labeled
"scouts" or "poachers."

The archetypes of "scout" and "poacher" are misleading,

but they capture the essence of the conflict that batters Costa Mlay. The stock route, for example, would require constructing a road bisecting the Selous Game Reserve, a 20,000-square-mile expanse of woodland and savanna that is home to the largest concentration of elephant and buffalo in the country, as well as one of the largest remaining populations of wild dogs in Africa. The infectious diseases of wildlife that have invaded the parks in northern Tanzania have not reached the Selous, but the cattle drive would introduce cattle-borne diseases to which the buffalo in the Selous have no immunity, while the herdsmen's dogs carry distemper and rabies that could wipe out the wild dogs.

The problems could be avoided by moving the cattle by train to Dar-Es-Salaam and then shipping them by sea down the coast. This method allows veterinarians to inspect, quarantine, and disinfect the cattle, thus preventing the spread of disease to the south, but it is also expensive and slow. Neither the Ministry of Agriculture, which approved the drive, nor the cattle ranchers seem willing to wait.

The stock road may serve a broader purpose than simply transporting cattle. Many conservationists in Tanzania and elsewhere in East Africa fear that building the stock road is just the first step toward cutting off the southern half of the Selous and opening it up to human settlement. The cattle drive thus threatens not only the animals in the Selous but the reserve itself. On the surface it would appear that Mlay, as Tanzania's chief conservationist, would be unable to support such a potentially destructive plan. With the Ministry of Agriculture and other ministries lined up in favor of it, however, he has no choice. Mlay, a trim, kindly man with an air of urgency about him, clearly feels uncomfortable about the stock road. He has already been put on the defensive by protests from the Wildlife Conservation Society of Tanzania, a local conservation organization, and he fears the controversy may spread to international groups, which contribute huge amounts of money for projects in Tanzania.

"The Selous is a large tract of land," Mlay says. "I hate the very thought that somebody intelligent should consider opposing the cattle drive. Seriously, [those opposing the drive have] conservation objectives that completely ignore reality. The people in the south need cattle, and if they have cattle they will not poach. If I sit in Dar-Es-Salaam and rule that cattle cannot come through the Selous because they might hurt the buffalo, it is a joke, a joke in very bad taste. I hate to think that anyone intelligent would want to stop or attempt to stop a move of national importance merely because the Maasai dogs accompanying the herds might spread disease to the wild dogs in the Selous."

Mlay's office in Dar-Es-Salaam reflects the dual nature of his job. Tucked into the corner of a stifling concrete building, the office's dominant feature is a pair of huge elephant tusks, weighing well over 100 pounds each. Mlay is quick to point out that the tusks are quite old, and were left by his predecessor. Elephant tusks make incongruous decorations for one of Africa's leading spokesmen for the ivory ban, but their presence is a perfect illustration of the two audiences, one African and one Western, that Mlay must please.

The pressure to support the cattle drive comes from within Tanzania, but Africans often must also balance their needs against the ideals of foreign governments and the international conservation community, as was the case with the campaign against the ivory trade. Mlay, for example, has a deep understanding of the changes conservation must undergo in terms of addressing the needs of rural people, but he cannot always be consistent in putting such changes into practice. While he supports efforts to integrate conservation and development, and to give those people living with wildlife a stake in conservation, he has also begun a regressive program in the village of Macao, southeast of the Serengeti National Park. A hunting company operating in the area, using a donation from an American businessman and conservationist, established a $30,000 fund to compensate villagers who pick up wire snares at the rate of $5 a snare. The money also goes to villagers who volunteer information leading to the arrest of poachers, or to the confiscation of a weapon or vehicle that has been used in poaching.

This reward scheme, essentially a bribe paid to rural Africans by rich Americans, stands in direct opposition to the trend toward involving local people in conservation in a meaningful way. The reward scheme cannot support itself, and will last only as long as the benefactor continues to sign the checks. Mlay, however, is wildly enthusiastic: "We collected more than one thousand snares over the first five months. We hope that this coming year we can attract $200,000, move it into protected areas beyond the original ones." As at the CITES meeting in 1989, when Mlay simultaneously gave an emotional plea to save elephants and supported sport hunting of them, so now he calls for local control over wildlife resources while relying on foreigners to pay off the villagers. Money was the driving force at CITES, in the village of Macao, and in the Selous: regardless of Mlay's personal sincerity, without funds (usually from wealthy foreigners) and political support from his own government, he can do nothing.

Western conservationists can afford to be single-minded in their efforts, but African governments—for good or ill—necessarily have broader concerns. That was clear in the plan to drive cattle across the Selous, and it is perhaps even more obvious in the southern African nation of Botswana. Botswana provides another dramatic illustration of the conflict that arises when Western conservationists working in Africa attempt to act on the assumption that conservation and development are mutually exclusive, and ignore the tension inherent in most conservation activities in Africa. As in Tanzania, American conservationists in Botswana played a counterproductive role.

Botswana's economy and culture are closely tied to cattle. Large areas of land are devoted to cattle ranching, and over 50 percent of Botswana's beef is exported to the European Community (EC) under special aid and trade agreements through which ranchers receive 60 percent more than world market value for their beef. This arrangement, while an economic boon to Botswana, also causes problems by forcing the country to abide by European import regulations that grew out of fears that beef from Africa might be contaminated with foot-and-mouth disease. Though scientists have never demonstrated how transmission occurs, Africa's wild animals, particularly buffalo, are reservoirs of the disease.

Concern over spreading disease from wildlife to cattle has played a large role in conservation and management efforts for many years. Beginning in the 1950s, the EC provided the funds to build a series of veterinary cordon fences at various locations in Botswana to protect the cattle.

Those fences became the focus of an international controversy, as they cut directly across the route of the most dramatic wildebeest migration outside the Serengeti. Botswana's wildebeest usually concentrate in the southwest part of the Kalahari, an arid savanna that fills the center of the country. Under normal circumstances the wildebeest do not migrate far, surviving on ephemeral pools of water and succulent roots instead of traveling great distances in search of water like their Serengeti cousins. Only the severe, periodic droughts that hit the Kalahari force the herds north and east toward permanent water sources such as Lake Xau. Starting in 1958, however, the route to the lake was blocked by the cordon fences. During a particularly harsh drought that lasted from 1979 to 1983, most of the migrating animals were unable to cross the fences and died of thirst or starvation. Botswana's wildebeest population was nearly wiped out.

The grisly scenes of wildebeest and other wildlife collapsing in the dust created an international media event, due in large part to the efforts of two American researchers, Mark and Delia Owens. The story of the wildebeest, the Owenses, and the fences embodies the conflict between Western attitudes about wildlife in Africa and the economic needs and interests of African governments. The furor over the fences focused on the Owenses—who carry on the tradition of Bernhard and

Michael Grzimek—and ignored the role that Western misperceptions played. The continuing fascination with such events also overshadows the important steps that countries like Botswana and Tanzania, finally shaking off the Grzimek legacy, have taken toward lasting conservation.

Like the Grzimeks, Mark and Delia Owens set out to study African wildlife in the most remote wilderness they could find. Their naive concept of wild Africa was a place with no distractions and no people. They thought they had found such a place on the Kalahari sands, which extend over 1,500 miles from the Orange River in South Africa to the rain forests of southern Zaire—the longest unbroken stretch of sand in the world. Though often called a desert, the Kalahari usually receives between 10 and 20 inches of rain annually and is more properly and evocatively called a "thirstland"; whatever rain does fall disappears into the thick sand or is rapidly absorbed by vegetation. The Kalahari thus has rain, but no streams and no permanent standing water.

The Owenses never discussed conservation priorities with the government of Botswana, nor did they seek to involve local people in scientific research or to train them in modern techniques for using natural resources. The result was first-rate scientific work of practically no conservation value. The Owenses set up camp in a dry riverbed in the northern part of the Central Kalahari Game Reserve called Deception Valley, and began studying the region's lions and brown hyenas. Until the wildebeest began dying along the fences, the Owenses had no contact with Botswana's government except to obtain work permits. It takes a great deal of time to collect data on the social behavior of desert lions and brown hyena in order to qualify for a PhD, and in reality this was the primary goal.

The Owenses paid lip service to the importance of conservation, yet they never used their expertise on lions and hyenas for conservation (save for a five-page appendix to their book). Instead, they jumped into a debate over wildlife and cattle about which they knew little, thus trading their scientific strengths for political controversy. Perhaps the greatest mistake the Owenses made was their failure to include Batswana—the collective term for all citizens of the country—in their work, caught up as they were with the vision of two dedicated scientists struggling against an evil government bureaucracy in order to save the Kalahari.

In the course of their studies, the Owenses laid claim to the "discovery" of the wildebeest migration in the Kalahari. Their assertion is misleading. In truth, both Africans and non-Africans knew of the migration long before the Owenses arrived in Botswana, but acknowledging that fact would have lessened the drama, described in their book *Cry of the Kalahari*, of Mark Owens at the moment of discovery, flying over the Kalahari in search of hyenas but finding instead herds of wildebeest on the move.

Even the more modest claim that the Owenses were the first to document the migration scientifically does not hold up under scrutiny. After five years of work on hyenas and lions, the Owenses did not suddenly switch gears and undertake a study of wildebeest. Rather, they told stories about what they saw from their airplane. These stories were only slightly more revealing than the anecdotes of early settlers and the bushmen. Between 1981 and 1984, D. T. Williamson, J. Williamson, and K. T. Ngwamotsoko carried out the first full scientific description of the wildebeest migration in the Kalahari, which required years of aerial surveys and in-depth analyses of soil and vegetation conditions. The Owenses did not participate in that research.

The Owenses had little success in stirring the government of Botswana into action to save the wildebeest, which is hardly surprising given their history of limited interaction with the country's conservation authorities. So the Owenses went public with their information. Conservation magazines such as *International Wildlife* and the German *Das Tier*, both of which employed the Owenses as roving editors once the story broke, published articles on the fences, and inevitably the popular press picked up on the story. The term "fences of death" became known worldwide.

When the Owenses pointed to the destruction the fences were causing the wildebeest, Botswana had to make a choice: remove the fences and clear the wildebeest migration route, or leave them in place and maintain an outlet for exporting beef, with a subsidy from the European Community. Since the cattle industry, along with the discovery of diamonds in the 1970s, propelled Botswana from terrible poverty to financial security in under a quarter century of independence, the government did not see the choice as a difficult one. It has now begun an effort to construct boreholes in the Kalahari to provide a year-round water supply for the wildebeest.

The Owenses unquestionably succeeded in attracting world attention to the plight of the Kalahari wildebeest. The positive impact of all this attention is unclear—the fences remain, and the wildebeest population has not yet rebounded (though there are now some encouraging signs following several years of good rains)—but the down side is all too apparent: the Owenses' activities set back conservation in Botswana by at least five years because the government grew increasingly wary of accepting international support for conservation activities. Faced with mounting criticism, the government of Botswana decided it had nothing more to lose; it declared Mark and Delia Owens prohibited immigrants and canceled their research permits. In the words of Dr. Quett Masire, president of Botswana; "If you cannot operate within the bounds of government, whom you are a guest of in this country, to work these issues out, then work elsewhere."

Conservationists in Europe and the United States clamored for the government of Botswana to allow the researchers to return to the country. The U.S. Embassy even became involved in negotiating terms. The Owenses were prepared to accept whatever stipulations the government wished to attach to their return, though they wanted to avoid the suggestion that they had made any concessions.

They were not granted new visas, however, so they began to search for a new area in which they could continue their studies. This search became the focus of a National Geographic Society television special. At one point during the film, the Owenses are in Zambia, looking for a research site in Kafue National Park. They seem to have radically changed their views on the role of local people in conservation, as they visit a village chief and we hear Mark Owens speaking about how important the cooperation of the villagers is to successful conservation in the area. But in the next scene, the Owenses are off once again, looking for a place as far away from these villagers as possible, where absolutely no people will clutter their idealistic vision of Africa.

The Owenses and the popular media in general oversimplified the conservation issues in Botswana. Even the veterinary fences, which seem so horrible at first glance, cannot easily be condemned. One fence, for example, forms a nearly 90-mile-long arc in the southwestern part of the Okavango Delta—a vast, reed-covered wetland that is perhaps Botswana's most precious wildlife area. This fence serves an unexpected but important conservation purpose. Constructed to keep buffalo who live in the delta out of neighboring cattle-grazing areas, the fence also keeps cattle out of the delta, which has been declared a cattle-free zone. The Okavango fence undoubtedly has prevented large-scale invasion of the delta by cattle, and has been an immense boon to such wildlife as buffalo, elephants, and the graceful, swamp-dwelling antelope called red lechwe. The government is now considering building a second fence near the Okavango, this one in the north. The plan has divided conservationists: some think the northern fence, like the southern, will keep cattle out of the delta, while others fear it will disturb migratory patterns of zebra, elephants, and wildebeest between the delta and the Linyanti/Chobe River system further north.

The Okavango Delta is one of the miracles of Africa. A procession of geological activity several million years ago redirected the Okavango River, which once flowed to the sea. The river now hits a dead end in the Kalahari sands. In this arid vastness, in the middle of the driest time of the year, a most unlikely event occurs: a flood. The rainy season in Botswana lasts from November to February; rains in Angola, where the Okavango begins its abbreviated journey to the sea, begin earlier and end later. The delta's gentle slope—it drops by just over 200 feet in 150 miles—and the thousands of channels choked by vegetation, mean that the floodwaters travel less than a mile each day and peak at the southern edge of the delta in July or August, though there has been no appreciable rain for five months.

The Okavango forms one of the few true inland deltas in the world, as well as an oasis the size of Massachusetts that may be the most beautiful spot on the continent. About 2 million years ago, seismic activity created a steep valley or fault which redirected the Okavango, Chobe, and Zambezi rivers to the south into a vast basin. This gave birth to the now-extinct Lake Makgadikgadi, at 23,000 square miles one of the largest lakes Africa has seen. Lake Makgadikgadi eventually overflowed and slowly drained. The Okavango Delta and the large, dry Makgadikgadi saltpans are the last remnants of this prehistoric lake.

The Okavango draws its water from the wet highlands of central Angola. After a nearly 200-mile trip down from the mountains, the Okavango fans out into the countless channels of the delta. The delta provides habitat for hundreds of bird species, including the striking malachite kingfisher, the rare slaty egret, and the even rarer shoebill. It is also the major surviving stronghold of the shy sitatunga, a medium-sized antelope which, alone among mammals, makes its home on the delta's floating reedbeds.

Everyone in the region, from farmers and basket weavers to lodge owners and diamond miners, has a stake in the future of the delta, so any management plan is guaranteed to cause controversy. Nearly all the challenges facing conservation in Botswana—indeed, in all of Africa—surface in some form at one time or another in the Okavango. The solutions remain elusive, but the Okavango and the area near the Chobe River just to the north demonstrate the futility of the kind of tactics used by Mark and Delia Owens.

Like many captivated by wild Africa, the Owenses overlooked the role of Africans. This omission seems all the more incredible given that local people, from the Tswana, Botswana's dominant tribe, to the San, the Bushmen of the Kalahari, have made use of the Kalahari and the far richer resources of the Okavango Delta for millennia. The balance between the delta and its human and animal inhabitants has always been fragile, however, and it may not last much longer.

Botswana has opened a second front in its war against cattle disease and has practically eliminated tsetse by spraying insecticide from airplanes. The tsetse eradication program led some conservationists to conclude that the government was preparing to drain the delta for cattle ranching. According to Nigel D. Hunter, deputy director of the Department of Wildlife and National Parks, that fear is unfounded. "The tsetse program was not intended to free the delta for livestock," says Hunter, one of the people most directly responsible for determining how Botswana should use its land. "The more reasonable approach will be to freeze development in the delta so that we can determine what we can do about use or non-use so that people can enjoy the delta and benefit from it without destroying it."

The delta's resources fill a variety of needs—agriculture, industry, crafts, livestock, hunting and fishing, building materials, tourism—which complicates management of the area. Communities around the northern reaches of the delta and along its western edge, for example, use the water for domestic purposes and small-scale agriculture. For now, the quantity extracted by these users and by scattered settlements and tourist camps within the delta is minuscule compared with the supply. More serious challenges, however, may be on the horizon.

According to Nigel Hunter, a booming tourist industry

poses the greatest threat to the Okavango Delta. "There is a growing concern about tourism," says Hunter. "Botswana is a young country, and many industries, including tourism, have mushroomed tremendously." In fact, the number of tourist camps operating in the delta has more than doubled over the last ten years. Some thirty thousand tourists pay Africa's highest park fees to visit the area each year, making tourism Botswana's fourth-largest source of income, behind diamonds, cattle, and copper-nickel mining. Soon, the few roads around the delta will be tarred, leaving it a two-day drive from Johannesburg.

Botswana's expanded tourist industry illustrates the problems facing governments and conservationists as they try to pull increasing revenues from wild areas while encouraging the wise use of natural resources. Tourism has brought increased foreign exchange to the country, but also problems of refuse and litter disposal, uncontrolled settlements, and large number of motorboats that disturb the delta's ecology. Planning and administrative processes Hunter terms "sometimes vague and sometimes chaotic" have compounded the problems of managing the delta.

Tourism has spurred the growth of Maun, a village at the delta's southern fringe that serves as the gateway to the isolated tourist camps. The demand for water in Maun now exceeds the capacity of the nearby Shashe River aquifer, which will have to be supplemented. One proposal has been to build two low dams to create a reservoir, allowing for better use of outflow for Maun and other villages. Two other dams would be needed to regulate *molapo,* the traditional method of floodplain farming in which growers move onto the floodplain after the water has receded and cultivate intensively for several months. The return of floodwater flushes away harmful salts and brings silt and detritus as natural fertilizers. Many African rural communities survive in this way, moving cattle and crops as falling floodwaters expose enriched bottomland and floodplains.

The proposed dams were originally intended to provide

water for agriculture, but the emphasis shifted to human water supply when little suitable soil was found in the southern delta. According to Hunter, dams at the delta's southern end have the potential to do far greater harm to the delta's ecology than other proposals to remove water from the northern delta. A slight decrease in flow in the north would be spread among the many channels and thus no single area would change substantially, while damming the seasonally flooded areas would completely choke off certain regions. The debate over how to use the resources of the delta without destroying it has raged on for years, and still no clear solution is in sight.

With the dry climate of southern Africa it is not surprising that Botswana, Namibia, and Angola, the three countries through which the Okavango flows, are interested in exploiting the river's resources. Namibia, for example, has already begun a project called the Eastern National Water Carrier, which will remove 2 percent of the flow of the Okavango River at the point where it crosses the border, and Angola may also have plans to use the river for hydroelectric power or agricultural development. An international agreement to protect the delta may be crucial, though Botswana's fiercely independent government has thus far been reluctant to join international environmental conventions.

Heavy industry presents another potential threat to the Okavango because of the huge demand for water. Approximately 90 miles from Maun, near the town of Orapa, lies the world's second-largest diamond mine. Diamonds were first discovered in Botswana in the late 1960s, and today they provide the country with its largest source of foreign exchange. Diamond mining, however, requires vast quantities of water to separate the gems from the sand, so the flow of one of the delta's main channels was increased by dredging.

A plan to dredge the river further into the delta collapsed at the hands of local people. The Tswana have longstanding democratic traditions—another reason that the refusal of Mark and Delia Owens to work with the local people seems so misguided. Chieftainships among the Tswana pass from father to son, but the chiefs rule by consensus. A village forum, called *kgotla* (pronounced HOTE-la) allows all the residents to voice their opinions about important issues or decisions. The *kgotla* remains a vital part of Botswana's political life, and the long history of citizens participating in government helps explain why Botswana is among the most democratic countries in Africa, with seven political parties and a vigorous parliament. An old Tswana saying still holds true: *"Kgosi ke kgosi ka morafe*—The chief is only the chief by the will of the tribe."

In January 1991, the government of Botswana invited the residents of Maun and nearby villages to a meeting about the proposed dredging project. Some seven hundred people attended, and one by one they rose to berate the government for the plan, which they feared would drain the delta dry. The scene is unimaginable in practically any other country in Africa. According to newspaper accounts of the Maun *kgotla,* one local fisherman said: "We believe this river has a life of its own. God gave it to us. It is not for man to kill it."

Botswana's democratic traditions provide a striking forum for local involvement in conservation. Such efforts are clearly shaping the future of wildlife conservation in Africa. Even Tanzania, for so long the bastion of preservationism, has finally escaped the ghost of Bernhard Grzimek and joined the movement toward local involvement. Two efforts, the Serengeti Regional Conservation Strategy (SRCS) in Tanzania and the Chobe Enclave Project in Botswana, reveal how these countries, with vastly different political and cultural roots, are taking a similar path to a new form of conservation.

In Botswana, the *kgotla* is the key. Through the *kgotla,* the villagers living in an area known as the Chobe Enclave, roughly 60 miles northwest of the Okavango Delta, help shape wildlife conservation. Surrounded on three sides by Chobe National Park (the Chobe River forms the northern boundary), this is a critical area for wildlife as well as a ready route for poachers. Yet the Department of Wildlife and National Parks rarely patrols the enclave, so increasing community involvement may be an effective means of curbing poaching.

Residents of the Chobe Enclave and other rural areas have benefited from recent changes in government policies. In an attempt to address the needs and aspirations of these communities, Botswana's government has reclassified some lands as Wildlife Management Areas (WMAs), zones where the primary activity involves wildlife management, and has partitioned the entire country into controlled hunting areas. Use of wildlife in these areas may range from total protection—as in the decision of the Tswana people to set aside a portion of their land as the Moremi Wildlife Reserve—to safari hunting in areas leased out to private concessionaires.

In a significant move, the communities living within some of these controlled hunting areas now can be given the rights to manage the resources found there. Rural communities are allowed to set up a decision-making group which develops a plan outlining types of use for a given area, methods of distributing funds, and zoning. The Department of Wildlife and National Parks still manages Botswana's wildlife by setting quotas for how many animals local people and safari hunters can kill, and the department provides technical expertise in developing the management plan. This program is changing the department from what was essentially a police force into an agency that provides training, agricultural improvements, and other forms of technical assistance which enable local communities to better manage their resources—often in those critical areas surrounding Botswana's national parks. As communities become more responsible for these resources, pressure on the parks will be redirected. Villagers can become the protectors.

Tanzania's Serengeti Regional Conservation Strategy (SRCS), which began to take shape at a conference held at the Serengeti Wildlife Research Centre in late 1985, has similar goals. The project seeks to contribute to village community development, increase the productivity of the land, and therefore ease the land hunger that threatens the Serengeti. The

SRCS now operates in twenty-seven villages in seven districts. As a first step, the Wildlife Department has given these villages a quota of animals they can hunt every year. Earlier efforts often required villagers to use rifles, which may be beyond their economic reach. Under SRCS, either the Wildlife Department will loan villagers a rifle or it will permit them to use traditional hunting methods that kill humanely. Village residents take full responsibility for the game meat, and each village has set up a committee to decide whether to sell it in Dar-Es-Salaam or divide it among the village households. The department sets the quotas, oversees how the villagers harvest that quota, and offers advice. But the major decision-making power remains with the villagers.

As SRCS matures, it will move beyond simply administering hunting quotas and will help local communities adopt farming and hunting techniques that do not deplete the natural resources of their lands. Development assistance to the underprivileged villages near the Serengeti will bring clean water, sanitation, roads, schools, and health clinics to those areas most in need, while securing natural resources over the long term.

Buffer zones, similar to Botswana's Wildlife Management Areas, are the most appropriate means of launching these development efforts. Improvements in land and animal husbandry, however, will only take place through the active and willing participation of the local communities. Tanzania's government will have to provide extension services in such specialties as agroforestry, soil conservation, establishment of tree nurseries, agriculture, and livestock production.

Both the SRCS and the Chobe Enclave Project operate in regions with little arable land. Half of the 730 square miles in the Chobe Enclave are taken up by the Chobe Forest Reserve, a region of deep sandy soils that are poor for agriculture but support vast stands of Rhodesian teak—the only tree of any value as a timber resource in Botswana, and one of the few in all of southern Africa. The enclave is also an important dry-season refuge for most of Chobe National Park's animals, including elephants, buffalo, sable and roan antelope, giraffe, and the associated predators.

Over twenty thousand elephants—almost one third of the country's total elephant population—live in Chobe National Park, and the habitat may not be able to support them all. Many of these animals cross back and forth between the park and the enclave. Without the opportunity to move to the enclave in search of water and grass, the elephants and other animals would almost certainly overgraze and destroy the national park. The trade-off is that the 4,500 people scattered among nearby villages and smaller settlements must compete with the wildlife for the use of available land.

Residents of the enclave have to struggle just to survive. Communal lands are restricted to a strip of relatively rich soil along the Chobe River. People living in the enclave are primarily farmers, though some also keep chickens, pigs, goats, and sheep, as well as some cattle. The biggest complaints heard from the villagers are about raids on crops by elephants, and on livestock by lions. Not surprisingly, these villagers share few of the Western sentiments toward elephants.

A tourist operation conducts both hunting and photographic safaris in part of the enclave. Foreign hunters pay steep license fees—between $500 and $1,500 per animal to the department, and $1,000 per day to the safari operator, who, under an agreement with the government, uses the money to fund wildlife conservation programs. Yet the villagers see few direct benefits from the lucrative tourist operation in the enclave or the park. The safari company hires a few residents as camp staff or trackers, but for most people their sole contact with the visitors to Chobe National Park is watching fancy four-wheel-drive vehicles pass through their villages, sometimes running over their chickens.

The village of Kachikau is typical. Filled with stoutly made round huts, the village has separate areas for crops and livestock. Grass fences provide some privacy, both from neighbors and from the main road—actually more of a sandy track—which bisects the village. Kachikau sits under a grove of Rhodesian teak, and also has a river frontage good for crops and grazing. It is in this village that the Department of Wildlife and National Parks first approached villagers about having more control over wildlife resources. According to Dr. David Lawson, head of the department's Wildlife Utilization Unit, "The villagers thought it was some kind of trick. The department usually tells them what they can't do or arrests them. It doesn't ask how it can help."

The village and the department needed to work together, because more and more animals were preying on livestock and crops, and the residents wanted them shot. Chief Julius Mologasele, speaking with the National Geographic Society, painted a bleak picture: "Lions are eating cattle. Elephants are coming for the destruction of the lands. People think elephants are too much. Some must be shot. We don't want animals to be finished in the country. Animals are food. You can't live without eating meat. We want the reserve to be farther from the lands of the people."

In light of the villagers' need, the department actively began a search for money to buy a new generation of electric fencing as a way to keep these animals out of gardens and livestock enclosures. A conservation group agreed to provide the necessary equipment, but it was up to the villagers to decide how best to deploy it and maintain it, and it was up to the department to teach them how to set it up.

Much of this was a show of commitment on the part of the department staff that they were serious about such a program, an indication of how much mistrust existed between Kachikau and this government agency. The next step was to develop a program of wildlife management by the Chobe Enclave communities. With its abundant wildlife, the area has great potential for innovative programs such as joint ventures between villagers and safari-hunting companies, game farming and ranching, and a village scout program.

The villagers living near Serengeti National Park face many of the same problems as those in Kachikau. As in Botswana, communication between Tanzanian park authorities and local communities has been largely nonexistent. The surest way of improving relations between the parks department and villagers living near protected areas is to guarantee that the revenues from wildlife reach the people who share their land with animals. Direct benefits from wildlife tourism—revenue and local development projects, for example—will reduce human pressures on protected areas, so long as the connection between these benefits and sustainable use is made clear.

In some ways, the SRCS harkens back to a system that existed in Tanzania, on paper at least, two decades ago. Throughout the mid-1960s and early 1970s, the government returned a portion of park revenues to district councils, the administrative bodies that represent rural villages. Costa Mlay, peering at a visitor over several four-foot pillars of file folders and reports that cover his desk, points out that the program rarely worked as intended. "The Wildlife Department used to go out at the end of every season and hand out checks for 25 percent of the total game fees collected to the district council. The district council was very happy, and they threw a party, but they did nothing for the villagers concerned. The district council had a budget: if that budget did well, everybody was happy; if it was in bad shape, then the district council took the money earned from wildlife, which should have been returned to the villagers, and spent it on things of little relevance to the subject at hand."

Mlay would like the SRCS to reverse this pattern. "We will only become believable if we are able to tell the villagers that the government is selling the animals within the park, and will send a percentage of that revenue back to the village to encourage village activities," he says. "For as long as we can show that these conservation areas represent a meaning and a value [to the local people], they will want them protected, and they will fight."

The fight may have already begun. At a recent session of Tanzania's parliament, the member from the Singida region in north-central Tanzania, south of the Serengeti, complained that although the region had beautiful natural areas, the Wildlife Department had not created any game reserves there. This was the first instance of rural Tanzanians volunteering their land for a game reserve.

The Singida region remains an isolated example, and Mlay recognizes that he must demonstrate the practical value of conservation if he is to enlist the support of rural people. "If a village is going hungry, they cannot possibly have the noble objectives of conservation and sustainable development, and we cannot hope to attract their interest, participation, or sympathy," Mlay says. He goes on to spell out in just a few sentences much of the history of conservation in Africa: "But precisely for that reason it was thought, completely mistakenly, that the ordinary villager had no interest in conservation, that it wouldn't possibly interest him, that his only interest in wildlife was meat, and meat not sustainably harvested but wantonly slaughtered. It was therefore decided quite deliberately that the villager has no other interest in wildlife except in gaining cheap—or for that matter free—meat, and that to try and interest him would be a waste of time, and therefore conservation had to be done without him, indeed had to continually fight him because he was threatening the wildlife. The philosophy that we the enlightened few think we can succeed without the cooperation of these people is very expensive, because then you are engaged in an endless war and you have not examined the root cause of that conflict and you will not be able to cure it."

Up until now Serengeti National Park has seemed at best irrelevant to the local people. "For all they care it could be on the moon," Mlay says, except that they have been arrested for entering the park illegally and hunting. Mlay believes that the increase in poaching reflects not just a need for food or income but also the frustration the local people feel about being excluded. Villagers in the Mara region sent an unmistakable message about that frustration when they stole a brand-new Land Rover from the regional commissioner, tore off the roof, and used it to carry the carcasses of poached animals. "It had got that bad," Mlay says. "Now we are introducing a completely new philosophy to them. They will need some time to know how to adjust to it, but they will adjust. We are saying, 'Let's not fight over it because this wildlife is ours, it's yours.' "

CHAPTER IX

▼ ▼ ▼

LIVING WITH CONSERVATION

It does not seem strange to me that I should protect animals . . . I have learned to do so from my parents. The animals are not bad. If they go we will suffer a great loneliness of the spirit.
> —Werimba Rutjani, of the Himba tribe,
> Kaokoland, Namibia

V*illagers living* near Zambia's South Luangwa National Park face an intriguing problem: how to live with successful conservation. Park rangers here struggle not only to keep poachers out of the park, but to keep the animals, particularly elephants, in it and away from the neighborhood gardens. Elephants seeking refuge from hunters are crossing the park boundary and moving in with the villagers, who now have a vested interest in protecting the sometimes troublesome beasts. The villagers, in cooperation with the National Parks and Wildlife Service (NPWS), have practically eliminated illegal hunting.

Yet ungrateful elephants have taken to trampling the gardens. The local people therefore must spend some dangerous nights in the fields, banging pots to scare off the crop raiders. Village women, who do most of the agricultural work, have begun to protest. Solve one problem, create another.

The gardens are safer than the park because hunters have little chance when entire communities decide they want to protect wildlife; an African village is a difficult place to be inconspicuous. Unlike Richard Bell's LIRDP, which also operates in the Luangwa Valley, the NPWS effort focuses solely on the wildlife management side of conservation to generate funds for rural development. Taken together, the efforts in Zambia, the even more far-reaching program in neighboring Zimbabwe, and the efforts around the Serengeti and Chobe Enclave, form the core of a style of conservation based not on an idealized vision of an Africa that never was, but rather on fitting wildlife management into the practical realities of life in a rural African village. The southern African approach in particular illuminates one possible future for conservation in Africa, and also provides a lesson about its past.

The most important early attempt to integrate local people's needs with modern conservation began in Kenya in 1960. A man named Ian Parker, then just four years into his career as a game warden, recommended reserving 3,000 square miles along the eastern border of Tsavo National Park for a tribe of renowned elephant hunters, the Wata. The Wata often earned their living by hunting the elephants within the park for their ivory, and they would need another source of income before they would stop. Under Parker's proposal, only approximately two hundred hunters and their families who depended on hunting for their livelihood would be allowed to live in the area on the park's edge, where a strict hunting quota of two hundred elephants per year would be enforced. The Wata would operate the scheme on a for-profit basis, keeping the proceeds from the sale of such products as meat, skins, and trophies, though by law all ivory belonged to the government. Wata elders and Game Department officials shared management responsibilities for the project, named the Galana Game Management Scheme, for the river that forms the eastern boundary of Tsavo National Park.

Parker soon found that the conservation philosophy of the Game Department itself presented a major obstacle to the success of the Galana Scheme. That philosophy, the familiar product of Western misperceptions about Africa, held that the department's concern was with animals, not people. "The fact that its major headache was people interacting with animals was overlooked," Parker writes in his book *Ivory Crisis*. The Game Department also decided that any revenues earned from safari hunting in the region newly opened by Parker and the Wata would go to the department, not to the Galana Scheme itself. The sight of white men hunting elephants under quotas meant for the Wata went a long way toward convincing the tribe that the Galana Scheme was not, as had been promised, being run primarily for their benefit.

The original goal was to use the Galana Scheme to benefit the Wata, but that goal faded as the problems of making the project profitable became clear. Although the scheme was eventually taken over as a private enterprise and continued to operate until 1976, when Kenya banned hunting, Parker admits that it was a sociological failure.

The failure of the Galana Scheme did not mean the death of the idea that local people should be involved in wildlife management, but it lay dormant for nearly twenty years. In 1983, Zambia's NPWS convened a workshop to develop a management strategy for a region just outside South Luangwa National Park called the Lupande Game Management Area, where both hunting and human settlement were allowed. Two divergent methods of conservation came out of the workshop. One was a broad resource development approach, involving many ministries and government agencies, that led to LIRDP. The other was a small-scale effort, operated by the Ministry of Tourism through the National Parks and Wildlife Service, that was based on the idea that the people of the Luangwa Valley should participate in the decisions regarding the region's natural resources. From this approach grew a nationwide scheme for conserving and managing wildlife, called the Administrative Management Design for Game Management Areas, or ADMADE. Technically, ADMADE in the Luangwa Valley falls under the aegis of LIRDP, which is a regional program. Both are examples of the movement toward using natural resources for the benefit of local communities.

The events leading up to the creation of ADMADE reveal a great deal about how attitudes to conservation have changed since the days of the Galana Scheme. Luangwa Valley contains four national parks and six Game Management Areas (GMAs), more than three times as large as the parks themselves. When Luangwa's parks were established in the 1950s by the British colonial government of Northern Rhodesia, villagers living within the parks were evicted and moved to the GMAs. Although the government assured them that benefits from wildlife would be forthcoming, the villagers received nothing in return for their land. The benefits from a growing wildlife tourist and safari-hunting industry went instead to private companies and their overseas clients.

The government claimed ownership of all the wildlife and began issuing hunting licenses at prices far beyond the means of the villagers. This signaled a major shift away from local custom. Traditionally, local chiefs owned all wildlife on behalf of their tribe. The chief controlled the allocation of land to households or clans for agriculture, as well as the use of forests and wildlife. One tribal leader, Chief Shikabeta of Luano Valley, summed up the traditional approach during an interview with Dale Lewis, an American zoologist working for NPWS: "The way we looked after animals in the past is different than today. A person could never kill an animal without informing the chief. A person who killed an animal would give the hind legs, rib cage, and insides to the chief. Particularly the eland: no one but the chief could hunt it and it was only hunted once a year. Anyone who killed an eland committed an offense. But nowadays it is different. Anyone can kill an eland. Long ago it was not so." The traditional system provided for communal needs and interests as well as conservation. Colonial game laws did not.

Both colonial and post-independence governments actively inhibited the ability of rural Africans to take control over their own lives. The damage has been at once spiritual and economic; villages have gradually fallen away from the economic mainstream, and now depend on urban centers for goods and services (e.g., food, clothing, and shelter) they once provided for themselves. African governments and international donors alike treat rural people in Africa like children.

The villages are often filled with inactive, bored men and overworked but powerless women. Conditions for wildlife conservation could hardly be worse. In Zambia, uncontrolled poaching during the 1970s and much of the 1980s killed nearly 95 percent of the country's black rhinos and over 50 percent of its elephants. Zambia tried to solve the problem in the usual manner, by stationing park rangers and game scouts in camps along the boundaries of national parks. This naturally provoked frequent conflicts between residents and park authorities. Villagers no longer regarded wildlife as a resource but only as a liability—someone else's property to be tolerated, stolen, or destroyed.

The villagers watched passively as commercial poaching escalated rapidly in the 1970s, though where poachers gave them small gifts or shared game meat, many people actively supported the poachers against the park rangers. The harder NPWS tried to enforce the game laws, the less cooperation it received from the local people. To make matters worse, NPWS shrank in size and effectiveness as the Zambian economy crashed along with the price of copper, the country's main export. Forced to recast its methods—law enforcement had not worked well to begin with, and fell off significantly with fewer men in the field—NPWS began to examine wildlife conservation in the context of human needs. A series of studies provided convincing evidence that wildlife could be conserved only if local residents regained some level of proprietorship.

Wildlife clearly had tremendous earning potential. While residents of the GMAs faced economic hardships—most grow traditional crops on small plots of land using a hand plow, though less than 10 percent of the land is arable—safari-hunting companies operating in the same area prospered. International safari hunting in a single GMA earned approximately $350,000 per year, more than four times the agricultural revenues of all the farming communities combined. Less than 1 percent of the safari revenue was returned to support local village economies.

Chief Malama, who ruled a large part of one GMA in Luangwa Valley, characterized the local attitudes for Dale Lewis: "Tourists come here to enjoy the lodges and to view wildlife. Safari companies come here to kill animals and make money. We are forgotten. . . . Employment here is too low, [the tourist lodge] employs only about four people and safari hunting employs no one. How can you ask us to cooperate with conservation when this is so?"

The NPWS workshop led to an experimental design for conserving and managing wildlife that was tested in the Lupande GMA. This pilot enterprise, known as the Lupande Development Project, ran until 1987. Like the Galana Scheme, the project provided direct training and employment in wildlife management for local villagers. In a significant improvement on Galana, however, revenues generated from safari-hunting companies operating in Lupande covered some of the costs of running the project itself, as well as the development needs of the community, as identified by traditional leaders in the villages. Another significant difference was that in Lupande, unlike Galana, sharing responsibility for wildlife management among local village leaders and NPWS led to much-needed dialogue.

Between 1985 and 1988, poaching rates in Lupande decreased at least tenfold, as the skills of the village scouts, with their intimate knowledge of the landscape, soon surpassed those of the NPWS regulars. Professional hunters who escorted overseas clients to hunt in the area reported fewer snares and animal carcasses. During their training, the village scouts also provided reliable sources of data on wildlife densities, population ranges, trophy harvests by privately owned safari companies, and crop damage from wildlife—information that had not been available prior to the work with village scouts.

The people in Chief Malama's area developed a protectiveness toward their wildlife, but elsewhere residents still believed wildlife was of little benefit to them. Thus, toward the end of 1987, NPWS expanded the Lupande management plan to eight other Game Management Areas. This expansion marked the official birth of ADMADE, which now covers nearly twenty GMAs in Zambia.

ADMADE has helped revive the role of the chiefs in wildlife conservation, and many have now taken matters into their own hands. Several have banned illegal firearms in their areas and have even mounted personal investigations into the rumored ownership of automatic firearms by their subjects. Chief Shikabeta of Luano has delivered stiff judgments to local residents found poaching by forcing them to shift to areas where wildlife does not exist. He also is advocating a wildlife reserve within his chiefdom, managed by his people.

Generating this protective attitude toward wildlife is the revenue being earned for local communities on an annual basis from the fees paid by safari-hunting companies (LIRDP also has a revenue-sharing arrangement with the GMAs). In 1988, ten ADMADE units generated $511,000 in revenues, while outside donor assistance amounted to $120,000, and that was before Zambia's Ministry of Finance allowed ADMADE to retain half of the fees from hunting licenses, instead of sending all the money to the national treasury. ADMADE treats conservation as a business, and the villages as economic entities. The profit margins of this business are increased by minimizing unnecessary managerial costs, such as expensive repairs to equipment misused by staff, by reducing resource costs such as illegal hunting or excessive late-season fires, and by maximizing the profits from wildlife. While photographic safaris will almost certainly contribute more money as ADMADE expands, for the moment safari hunting represents the most profitable approach to financing conservation in Zambia.

This bears little resemblance to the usual methods of wildlife conservation, which may pose a problem. ADMADE's future depends not only on its results but on the acceptability of its methods in the West. While Zambians have embraced ADMADE, contributors to conservation organizations do not think of African wildlife in economic terms. Equally important, the growing animal rights movement in Europe and the United States may force international organizations—important sources of technical and financial support for projects like ADMADE—to drop safari hunting from their conservation toolbox.

The large conservation groups find themselves caught in the middle of a deepening gulf. As Africans become more engaged in conservation, programs like ADMADE will incorporate traditional views about hunting, while in the West a relatively small number of animal rights activists may push a conservation agenda that demands the elimination of all hunting. Conservation's middle ground, the practical approach which leaves open the option of hunting some animals if that seems to be the best way to save entire species or ecosystems, may not hold.

The ethical standards which support the argument for animal rights do not apply in Africa. Some people in the animal rights movement argue that it is only a matter of time before African culture "evolves" to a point where Africans will accept the value of strict preservationism. Not only does this attitude endorse the imperialist assumption that Western culture is more advanced, it also implies that the West has a moral duty to intervene until Africans recognize the folly of their ways. Imperialism takes many forms, perhaps none more insidious than when it comes in the guise of an ethical concern for animals.

Another brand of ecological imperialism, without the moral imperative, lurks beneath the attitude that the African experience must parallel that of the West. Africans will not begin to protect their natural heritage until they have destroyed nearly all of it, this argument goes, so the West, with little wilderness of its own to defend, has an interest in protecting those parts of the environment that Africans would destroy, and foreign interests will have to subsidize parks and other protected areas in Africa. This attitude—neatly expressed in the Introduction of this book by Roderick Nash's comment about buying the Serengeti—ignores the fact that few parks in Africa depend solely on subsidies from abroad. It also ignores the vast amounts of money that would be needed to support all of Africa's parks, an investment far beyond the current international support for African conservation.

Zimbabwe's efforts to save the black rhino provide a revealing illustration of both the costs of conservation and the necessity of involving local people. Over 1,700 of the roughly 3,800 black rhino remaining in the wild live in Zimbabwe. The country's aggressive program of patrols and anti-poaching squads thus seems to have been successful, but the Department of National Parks and Wild Life Management (DNPWM) is being pushed to the limit. Many conservation-minded people blame this dire situation on the international trade in rhino horn: the horns command high prices in Arab countries, where they are used as handles for ceremonial daggers, and in the Far East, where crushed rhino horn is believed to be a cure for a wide range of diseases (few people in Asia consider rhino horn to be an aphrodisiac, contrary to popular belief).

Yet, for Rowan Martin, the department's blunt deputy director, the problem boils down to simple economics: how much does it cost to save a rhino and who will pay? "All this emphasis on stopping trade in rhino horn is bullshit," says Martin, never a man to mince words. "The problem is can you conserve your rhino where you are. Trade is irrelevant. We have played the game of fourteen years of a trade ban, and it makes no difference whatsoever to the conservation of black rhino because you have to stop the killing of black rhino, not kill the trade. The rhino horn trade is alive and well in Asia. I found it in all the medicine shops. They are crushing up won-derful Ming Dynasty rhino horn carvings for medicine. The answer is to get control at your end."

Martin is a soulmate of Richard Bell. Like Bell, Martin's attitudes toward wildlife management often drive traditional conservationists to distraction. He manages, however, to convey an almost inspiring air of certainty about his theories. As we sat one morning in his drab office in Harare, Martin, his voice made gravel-rough by chain smoking, advocated reinstituting the trade in rhino horn, and said he would allow many more game ranches—private, commercial operations that raise wild animals for safari hunting, meat, skins, and trophies—with sales of live animals between them. The number of these ranches has been growing steadily in Zimbabwe since the early 1970s. Yet Martin's vision of auctioning off rhino or sable antelope to private landowners so they could charge people to shoot them with a rifle or even a camera would likely send the animal rights community into a frenzy. Martin relishes this prospect, and he expresses great faith in sport hunting as a means of raising money for conservation. Implementing any one of these ideas would provoke angry opposition from various quarters, but Martin gleefully argues for all of them simultaneously. Martin's distaste for international conservation groups is palpable: he refers to them as "a bunch of puppies sitting in plush offices who don't know a thing about what goes on in Africa."

Martin has staked out extreme positions with such vigor that he is now unable to change without losing credibility. His rhetoric has become incendiary, but beneath the bluster lies a method of conservation that incorporates age-old tactics, as well as a number of new ideas destined to become part of mainstream conservation. Zimbabwe's response to the rhino crisis thus far, for example, has been entirely conventional. The government has intensified law enforcement, enacted emergency measures such as hunting bans, and removed rhino from vulnerable areas. It might work, but only if there is enough cash on hand to support it.

Martin calculates that rhino conservation requires one ranger per 20 square kilometers, at a cost of $190 per square kilometer. "We are putting in about $85 per square kilometer, with the expected results," he said. "Everybody is stretched very thin. The success is not quite what we would like the success to be, but we are holding our own. The rhino are not increasing, the rhino are not decreasing. They are very delicately poised: a little bit of loss of morale—the guys in the field are getting war-weary—and the whole thing could just tip very easily. To get the recurrent expenditure up, what are your options? Live forever with handouts from the international conservation community? They are not used to what these costs are. Our government puts in $15 million per year. The total contribution from all world aid doesn't add up to a half a million bucks a year. Stop all the talk about international groups being any bloody use to conservation in Africa. They can't come close to what governments put into conservation."

Martin's solution: open the trade in rhino horn. "The sooner we get black rhino off the specially protected species list the better, so we can reopen the legal trade and farm rhino for their horn." The idea won't win many converts outside Africa, but it puts the conservation issues in dramatic relief. Martin's calculations show that raising rhino for their horn will produce over $50 per hectare, far more than cattle or other standard agricultural uses. "Why aren't we doing it?" Martin asks. "We could have a small quota for sport hunting, supply live rhino for captive breeding programs in other countries, and sell the things, all on a sustainable basis. Our conservation problems would be over."

Even Martin recognizes the extraordinarily long odds against any attempt to remove the rhino from the endangered species list. Yet his conservation calculus is powerful, and applies to elephants as well. Sub-Saharan Africa covers roughly 5 million square kilometers and contains on the order of 500,000 elephants. Perhaps half of the elephants live in state protected areas, which add up to 500,000 square kilometers. Martin argues that elephant conservation requires a minimum of one trained and equipped ranger per 50 square kilometers, or ten thousand men in the field at a cost of $100 million just to protect elephants in parks and reserves. Those figures dwarf the resources of Africa's parks departments. South Africa aside, the rest of the continent probably spends less than $50 million on wildlife conservation.

The situation gets vastly more complicated outside the protected areas. The first question is, who owns the wildlife? If the state claims ownership, then conservation programs will fail, Martin believes. He argues there may be a chance if the people who own the land also own the wildlife, and if those people can take control over conservation efforts. If the land is communally owned, as in much of rural Africa, there must be institutions that allow people to utilize their wildlife and provide access to markets. Government bureaucracies will kill conservation outside the parks, as will international restrictions.

What should a responsible government do? According to Martin, simply this: Take the annual wildlife budget and divide by 200. The resulting figure is the number of square kilometers that can be adequately protected as conventional national parks. That land—no more, no less—should be protected no matter what, even if it never raises a dollar in tourist revenue, because it contains the country's most precious natural and cultural monuments. The rest of the land is up for grabs.

Calculations like these reveal the depth of the problems facing some African countries. In Zambia, for example, the total protected area is five times the size that the country can actually support, according to Martin. It is therefore no surprise that many of Zambia's parks have few guards, poor roads, and no tourists. Martin's proposal of limiting the protected areas to those few that can be saved and letting wildlife compete with agriculture and livestock on the rest of the land strikes many conservationists as defeatist. The approach seems to give up on the majority of Africa's animals; but the appearance may be misleading.

Wildlife is in fact one of the most productive uses of land in Africa, particularly in semi-arid areas. People living near protected areas thus would be wise to preserve their wildlife, rather than killing it off so the land could be used for something else. Mass wildlife tourism, as in Kenya, produces $100 per hectare, while more exclusive tourism brings in $50 per hectare. Sport hunting generates $10 per hectare, double that of commercial hunting for meat and hides. Cattle ranching for beef on Zimbabwe's semi-arid pasture is actually a drain on the economy, costing $5 per hectare.

"Far from being something you go for as a last resort in your marginal areas, wildlife will outcompete domestic livestock every stage of the way, right up to your most fertile areas, in terms of dollars per hectare," Martin argues. These benefits only flow when people can use the wildlife in every imaginable way, from tourism to tanneries. Most conservation programs, according to Martin, only make it more difficult. "I think one of the biggest disservices that's been done is the whole confusion over what conservation is doing," he says. "The irony is that where conservation hasn't intruded, wildlife has done very well. But people have come in with their muddled thoughts about protected species, preventing people from using wildlife and thus saving it. I now in my old age believe that legal protection of anything is bad news, it never addresses the problem."

The pieces of Martin's argument fit so neatly that it has the ring of a Just-So Story: given the freedom to use wild animals, people will choose the course that both makes money and allows the animals to thrive. Simple, right? Perhaps. One obvious problem will be convincing both governments and rural people that wildlife is a better bet than cattle. Everyone knows the value of a cow; only ecologists know that in the long run cattle could eat themselves out of existence in some parts of Africa. Governments have told rural Africans that they would benefit from wildlife many times before and nothing has come of it. So, given the choice, most people will opt for cattle over wildlife every time.

Martin paints the problems facing conservation in black and white: economics versus aesthetics, the myth of wild Africa turned on its head. In balancing conflicting needs of human beings and wild animals, however, the solutions turn out mostly gray. The government of Zimbabwe expects that by the turn of the century nearly half the country will be raising its cash from wildlife, so obviously the animals will have to be tightly managed. This makes conservation a less than romantic endeavor, and requires the conservationist to become something more akin to a World Bank bureaucrat than to a modern St. Francis roaming the wild frontier.

Dr. David H. M. Cumming represents an intermediate stage in the transition from crusader to manager. A thoughtful, quiet man—Rowan Martin without the barbs—Cumming runs WWF's Multispecies Project in Zimbabwe, after many years of working for the Department of National Parks and Wild Life Management. In the 1970s, Cumming worked with Martin, the economist Norman Reynolds, and ecologist Russell Taylor, and the four men began to push for involving more local communities in wildlife conservation. They grew increasingly concerned over changes they saw occurring in the landscape, and became convinced that rural Africans hold all the keys for successful conservation.

"The prevailing view in conservation is that you set land aside," Cumming said one hot afternoon in Dar-Es-Salaam, where he was helping to develop a community wildlife management plan. "As soon as you have that view, it implies that somebody is going to have to carry the opportunity costs of setting that land aside. [Sub-Saharan Africa] has set aside an enormous land area. Apart from Alaska, nowhere else in the world has an area as large as this been set aside. Now who is going to carry the costs of that? The rural communities? Is it going to be the African states? Is it going to be the world?"

"The world" can no more afford to run Africa's parks than can the Africans, so the answer must lie elsewhere. Unless the protected areas become embedded once again in the economic and aesthetic life of the local culture, they will disappear, if for no other reason than simply because of the enormous pressure of growing human population.

"We have got to find land uses that are sympathetic to the continuation of these protected areas, to the continuation of having large and dangerous animals running around all over the place," Cumming argues. From an ecological perspective, those large and dangerous animals require a healthy habitat big enough to support them, so preserving large mammals also means preserving the rest of the biological diversity that goes with them. Like Martin, Cumming believes it is worth using the large animals for economic ends, because that can carry so much else with it. "If people are genuinely concerned about conservation as opposed to protecting elephants or rhinos or some particular animal they happen to be hooked on, then they need to think very seriously about how comfortable they are with people hunting elephant, using the meat, the ivory, the skins. For if people outside Africa make each of these animals into a symbol of conservation and human rights, for which there is no value other than the aesthetic value, they are in a sense condemning these animals to death in Africa."

Cumming sees something of a double standard in the Western attitude. "Go to North America and ask people about reintroducing wolves to Yellowstone National Park," he said. "What sort of reaction do you get? And yet the same people have the nerve to say to Africans, 'You keep your elephant and your rhino, in the number that we think you should.' In other words, Africa should have a million elephants or more, rather than 250,000 or whatever. 250,000 is a long way from extinction, when you compare it with the grizzly bear. How many grizzlies are there in the lower forty-eight states? A couple hundred?"

Cumming began his career in the Sengwa Research Area,

and he set out for that remote post with the myth of wild Africa firmly in mind, even though his family has lived in Africa for generations. "There were no roads, there weren't even many people, and I had this feeling initially of exploring wildest Africa," he says now. Cumming began digging into the history of the area, and he found that forty years before it had been well settled. He met elderly people who took him to all their old village sites. In a few years Cumming's myths were shattered.

When Cumming arrived in Sengwa, the elephant population had grown so large that the animals were wreaking havoc on the woodlands. The old men in the region had never seen anything like it, because at the turn of the century, when they were young, the elephant population had not yet recovered from the onslaught of the great white hunters. By 1890, Zimbabwe had less than four to five thousand elephants left. Today, there are more than fifty thousand.

The hunters and sleeping sickness cleared most of southern Africa of animals and men by the end of the nineteenth century. The type of human sleeping sickness found in the region is caused by a particularly nasty organism called *Trypanosoma rhodisiense,* and it can kill in a week, unlike the chronic West Africa version. The combination of this virulent disease with the slave trade, and the extreme poverty that came about through the rinderpest epidemic of the 1890s, not only greatly reduced the size of the African population but also left it weak and demoralized. That condition persisted until the 1940s, so large areas of once agriculturally productive lands were abandoned. "Over the past fifty years, people have seen these lands as the last wilderness of Africa, without realizing that it is anything but," Cumming said.

The other key figure who joins Cumming, Martin, and Taylor in Zimbabwe's efforts is Marshall Murphree, a professor at the University of Harare, and director of the university's Center for Applied Social Sciences (CASS). Murphree has long studied the role of rural communities in wildlife conservation throughout southern Africa, and he is one of the most respected thinkers working in African conservation today—a colleague says that if there were one thousand like him, Africa's problems would be over. Murphree's weathered looks and gentle manner reflect the years he has spent working in Zimbabwe's rural villages. As we sat one evening on the spacious veranda of his Harare home, surrounded by a boisterous family of Rhodesian ridgebacks (the large dogs bred to hunt lions), Murphree sketched the outlines of his philosophy.

"If your goal is conservation writ large, then for all its defects, setting up protected areas is the way to go," he says. "National conservation concerns cannot be financially based. You have to pay for them out of the public purse, and pay whatever it takes. But outside the crucial protected areas, wildlife must pay its own way." Murphree thus strikes a balance between preservationism and economics that recognizes both the desire for inviolable natural enclaves and the needs of the human population.

Murphree's position comes as something of a surprise, given the perception among conservationists that southern Africa is leading the charge away from traditional practices like national parks. Murphree in many ways resembles those millions of people who watch "Nature" every Saturday, but out of his deep love for Africa's wildlife he has carefully constructed a modern theory of conservation economics. A key element of that theory is that the combination of diminished access to land and exclusion from legal access to wildlife resources spells disaster for a rational, community-based system of wildlife management. Worse, Murphree says, "for over half a century, the cultural perspectives of an earlier era which linked wildlife conservation with sustainable exploitation have been suppressed."

In trying to put this perspective into practice, Murphree, Cumming, and their colleagues got an inadvertent helping hand from Zimbabwe's government. In the mid-1970s, the international safari business began to expand, and gradually became an important source of foreign currency. To encourage the growth of the safari market, the legislature in 1975 passed the Parks and Wildlife Act, which gave landowners the right to exploit wildlife on their land for their own benefit. Though aimed mainly at commercial farmers, the act contained the seed of community involvement.

Roughly 45 percent of Zimbabwe is communal land, home to two thirds of the population. Often located on the boundaries of national parks and safari areas, communal lands also contain much of the country's wildlife. No individual owns land in the communal areas, but since the 1975 Act, the country's sixteen district councils—administrative bodies which each have authority over roughly one hundred villages—can be designated the "appropriate authorities" for managing wildlife. In other words, a district council can take legal responsibility for managing wildlife on its land, much as a private landowner operates a commercial game ranch. The potential of this authority to bring rural Africans into conservation remained largely unexploited for more than a decade; only about half of the $3 million earned from wildlife in the communal lands between 1980 and 1987 was returned to the local communities, and by mid-1988 no district council in a communal area had been granted the legal status as an appropriate authority for wildlife.

In the mid-1970s, the WINDFALL program (Wildlife Industries New Development for All) marked Zimbabwe's first attempt to return the benefits of wildlife to local communities. Much like the Galana Scheme of the early 1960s, under WINDFALL meat from culled animals was to be made available to villagers, and revenues from safari-hunting concessions were to be returned to the district councils. And again like Galana, the program fell flat. Little meat found its way back to the villages, and only a few dollars filtered through the bureaucratic tangle to district councils, let alone to original communities. The communities that shared their land with wildlife saw the loose change that came their way as a government handout, since WINDFALL had failed to convey any sense of the relationship between the cash and the management of their wildlife resources. Local people did not participate in decision making, and thus they had no awareness of local proprietorship.

The conservationists went back to the drawing board. The result was an outline for a new program called CAMPFIRE—Communal Areas Management Programme for Indigenous Resources. The plan contained two key insights: first, that people living with wildlife pay the price for conservation—threat of injury by dangerous animals, damage to crops, and so forth—and so must reap the benefits; and second, that these people have the collective capacity to manage their natural resources. The second insight was the more important of the two, and marked the greater departure from past thinking. CAMPFIRE seeks to restore localized custodianship, fusing ecological responsibility and the communal interest characteristic of traditional African cultures.

The CAMPFIRE plan envisions a system of natural resource cooperatives with essentially the same rights and obligations as private owners of commercial ranches, all inhabitants of the community being shareholders. Profits from the enterprise may be used for communal benefits or dispensed to individuals. Zimbabwe's government endorsed CAMPFIRE almost immediately—the principles have been incorporated in the manifesto of Zimbabwe's ruling political party—but bureaucratic in-fighting slowed progress to a crawl. Some of the district councils are unwilling to let money go back to local communities. The bureaucratic urge to keep control is a pitfall for nearly all rural development plans, since by their nature bureaucracies balk at the prospect of handing their authority over to the rural population. The pattern is so ingrained that rural people now expect the central government to provide all the necessary money and services. "You go to these people and for the most part they are expecting government to do everything for them," says Cumming. "In a sense, the trick of rural development in Africa is to make rural communities realize that they can do things themselves."

Finally, in November 1988, two district councils, Nyaminyami and Guruve, both in the Zambezi Valley, were granted the authority to "do things for themselves." Nyaminyami surrounds Matusadona National Park on three sides (Lake Kariba forms the park's fourth boundary) and is among Zimbabwe's poorest districts, with a hot, dry climate and shallow soils. Yet people continue to move into the area because of overcrowding elsewhere in the country and because the tsetse that once infested Nyaminyami has been eradicated. Malnutrition and protein deficiency run high, and the most basic services are lacking.

Wildlife is Nyaminyami's one great resource. The district boasts large populations of elephant, buffalo, and impala, and smaller numbers of other mammals and birds. Nyaminyami was the first district to apply for the right to manage its wildlife under CAMPFIRE, and created the Nyaminyami Wildlife Management Trust to take on the task. The motivation for Nyaminyami's interest in CAMPFIRE was purely economic, but the district also accepted responsibility for law enforcement and protection of wildlife. In the first year of operation, the Wildlife Trust brought in a profit of about $30,000 to Nyaminyami from safari-hunting concessions, cropping operations, and the sale of meat and skins from animals killed because they were raiding crops or livestock. With additional support from a local foundation, the Zimbabwe Trust, Nyaminyami had over $125,000 to distribute to district residents. The district council tried to keep much of the money to fund its own development projects, but after some haggling each of the district's two thousand households received roughly $50—nearly a quarter of the average annual income.

CAMPFIRE scored a clear financial success in Nyaminyami, and the district also did an excellent job of ecological management. So far, however, CAMPFIRE has not been able to attract full participation in the program. As Richard Bell has found with LIRDP in Zambia, Zimbabwe is learning that generating full participation in a conservation effort is a complicated business. Few people in local government below district council level take part in the debates over policy or how money should be spent. As a result, people in the villages still do not feel that the wildlife belongs to them. While they once felt that the government or the Wildlife Department owned the animals, now they believe the animals belong to the Wildlife Trust.

This at least brings the control of wildlife several steps closer to individual rural Africans, but more needs to be done before CAMPFIRE fulfills its promise in Nyaminyami. The performance in Guruve District, the second to be granted management authority, has been worse. Only about one quarter of the money earned from two safari-hunting operations— one run by the district council itself—has reached village residents, and several wards have received nothing at all. The district council has kept most of the money to meet its own budget, in a disturbing parallel to the days before CAMPFIRE when the central treasury kept the money. In any case, the local people do not really care whether the money remains in Harare or with the local district council. The villagers only know that they still see no direct benefit from wildlife, and many have already concluded CAMPFIRE is nothing more than empty promises.

District councils are becoming increasingly aggressive in their attempts to extend their authority over wildlife. Most districts in the Zambezi Valley incorporate both communal areas with high population densities and little wildlife, and areas with low human populations but rich wildlife resources. The district councils are dominated by councilors from wards that have no wildlife and thus pay nothing for conservation and produce no revenues from wildlife utilization. The influence of the councilors from these wards has aroused suspicion and mistrust among wildlife-rich but developmentally backward areas. "Council is a thief," one ward authority said. "It takes our revenues away from us with one hand and offers nothing but food-for-work drought relief handouts with the other."

That may be something of an exaggeration. Most people in

the villages recognize the benefits of community projects—schools, clinics, grinding mills, and improved roads. CAMP-FIRE's goal, however, is to provide income to households. The obvious route would be direct involvement with the safari-hunting industry, the most economically productive mode of wildlife exploitation. The wards and villages lack the management skills necessary for this industry, so local government will have to negotiate transitional contracts with safari operators. DNPWM now awards safari concessions on communal lands only after taking advice from district councils; as a consequence, some safari operators have been excluded from these contracts, while others, foreseeing future changes in the structure of proprietorship, have begun to consider the possibility of acting as employees of councils, filling dual management and training roles.

Building bridges between private enterprise and communal lands will be vital for the success of CAMPFIRE. On paper, the match seems ideal; the safari operators have the expertise, the villagers own the resources. In practice, however, such arrangements may prove to be complex, particularly since no one in the villages, the university, or the Department of National Parks has much experience establishing joint ventures with big business. Doris Jansen, an economist with WWF's Multispecies Project, has begun training district councils in negotiating contracts—a far cry from the usual conservation activities WWF sponsors. If the bridges collapse, there is a risk that the benefits from wildlife will be seen, once again, as going primarily to the rich elite.

The growing pains CAMPFIRE has experienced illustrate how difficult it is to break the mold of traditional conservation. Zimbabwe has all the tools in hand: a policy of decentralization, suitable legislation, a resolute and well-run Department of National Parks, talented conservationists, and a Ministry of Natural Resources and Tourism with the courage to experiment in genuine collaboration with district councils in wildlife management. At the same time, rural people are beginning to assert claims over local resources, and a coalition of non-government organizations—the Zimbabwe Trust, WWF, CASS—sensitive to local initiatives, provides carefully orchestrated support that emphasizes local management's abilities rather than donor aid. With all this working in its favor, CAMPFIRE languished for eight years, and still struggles to overcome entrenched interests and patterns of behavior.

Despite the problems, other district councils in the country have lined up for appropriate authority status—twenty-six district council or community wildlife projects were in either planning or implementation stages in 1991. "The interesting thing that is happening with CAMPFIRE is that in the early 1980s it was us plugging to get rural communities interested in wildlife as a land use," Rowan Martin says. "Now, they are coming to us."

The fate of CAMPFIRE is ultimately a political question. The government of Zimbabwe must decide both how to use the country's land resources and how much power to cede to its rural people. Few African governments have been willing thus far to truly empower a majority of their citizens. In Zimbabwe, the government has not followed up on its official rhetoric supporting decentralization, but gradually President Robert Mugabe and his ministers seem to be realizing that they are going to have loosen their grip on the country if they want to conserve its natural resources. One of the slogans that appears in many of the CAMPFIRE policy documents is: "It's no longer conservation *against* the people, but conservation *for* the people." Given the neo-colonial implication of "conservation *for* the people," David Cumming tactfully suggested that the slogan should be "Conservation *with* the people."

For Marshall Murphree, successful wildlife conservation ultimately depends on profound political changes. He foresees a system of collective management of natural resources, which to some may sound like state socialism. Murphree points out, however, that neither state control nor complete autonomy on the part of the individual landowner can last. In Kenya, for example, all land will soon be under private title, but thousands of small farms would be ecologically disastrous. So now the government is trying to convince the landowners to manage their land collectively. Zimbabwe is trying to avoid this dilemma through a wildlife management program Murphree describes as a form of corporate communal capitalism; a system of shares and dividends targeted at individual households, not communities. "Like most development plans, schemes for the decentralized proprietorship of wildlife resources in Zimbabwe are not immutable," Murphree points out. "They are likely to change continuously in their context and direction. In effect, they are experiments in socio-ecological engineering."

To its supporters, the CAMPFIRE experiment has already become indispensable. "Without CAMPFIRE, without the initiatives that have been taken, there really would be absolutely no hope for wildlife outside of protected areas other than on commercial ranches," David Cumming says. "The time I feel most optimistic is when I am in the villages. The changes that are needed will come about when the people decide they are important."

CHAPTER X

▼ ▼ ▼

GORILLAS
IN THEIR MIDST

There are many more difficult issues in conserva-
tion than the mountain gorillas. Mountain gorillas
are easy, that's the bottom line. They live in a won-
derful place, which lots of people are going to visit.
As long as the country doesn't go to hell there will be
tourism. It will pay all the costs.

—Bill Weber

In early January 1977, a somber Walter Cronkite reported to the nation on the death of a gorilla. The gorilla's name was Digit and it had been brought to world attention by Dian Fossey, who was studying gorillas in the equatorial African nation of Rwanda. Digit had been killed by poachers, Cronkite announced, its head and hands cut off to be sold to tourists. That the death of a single gorilla in a tiny, faraway place was worthy of the CBS Evening News was amazing enough, but that was only the beginning. Dian Fossey and the mountain gorillas went on to capture the hearts and minds of millions of people, to the point that she became a symbol for conservation in Africa.

If the Serengeti plains embody the Western image of Africa, then Dian Fossey personifies the ideal conservationist: a dedicated white scientist forced to take a stand against vicious poachers, with only a few loyal Africans at her side. Nowhere is the tendency to portray conservation as a morality play more evident. But Fossey does not fit that role. In fact, had she lived, Fossey may well have failed to secure a safe future for the gorillas she often considered her own. The mountain gorillas provide a case study in the contrasts between old-fashioned conservation and the new methods that are beginning to take its place. Unlike CAMPFIRE and other efforts in southern Africa, which begin with people outside the parks, conservation of the mountain gorillas begins within the park, and with a single species.

Dian Fossey achieved greater celebrity than nearly any conservationist working in Africa, and no one save for Jane Goodall is as closely associated with the object of her studies. The intimate relationship between Fossey and the gorillas, along with some skillful editing and film making by the National Geographic Society, created a compelling story that attracted tremendous interest in conservation efforts focused on the gorillas. Yet the source of Fossey's public support, her emotional attachment to the gorillas, was also her undoing. In the end—her health failing and her behavior increasingly bizarre—Fossey herself became the dominant issue, and the gorillas paid the price.

Fossey fought a lifelong war to save the gorillas, and for her single-minded courage she became something of a hero and an endlessly attractive subject for biographers. But the descriptions of Fossey as a troubled and fascinating individual tend to overlook Fossey as a conservationist, and most accounts of her life settle for the comfortable but incorrect assumption that without her there would be no mountain gorillas left. Fossey herself believed that to be true: "I am going to die and the gorillas will all die around me," she predicted in the late 1970s. "They will all be gone within ten years."

Fossey was correct in her assumption that no one else would take up the fight using her often outrageous tactics aimed at stopping the poachers—torture, kidnapping, burning huts, even casting herself as a sorceress—but quite mistaken that the gorillas would perish without them. Fossey failed to see that such methods could not last. There are more mountain gorillas now than at any time in the past twenty years, and not one has been killed by hunters since 1984, because of the conservation efforts of the Mountain Gorilla Project, an ambitious effort to conserve the gorillas and their habitat. The project consists of improved park security, a tourism program based on tightly controlled visits to the gorillas that fund park management and provide the local people with an economic incentive to protect the park, and a conservation education program to increase Rwandan awareness of and interest in their wildlife. Fossey opposed the project and its methods.

Yet it would be unfair to judge Dian Fossey by current standards of integrating conservation and development, and it was her efforts to attract world attention to the gorillas that helped convince a number of organizations to create the Mountain Gorilla Project after several highly publicized gorilla killings. When Fossey arrived in the Congo to study gorillas in 1967 (the country became Zaire in 1971), her sole qualification was that she had sought out Louis Leakey and piqued his interest. Leakey believed that the best person to study primates in the wild was a scientifically untrained woman, as he felt women were more careful observers of behavior than men. Fossey was the second of Leakey's protégées to be successful—the first, Jane Goodall, has studied chimpanzees in Tanzania for over thirty years, and a third, Birute Galdikas, studies orangutans in Sumatra.

Leakey's theory about women making better students of primate behavior than men may or may not be correct, but Fossey does not provide an appropriate test case. While no one had conducted in-depth studies of chimps and orangutans in the wild until Goodall and Galdikas, Fossey was following the enormous footsteps of George Schaller, the dean of field biologists, who had studied mountain gorillas for eighteen months in 1959 and 1960. Schaller had already described much of gorilla behavior, so the next step should have been a meticulous study to fill in the details. Fossey was not the person for the job. As Schaller puts it: "It is clear that Louis Leakey acted irresponsibly when he sent someone to study gorillas who was wholly untrained and inexperienced (as well as physically unfit, with almost no money and unable to speak a local language) alone into the forest to conduct a scientific study." While Schaller provided the first careful study of gorilla behavior, the apes had been described long before. The first European to see a gorilla in the wild was a missionary in West Africa, Dr. Thomas S. Savage, in 1847, but the French-American explorer Paul du Chaillu gave a fuller description after traveling in the region in the 1850s. Mountain gorillas, however, were unknown until the turn óf the century, when a German explorer named von Beringe shot two while climbing Mt. Sabinyo, on the far eastern edge of the Belgian Congo, in 1902. For his efforts, this otherwise unknown adventurer achieved taxonomic immortality: the scientific name of the mountain gorilla is *Gorilla gorilla beringei*. Over the next twenty years, numerous expeditions traveled to this remote region to hunt or capture gorillas, and at least sixty gorillas were killed.

Carl Akeley, a collector and sculptor for the New York Museum of Natural History, shot four gorillas himself, and they remain on display in the museum's Central Africa exhibit. Akeley was so taken by the gorillas and their habitat that he launched a speaking tour and lobbying campaign to protect them. His efforts included a book, *In Brightest Africa*, published in 1923. In it, Akeley reveals the contradictions that plagued him and other conservationist hunters and collectors such as Theodore Roosevelt (to whom Akeley dedicated his book). Like Roosevelt, Akeley tended toward the romantic: "In the midst of a forest, a land of beauty, we overlooked a scene incomparable, a scene of a world in the making, while our great primitive cousin lay dead at our feet. That was the sad part."

The best way to protect the gorillas, Akeley believed, was to create a park around their mountainous habitat, a 37-mile-long chain of volcanoes (a few are still active) stretching east to west along the present-day borders of Zaire, Rwanda, and Uganda. Called the Virunga (the Swahili word for "volcanoes"), the volcanoes are part of the Zaire-Nile divide: rain falling on one side flows into the Zaire River, while rain on the opposite slopes eventually reaches the Nile. The Virunga consist of eight principal peaks rising to between 10,000 and 15,000 feet, and scores of smaller calderas. The slopes of the volcanoes are bathed in nearly constant mist and rainfall, creating thick stands of bamboo at the lower elevations which merge into semi-closed forest higher up, finally giving way to the unique subalpine flora of giant, shaggy forms of the common bell-flower and *Senecio* above 10,500 feet. Only the hardiest grasses, mosses, and lichens survive the cold and exposure on the summits above 13,000 feet.

Akeley directed his efforts to protect the beautiful montane forests and the gorillas toward King Albert of Belgium, colonial ruler of the Virunga. The king was receptive, in part because he had just attended a conference on national parks at Yellowstone, and in 1925 he created Albert National Park, the first national park in Africa. The original park covered only three of the mountains, but it was expanded in 1929 to include the whole chain. In celebrating the creation of the park, the king's ambassador, Baron Cartier de Marchienne, told Akeley and his supporters that the park would "make the world safe for mountain gorillas."

Akeley returned to Africa to study gorillas, but died of malaria soon after his arrival. Thirty years later, George Schaller conducted his research from Akeley's original cabin at the base of Mt. Mikeno, in the Congo. After the Congo and Rwanda became independent in 1962, Albert National Park was split into the Parc National des Virunga in the Congo and the Parc National des Volcans in Rwanda. Mountain gorillas also live in Uganda's Impenetrable (Bwindi) Forest, though this species may be distinct from those in Rwanda and Zaire—a rather obscure question that taxonomists will debate for years. All told, the 162 square miles in the three parks cover most of the Virunga ecosystem.

Mountain gorillas are the easternmost of the three gorilla

species. The lowland gorilla, *Gorilla gorilla gorilla*, occurs from the Atlantic coast to roughly 500 miles inland. About 1,000 miles further east, a second subspecies, *Gorilla gorilla graueri*, lives in scattered pockets of forest in highland (eastern) Zaire. These are called Grauer's gorillas or sometimes eastern lowland gorillas, even though they live at all elevations along the mountainsides. The mountain gorillas of the Virunga live still further east, across a rift valley that contains Lakes Albert and Edward.

Mountain gorillas are better known than their cousins, as researchers can follow them much more readily in montane vegetation, which is substantially less dense than in the often impenetrable lowland forests, and thus can quickly habituate them to human presence. Virtually everything scientists know about the genus *Gorilla* comes from field studies of the mountain subspecies, but none are currently in captivity (two mountain gorillas lived for nine years in the Cologne Zoo, dying within a month of each other in 1978). Schaller, in both his scholarly report *The Mountain Gorilla,* and his popular account *The Year of the Gorilla,* goes to some lengths to dispel the King Kong myth and to describe gorillas as gentle and placid. Conflicts among gorillas, when they do occur, are usually resolved without violence through ritualized threat displays such as chest beating, roaring, and bluff charges. Wild, unhabituated gorillas use similar displays to keep humans at a distance. Gorillas will attack if threatened or if taken by surprise, particularly when newborns are present, but despite the gorillas' incredible strength—they can snap off thick tree limbs in their hands—such attacks are rarely fatal.

Mountain gorillas live in large, stable family groups consisting of at least one mature male, called a silverback because of his distinctive patch of silvery-gray hair, several young adult males called blackbacks, anywhere between two and six females, and their offspring. An average group of nine or ten gorillas will move irregularly through home ranges averaging roughly 4 square miles. Gorillas, however, are not territorial, as the home ranges of various groups overlap and encounters between groups are not uncommon.

Gorillas spend the night in large nests made of nearby branches and vines, and all juvenile and adult gorillas build a new nest each night. This habit simplifies the task of gorilla census takers, who do not have to rely on actually seeing the gorillas (wild gorillas are quite reclusive) and instead can count the nests. Two researchers who have become experts at counting gorillas are Bill Weber, who is now assistant director of conservation at Wildlife Conservation International (WCI), the conservation arm of the New York Zoological Society, and Amy Vedder, an ecologist with WCI. Either Weber or Vedder (they are married) has been involved in every gorilla census since 1978. Weber, a quietly intense man who is built like a lumberjack, notes that night nests only make censuses possible, not easy. A count requires following gorilla trails up and down countless ravines, examining a succession of nesting sites until the size and composition of each gorilla group becomes clear. This labor-intensive but reasonably accurate process indicates that the gorilla population stands at approximately 320 gorillas in the Virunga, up from about 275 in 1971, though still down from Schaller's rough estimate of between 400 and 500 in 1959. (Ballpark estimates for the other two subspecies, which also build nests but are much more difficult to count because of their habitat, are as many as 40,000 lowland gorillas and perhaps 1,000 Grauer's gorillas.)

The mountain gorilla population has continued to grow, and Weber for one is amazed at the increase, considering that gorillas mature slowly, and each female will have just three or four infants that survive to adulthood. Without poaching or encroachment on their habitat, says Weber, the gorilla population could increase at a rate of nearly 2 percent per year.

Weber is just one of a long line of researchers who have studied mountain gorillas. Indeed, few animals have been examined as closely over as long a period of time as the mountain gorillas. It is tempting to take this wealth of information for granted, but when Dian Fossey arrived in Africa, nothing had been done in the seven years since Schaller's study. Like Schaller and Akeley, Fossey began her work on the Congo side of the Virunga, but political unrest soon forced her to shift her research to Rwanda. There, on a saddle at 10,000 feet between Mt. Karisimbi and Mt. Visoke, just three hours walk from the Kabara meadow where Carl Akeley is buried, she founded the Karisoke Centre for Mountain Gorilla Research. Save for short stints away earning her doctorate at Cambridge or teaching in the United States, Fossey would spend the last eighteen years of her life at Karisoke.

Fossey had relocated to what was rapidly becoming an island of wilderness in the most densely settled country in Africa. Rwanda's population has increased sevenfold since 1900, to the current level of over 7 million. The country's dwindling supply of arable land supports nearly seven hundred people per square mile—a density comparable to India— and at the current growth rate all available agricultural land will be gone by 1995. The situation may be even more desperate, says Weber: if one assumes that each family needs just under five acres of land to produce surplus food and allow for some degree of development, Rwanda has been overpopulated since 1977.

With nearly all suitable arable land under cultivation, farmers are converting pastureland to cropland, cultivating marginal areas, and clearing the forests along the Zaire-Nile crest. The threatened forests are not nearly as rich biologically as lowland tropical forest—"most deserts are more diverse than the Virunga," says Bill Weber—but they are of tremendous conservation importance. The montane forests protect vulnerable volcanic soils from erosion and provide a critical habitat for distinctive fauna adapted to life at high elevations. In addition to the mountain gorilla, the Virunga provide habitat for more than one hundred species of birds, including such rare ones as the Ruwenzori turaco and the scarlet-tufted malachite sunbird, as well as golden monkeys, the nocturnal Bosman's potto (a slow-moving relative of the bushbaby), golden cats, leopards, and tree hyrax, a hamster-size mammal whose closest living relative is apparently the elephant.

Dian Fossey spent 11,000 hours—or over fifteen solid months—observing gorillas in these forests, and her attention rarely shifted from the great apes to the wider environment. Early in her research, this tunnel vision enabled Fossey to make some major contributions to understanding gorilla behavior, particularly regarding infanticide and the migration of females between groups. Fossey studied under the distinguished ethologist Robert Hinde—a protégé of Niko Tinbergen—and earned a doctorate from Cambridge, but she never adopted the basic scientific and statistical techniques for studying animal behavior. Despite the vast quantities of observational data Fossey collected, Schaller's *Mountain Gorilla* remains the standard text on the subject. Fossey's reputation would be made in the popular press, but not among scientists.

Fossey's greatest failing as a scientist had less to do with training than with temperament. She was not at all interested in maintaining a distance between herself and her subjects, thus rejecting perhaps the most fundamental principle of ethology. Fossey quite simply wanted to live with gorillas, to spend time in their company, more than she wanted to study them. She played with the gorillas, she groomed them, she treated them as her peers. The roots of this emotional tie to the gorillas go deep into Fossey's personal history—described in even-handed detail by the journalist Harold T. P. Hayes in his book *The Dark Romance of Dian Fossey*—but the reasons for her behavior are less important in terms of conservation than the effects her behavior had on efforts to save the mountain gorilla.

Fossey dismissed science as "theoretical conservation." She had a point: as in the Serengeti, scientific research on the gorillas, no matter how sophisticated, would contribute little by itself to wildlife conservation. The solution, again as in the Serengeti, would have been to use behavioral data to bolster the management of the protected area in which the gorillas lived. Fossey, however, was as uninterested in park management as she was in the details of scientific research.

Fossey's narrow focus on gorilla behavior excluded the possibility of studying the Virunga ecosystem as a whole, and prevented her from recognizing any role for human beings in the forests other than as poachers. Fossey forbade students working at Karisoke from doing anything but research on the gorillas. When Fossey left Karisoke in 1980 to take a visiting professorship at Cornell University (during which time she wrote the immensely popular book *Gorillas in the Mist*), Richard Barnes, a cautious, precise scientist who had studied elephants in Tanzania, directed the research center. Barnes, like Fossey, did his academic training at Cambridge, but the similarities ended there. Indeed, the two could hardly have been less alike, in everything from temperament to scientific method to relationship with Africans. Barnes attempted to broaden Karisoke's scope beyond the gorillas, and when Fossey returned to Karisoke in 1983, she was furious with the changes. Fossey had been expected to stay only for a brief visit, but it soon became clear that she was back for good, and Barnes felt he had no choice but to leave his post as director.

Gorillas in the Mist and the National Geographic documentary had shown Fossey the power of the public attraction to the gorillas, and she knew that what fascinated people and inspired them to contribute to saving the gorillas were her stories about gorilla behavior, so the ecological details were unimportant. As Bill Weber puts it: "What is most interesting about gorillas and chimps is what they do and not what they eat." The same can be said for elephants, whose leading public champion is Cynthia Moss, an authority on elephant behavior. While marvelously effective at raising funds for conservation, a study of animal behavior is in truth only the first step in designing a lasting conservation program.

Fossey never learned this lesson, and Karisoke reflected her attitude, ignoring until recently even such important elements of the Virunga ecosystem as Cape Buffalo, a common and extremely dangerous animal that also has a fondness for eating the crops grown in local villages. Karisoke also suffered because Fossey abandoned any pretension of scientific research after Digit—her favorite of all the gorillas—was killed in 1977, and turned all her energies to halting poaching. During one eighteen-month period in the late 1970s, Fossey went out to see the gorillas only six times.

Fossey never had good relations with Africans; she called them "wogs," or, oddly, "apes." She misinterpreted the African attitude toward wildlife as cruelty, and a friend has said that Fossey felt compelled to buy every animal she saw in Africa to save it from torture. Digit's death caused Fossey to step up her campaign of what she called "active conservation." Richard Barnes has a better name for it: "confrontational conservation."

A tall, hot-tempered woman, Fossey had intimidated the gentle local people, and she would torture those poachers she could catch, whipping them with stinging nettles, putting nooses around their necks, kidnapping their children, and burning their possessions. She also waged a psychological war, which included terrifying suspected poachers into believing that she was a sorceress capable of casting spells—much as early explorers, using everything from gunpowder to false teeth, tried to convince Africans that they had supernatural powers. Such tactics led Barnes to comment that he "couldn't believe she was getting away with what she was doing up there in the late twentieth century." But most of Fossey's supporters outside of Africa believed that hers was the only method available, committed as they were to the notion that Africans were the sworn enemies of wildlife.

Some Africans in Rwanda had instead become the sworn enemies of Dian Fossey. Most of the gorillas killed by poachers from 1978 on were the ones in her favorite study group. The poachers specifically sought out these particular gorillas, waiting for a time when they knew no researchers would be around before killing them. The poachers were sending a clear message to Fossey, and it was now equally clear that she had become a major threat to the gorillas' survival. Yet Fossey had already established herself, in her own mind and in Western public opinion, as the only person fully capable of saving mountain gorillas from extinction.

Fossey felt she had good reason to be concerned, but she misread the data. Although the most recent surveys by Amy Vedder and Bill Weber indicate a steadily growing gorilla population, throughout the 1970s the numbers were headed in the opposite direction. The gorilla population had declined to an all-time low of roughly 254 by 1981. The steepest decline occurred on Mt. Mikeno in Zaire, and was due mostly to hunting. Since Fossey had such extensive firsthand experience with poachers, it seemed to her that poachers were systematically wiping out the gorillas. She was mistaken. Bill Weber points out that most of the hunting had rather obvious political roots, and the hunters were not those usually labeled as poachers, as they had little financial stake in their prey. Until 1967, regional, national, international, and private mercenary armies vied for control of the Congo. All these forces lived off the land, taking what they needed from the local population. People living near the volcanoes turned to the park after their crops had been stolen or destroyed. Many gorillas were slaughtered and eaten, and twenty-six park guards were also killed trying to defend the park.

The pressures that led to heavy poaching in Zaire did not exist in Rwanda. Organized poaching in Virunga is a relatively recent phenomenon. Neither of the indigenous ethnic groups—the Hutu and the Twa pygmies—traditionally hunt gorillas, and Rwanda avoided the political turmoil that plagued the Congo. Around 1973, one or two bands of Twa began killing and capturing gorillas. Many were killed for their skulls, which were sold to collectors and museums, and their hands, which became ashtrays for the tourist trade, while live young were captured for sale to foreign collectors. According to Bill

Weber, demand for gorilla curios continued until 1978, when nine gorillas were killed, but since then the market—fueled by "outlaw" museum or zoo collectors—has vanished or been forced far underground by government law enforcement campaigns.

Pressure to convert parkland for agriculture or other uses posed a more serious long-term threat to the gorillas than poachers. The size of the original Albert National Park has been steadily shrinking, particularly in Rwanda. In 1958, Belgian authorities took 18,500 acres—almost a quarter of the park—for an agricultural settlement program, and the government of Rwanda cleared another 25,000 acres in the late 1960s for a cash crop venture focused on pyrethrum, a plant from which the natural pesticide pyrethrin can be made. The pyrethrum scheme collapsed, but five thousand families remain settled on what was once parkland. This leaves only 30,000 acres protected and raises the park's lower limit to an altitude of just under 9,000 feet, squeezing the gorillas into the narrow band between 8,800 and 10,800 feet where they would find the best forage. What remains of the park amounts to one half of 1 percent of Rwanda's land.

By 1978, much of what we know about gorillas had been discovered, but Weber and Vedder recognized that no one had focused either on conservation beyond anti-poaching patrols or on the roots of the gorillas' endangered status. There had been no serious effort to communicate or cooperate with the government or local people, those ultimately responsible for the gorillas' survival. So the two scientists undertook a broad, interdisciplinary study designed to address the demographic, ecological, and socioeconomic factors in the gorillas' decline.

The first priority of the study—which would provide the baseline data for the Mountain Gorilla Project—was traditional conservation biology: how many gorillas remain, what resources do they need to survive, and how viable is the population? The results of their census, completed in 1978, basically indicated that the drastic decline that had begun in the

1960s had come to a halt—supporting Weber's theory that isolated hunting motivated by civil disturbances in Zaire and large-scale conversion of parkland in Rwanda were the primary causal factors in the gorillas' decline. The total population remained small, with approximately 268 individuals. In a sign of continued stress, the percentage of young had continued to drop, though not as steeply, and the groups were smaller. The gorillas' reproductive rates remained high, however, and the population's requirements for food and space did not exceed the available supply. Weber and Vedder concluded that the population could theoretically double in thirty years.

While the gorillas seemed generally healthier than they had five or six years earlier, the results of the census were far from rosy. Fossey, however, tried to suppress the census because it contradicted her gloomy predictions—based on little evidence, given that she rarely left her cabin any more—that there were already less than two hundred gorillas remaining. Weber's survey was as accurate as anyone could hope for, but the news wasn't bad enough for Fossey. As with elephants, gorilla counts had become the means for creating panic among the conservation-minded, and thus raising money.

In the midst of their gorilla census in 1978, Weber and Vedder learned that the Rwandan government was planning to take over 12,000 acres of the park for cattle grazing, which would reduce the gorillas' habitat to three isolated islands. They knew that they had to come up with a money-making alternative to cattle grazing, and they had to do it quickly. Tourism seemed to be the approach that would show financial returns in the shortest amount of time, though they were not entirely comfortable with the idea of tourism as a conservation tool. "Faced with a proposal to put in five thousand head of cattle and take another 5,000 hectares of the park, tourism made total sense," says Weber. "You didn't have to put in that many tourists to outcompete the cattle, just on a purely economic basis. You are not going to generate Wisconsin levels of milk production on any of those lands with any of those cows."

Fossey adamantly opposed tourism, which she ridiculed in her book as one of "the Zs of theoretical conservation." She called tourists "idle rubberneckers," and once fired several shots over the heads of a party of Dutch tourists who had come to Karisoke uninvited. Fossey had found that *Gorillas in the Mist* gave her new authority, and she became even more convinced that only her methods would work. Richard Barnes and others tried to prevent Fossey from returning to Rwanda after her teaching stint at Cornell, believing that her opposition to the Mountain Gorilla Project and her attitudes toward Africans could only do harm to gorilla conservation. Their stance was absolutely correct as far as the gorillas were concerned, but Barnes and the others had a poor sense of public relations. The Rwandese ambassador to the United States would not go along. "How can I refuse Dian Fossey a visa," the ambassador asked, "when just down the street people are lining up to hear her speak and to buy her book?"

Fossey returned to Karisoke in June 1983, and once again took up her war with the poachers. The next victim, however, was not another gorilla but Fossey herself. The day after Christmas, 1985, someone cut through the tin sides of Fossey's cabin and killed her with a *panga*, the large machetes used to clear paths through the forest. Theories about her murder abound—Fossey had made many enemies—and the truth will likely never be discovered. The Rwandan authorities clearly wanted to put the matter behind them as quickly as possible. Wayne McGuire, an American student at Karisoke, found Fossey's body, and he was eventually tried in absentia, convicted, and sentenced to death by firing squad, the motive being theft of Fossey's research notes. The trial lasted twenty-five minutes.

Many people in the United States and Europe tried to make a martyr of Dian Fossey, who died protecting the helpless gorillas. Bill Weber has a different view. "She didn't get killed because she was saving the gorillas," Weber told the journalist Alex Shoumatoff. "She got killed because she was behaving like Dian Fossey."

The Mountain Gorilla Project was well under way at the time of Fossey's death. With funding from the African Wildlife Foundation, the Flora and Fauna Preservation Society, and the People's Trust for Endangered Species (PTES), the project sought to establish a sound tourism program. But first Weber, Vedder, and the other project organizers had to overcome some rather inappropriate attitudes among both the local people and the government.

The most direct means of changing the negative outlook among the villagers has been to educate them about the real economic values of an intact forest, particularly its role in watershed and soil protection, and to tell them about the need for a reserve for the gorillas, the nature and endangered status of gorillas. The Mountain Gorilla Project's education effort reaches the general public by traveling the country, showing films, giving lectures, and broadcasting radio programs. The education program has reached hundreds of thousands of Rwandans, mostly in primary and secondary schools and universities, but also through meetings in the villages bordering the park. As a result, mountain gorillas have become part of the popular culture. They are the subject of songs, and they appear on stamps and business logos.

The government also needed to understand the earning potential of the gorillas. "We found that Belgian and German technical assistance had locked into classic African tourism, in which you must travel in a zebra-striped minivan through grasslands and watch lions yawn," says Weber. "When we went in and said we think there are people who will want to come here and walk around the mountains, they really thought we were nuts, and the head of the Rwandan parks service at first turned it down. He said it just wasn't workable. And the next time we suggested it, he asked if I thought there were enough crazy *mzungu* [the Swahili equivalent of gringo] who will want to come crawl around Green Hell National Park. . . . We felt it was safe to say something like one thousand [tourists per year] and pretty soon you might get two thousand." The most recent figures show that over seven thousand people now visit Parc National des Volcans each year to see the gorillas.

In 1978, a tourist could search for gorillas for a week at the cost of just one $5 entry fee, but fewer than five hundred people per year came to the park. In any event, without guides and habituated groups of gorillas, they had little chance of finding much wildlife. In the first year of the Mountain Gorilla Project, park visits jumped over 50 percent, visits to gorillas went up over 100 percent, and total park revenues increased 330 percent. For the first time ever, the number of foreign visitors surpassed that of residents. Following the first year, the proposed cattle project was moved to another site.

Once it became clear that tourism would bring in substantial revenues, the government pressured the Mountain Gorilla Project to increase the number of people who could visit the gorillas at one time. Early on, though, the dangers of taking large groups into the forest became apparent. One weekend about three months after the project began, Weber says, sixteen people showed up at once. Weber resisted taking such a large group to see the gorillas, but the tourists had driven a long way from Kigali, Rwanda's capital, and they would not take no for an answer. After two hours on the trail, just moments after glimpsing a female and a few infants in the trees, one of the hikers fell cursing into the nettles. The silverback screamed, and the gorillas were gone. Taking two of the group with him, Weber decided to go find them again. "I went about 20 yards away, crawled into this little tunnel of vegetation and the silverback was sitting right there. I looked at him and he wasn't who I thought he was, we had followed the wrong group, a totally wild group. I was down on all fours, and he had had it with sixteen white apes crawling after him for the last two hours. He was fed up. He didn't make any bluff, he didn't do anything. He just reared up, grabbed a hold of a tree trunk, bit both sides of my neck, broke two ribs. That made it easy to go down to park headquarters and say, 'I'll go back out there, but we have to set up some standards.' Two groups had crossed trails, and they were almost identical in size. It was very bad luck, but at the same time it did help make a point we were having trouble making otherwise."

From that point on, tourist groups were limited to six people (it has since been expanded to eight) because that was the maximum number that the silverback would be able to see all at once in the fall season, when the bamboo is shooting and the forests are particularly dense with vegetation. Visits are limited to one hour, and now cost $200 per person. Four of the twenty-nine mountain gorilla groups have been habituated to tourists in Rwanda, and four more are reserved for research. Four groups have also been habituated in Zaire, which has adopted the Rwandan tourist standards for both mountain gorillas and Grauer's gorillas in Kahuzi-Biega National Park. Gorilla tourism generates nearly $1 million per year for Rwanda, a portion of which is returned to the park to cover management costs. Foreign tourists spend about $3 million annually in the country, and tourism has moved ahead of all but coffee and tea as a source of foreign exchange.

Tourism provides the funds needed to keep the park and the gorillas secure. Before the Mountain Gorilla Project began, Weber and Vedder recognized that illegal hunting in the park had to be stopped. Since they refused to take on Fossey's private war, they looked instead to the Rwandan Office of Tourism and National Parks (ORTPN), the government agency responsible for managing the park and the gorillas. What they found was less than encouraging: park staff consisted of just twenty guards and minimal administrative employees, and they needed equipment, training, and motivation. The Mountain Gorilla Project developed a system of mobile patrols, supplying the guards with uniforms, camping equipment, and transport for three- to six-day foot patrols.

The anti-poaching forces grew with revenue from tourism, and now total seventy full-time guards paid by ORTPN, or one man for every 2 square kilometers, making Parc National des Volcans one of the best protected areas on earth. "And [the Rwandan government] pays their salaries," says Weber. "It's not the African Wildlife Foundation or us or the Germans or anybody else. The Rwandans pay them and they are paid over $1,000 a year." Park guards across the border in Zaire, in contrast, are paid a little over $100 a year.

The patrols have eliminated interest in obtaining live animals or gorilla skulls and body parts. Gorillas still often get caught in the snares set for other animals—for all their intelligence and opposable thumbs, gorillas have not figured out how to untangle a snare. In 1988, for the first time in five years, a gorilla died as an indirect result of poaching when a young gorilla ensnared in a duiker trap subsequently died of an infection.

The gorilla tourist industry funds nearly all of the management activities in Parc National des Volcans, and protecting the gorillas in turn protects the entire Virunga ecosystem. Gorillas are perhaps the leading example of a flagship species; they attract attention and support, and conservation efforts aimed at the gorillas also conserve hundreds of other species—insects and plants, in particular—that are biologically vital but of little interest to the members of international conservation organizations. "Gorillas are virtually without question the only reason that the Virunga ecosystem, at least the forested part of that ecosystem, still exists," says Bill Weber. "Frankly, the Rwandans could farm all of the saddles in between all of the peaks, and they could certainly graze it, and if they wanted to, the whole thing could go."

Tourism had been a source of increasing revenues for Rwanda over the past decade. Now, however, the industry is operating at near capacity year-round, and during the peak tourism months demand far outpaces supply. The pressure to increase the revenues by whatever means—raising prices or enlarging the groups—is already being felt. In 1988, the government abandoned the two-tiered system for gorilla visits under which Rwandan citizens had paid just a fraction of the prices charged for foreigners. Everyone now pays the same

$200 fee; since the average Rwandan earns just $260 year, few local people will visit the gorillas, and the goodwill toward the park may fall. Allowing more tourists into the park to see the gorillas may threaten the Virunga ecosystem, though so far predictions that any level of tourism would harm the gorillas have not been born out. Indeed, in the latest census, the groups visited by tourists had the highest percentage of young, possibly because tourists deter poachers.

Of more serious concern, gorilla conservation now rests with tourists, a notoriously fickle lot. Many events, such as the Persian Gulf War, which put a damper on worldwide travel, or the civil war that broke out in Rwanda in October 1989, curtail tourism. "Tourism is a very sensitive industry," Weber says. "If it is managed poorly, over time word will get back [to international travelers]. Quality control is important, especially where you are asking people to pay $180–200 just for this one-hour experience. All of these places are going to try and squeeze one more golden egg out of the goose." Such heavy reliance on a single source of income is particularly risky in Africa, where civil unrest always seems just around the corner.

Tourism in Rwanda picked up slightly after the rebels and the government signed a cease-fire, but the lasting effects of the war may not be known for some time. Both sides in the conflict expressed concern about the safety of the gorillas, and there is no evidence that any gorillas have been harmed. The gorillas seem to have generated considerable political support, as everyone involved in the conflict recognizes their earning potential and the international interest in their survival. Gorillas have become powerful propaganda tools: the government claimed gorillas were being harmed by the rebels, who in turn said that the government was planning to bomb the park with napalm.

If nothing else, the concern for the safety of the gorillas in the midst of a war shows how successful the Mountain Gorilla Project has been. In addition to generating phenomenal levels of national income, gorilla tourism generates money that creates a fair amount of local employment. As park protection improved with better funding, however, the local people were forced to give up more and more of the resources they once had taken from the park. The government rejected a revenue-sharing proposal, wanting to keep the huge tourist revenues for the central treasury. At the same time, the government identified rural communities as the engine of national development.

Still, the attitude of local people toward the park has changed dramatically since the Mountain Gorilla Project began. Bill Weber probably knows the local attitudes better than anyone outside of Rwanda, as he has been conducting surveys about local knowledge of conservation for over a decade. He found when he began his work in 1978 that while the rest of the world has learned about gorillas, little of the information that was being collected had been conveyed to the local people. No Rwandan scientist had seen, let alone studied, the gorillas, and there was no effort at broad public education. A majority of the farmers living near Parc National des Volcans believed the park should be opened to agriculture even though steep slopes, shallow soils, heavy rainfall, and high elevation combine to virtually eliminate any possibility of productive agriculture. Thus they gave little weight to the non-consumptive values of conservation.

Weber's most recent survey of local attitudes reveals the impact of the education efforts of the Mountain Gorilla Project. The farmers are now more likely to cite non-consumptive values of park and wildlife conservation. Less than a third of the local farmers now want to convert the park to agriculture, and more than 80 percent of all farmers thought both the country as a whole and their region benefited economically from tourism.

The Mountain Gorilla Project is not without problems, particularly the continued prominent role of expatriates, the lack of revenue sharing with local communities, and the incomplete transfer of information and expertise to Rwandans. But the

project has been a dramatic success in most respects, and the
staff is cooperating with similar projects in Zaire and Uganda.
The question remains whether the experience in Rwanda
can be replicated elsewhere in Africa. The answer may be crucial, given the extraordinary explosion of interest in the idea of
eco-tourism. Suddenly, attracting tourists has become the
panacea for Africa's ills. Bill Weber cautions against taking too
much from the experience with mountain gorillas and apply-
ing it elsewhere, particularly outside of East Africa, where the
tourist resource is not as great as in Rwanda. "The lesson most
people draw from the Mountain Gorilla Project is that parks in
Africa will pay for themselves, you just have to develop tourism. No. Most of them will not pay for themselves—they won't
come close to paying for themselves—through tourism. Once
you drop out of the mountains and go into Zaire, Congo,
Gabon, Cameroon, the tourism potential disappears. That is
where you get into much more challenging situations. I think
people in conservation have to be far more creative than we've
been in the past."

The lesson to be drawn from the Mountain Gorilla Project,
Weber believes, is that conservation efforts must weigh the
importance of a wide variety of considerations unique to each
location: social, economic, and political factors, biological concerns such as the size of the reserve, current management
practices, funding availability, Western interest that might
generate money, alternative uses for the reserve, competing
values for the land, and so on. Weber talks about "balancing
the conservation equation": evaluating the various interests in
a particular area and then putting them together in such a way
that they favor conservation.

"Sometimes that solution will be a protection scheme,
sometimes it will be multiple use with a core protected area,
sometimes it's simply going to be a better form of logging than
was there before," Weber argues. "That to me is what is
missed an awful lot when people look at the Mountain Gorilla
Project. What it was at its time was a very creative, interdisci-

plinary approach to solving a difficult problem, and that approach can be applied anywhere, and it is being applied in other places, but the solutions will be very different." The two constant factors in these varying solutions are the needs and attitudes of the people who share their land with wild animals. Perhaps the real tragedy of Dian Fossey is that she never grasped this basic truth.

▼ ▼ ▼

CHAPTER XI

CONSERVATION WITHOUT MYTH

*Nobody works here any more. Nobody listens to me
as they used to. The young are leaving, and the
elephants and gorillas run freely through our gardens destroying what little we grow to eat.*
—Chief Mboula Thaophile, Nioungou village,
Gabon

The *Ivindo River* flows through the forests of northeastern Gabon and into a piece of mythic Africa. The
forest seems to close in all around the river: dense vegetation
crowds the bank, blocking any view beyond the river itself, and
mist hangs low over the water. Hornbills and gray parrots
screech, monkeys call, and chimpanzees scream bloody murder. Night comes with the sudden quickness typical of the
tropics, and then the tree hyrax looses its bizarre territorial cry,
a sound like the rusted hinge of a huge gate slowly opening,
followed by the expiring wails of a soul in torment. There are
no people. This forest may truly be the heart of darkness.

The forests convey a sense of permanence and immutabil-
ity. From within, all tropical forests are overwhelming, but
some, like the Amazon—the disappearance of which has been
discussed so often that it seems to have already happened—
reveal the inherent fragility of the forest ecosystem more readily than others. The solidity of Gabon's forests is not an illusion. Settlers are converting Gabon's tropical forests to other
uses at the slowest rate in Africa. Half a century from now,

Gabon will probably have five times as much forest per person as anywhere on the continent. With those forests comes a wealth of wildlife: the area is crisscrossed with well-used elephant trails. In the dense undergrowth the elephants are difficult if not impossible to see, but they are often heard pushing their way through the bush. Monkeys are more obvious, hooting alarm calls from high in the trees. Chimpanzees are seen occasionally, as are gorillas, who move from tree to tree looking for ripe fruits which make up most of their diet in the lowland forests of Central Africa.

A census of western lowland gorillas and chimpanzees in Gabon resulted in population estimates of 30,000 and 60,000 for the two species—higher than the previous estimates of the species' entire continental population. With a total of twelve diurnal primates, northeast Gabon is one of the most diverse regions in Africa. Recent surveys also indicate there may be on the order of 50,000 elephants in Gabon, and that the population is maintaining its numbers if not actually increasing.

In northeast Gabon, the forest animals remain unused to humans. Unlike their cousins in other, more heavily traveled forests in Africa, where monkeys usually scatter at the first hint of people, the monkeys here do not run away, but follow travelers through the forest as if to get a closer look at the strange beings on the ground. Mandrills—large, brightly colored forest baboons that usually shun people—pass through the middle of a busy campsite full of tents and tables.

With huge areas relatively untouched by man, and thousands of rare animals at play and unafraid in the forests not only in the northeast but in unpopulated areas across the country, Gabon begins to sound like wild Africa come to life. Gabon thus elicits the expected and age-old response from some conservationists: Dr. Thomas E. Lovejoy, Assistant Secretary at the Smithsonian Institution, says, "The entire country should be declared a national park."

How did a country the size of Colorado end up with such a staggering wealth of wildlife? A flight over the countryside reveals the answer in short order: long stretches of uninhabited tropical forest, endless carpets of thick vegetation that show little sign of human influence. These areas are neither parks nor reserves. Indeed, they are not under any special management regime at all. In Gabon as elsewhere on earth, where population densities are low there is little human impact on the environment, and animals and habitats thrive.

The demography of a country such as Gabon argues for creating a long-term program of integrating environmental management with development, and opens the door to designing conservation programs before a crisis forces the issue, and before misguided efforts become entrenched. Ironically, Gabon, a country with few people, illustrates the importance of incorporating the needs and desires of people into conservation. With so few pristine environments like Gabon left on earth, however, the remaining jewels also attract dozens of governments and conservation organizations, many of whom are more interested in how their projects look to interest groups at home than in whether the projects actually work.

While the international conservation community has shown a growing interest in working in Gabon, the Gabonese government itself has been less enthusiastic. Conservation in Gabon, to the extent that it exists, consists less as an acknowledged policy that allows for interactions between potential wildlife resource users than as a response to environmental realities— probably the most natural conservation policy of all. It is based on low human population and slow population growth, and an abundance of forest resources. Gabon seems at a glance to be a conservation success story. In fact, the Gabonese have only begun to acknowledge the importance of conservation.

The forest blocks of northeastern Gabon and adjacent parts of northern Congo, southeastern Cameroon, and southwestern Central African Republic, are among the most remote areas in Africa. Reaching them requires travel by dugout canoe on the numerous rivers penetrating the dense forest, or on foot, the same methods used by the early explorers. The

French-American explorer Paul du Chaillu, who visited Gabon in the 1850s, spent four years making three long journeys into the interior. Du Chaillu always traveled on foot, unaccompanied by other white men. He gave a stoic description of the hardships: "I suffered 50 attacks of the African fever, taking, to cure myself, more than fourteen ounces of quinine. Of famine, long-continued exposures to the tropical rains, and attacks of ferocious ants and venomous flies, it is not worthwhile to speak."

During his travels in Gabon, du Chaillu was also the first European to describe the gorilla in the wild:

> The underbrush swayed rapidly just ahead and presently before us stood an immense male gorilla. He had gone through the jungle on his all-fours; but when he saw our party he erected himself and looked us boldly in the face. He stood about a dozen yards from us, and was a sight I think I shall never forget. Nearly six feet high with immense body, huge chest, and great muscular arms, with fiercely glaring large deep grey eyes, and a hellish expression of face, which seemed to me like some nightmare vision: thus stood before us the king of the African forest. He was not afraid of us. He stood there, and beat his breast with huge fists till it sounded like an immense bass-drum, which is their mode of offering defiance; meantime giving vent to roar after roar.

As with the other African explorers of his day, du Chaillu played to a European audience that craved tales of adventure. In fact, du Chaillu's editors refused to publish his account of his journey, *Explorations and Adventures in Equatorial Africa,* until he had revised it twice so it met their high standard of sensationalism. They knew the European marketplace, if not the African forest: the book, finally published in 1861, sold over ten thousand copies in two years.

The far northeast of Gabon remains as inaccessible today as in du Chaillu's day. Only major expeditions which carry large amounts of food and camping equipment can penetrate the interior of the country. Travel up the Ivindo River has been hastened by the advent of the outboard motor, but a trip deep into the interior can take three days just to reach the jumping-off point.

The Ivindo, the second-largest river in Gabon, rises on the common borders of Cameroon, the Congo, and Gabon, and flows southwest, collecting the vast amounts of water held by the tropical forest. The Ivindo meets the Ogooué, Gabon's largest river, in mid-country. It is the main highway of the northeast region, yet one sees few people. Small villages—clusters of grass huts, the occasional gleam of a metal roof, rows of cassava and plantain hugging the bank—appear around bends in the river, surrounded by the ever-encroaching forest. Dogs bark, people wave, and then the village is gone, replaced once again by the forest. While one bank of the river is high firm ground, covered by mature trees, the other is often flooded. Short and stumpy trees rise out of the river, limiting access to the forest.

Leaving the Ivindo for the smaller rivers that penetrate the interior, water flows faster, the banks crowd in, and villages disappear altogether. The only signs of humanity are the occasional fishermen or the remains of their camps. Even the hunting and fishing camps disappear along the farthest reaches of these streams, as establishing such distant outposts would take too long and cost too much for rural people of limited means.

This was not always the case. As in much of East and southern Africa, in Gabon what now appears to be pure wilderness, unchanged since the last Ice Age, was once settled and farmed. At the turn of the century, northeastern Gabon was well populated by a number of family clans that had moved into the region from Cameroon.

The villages would not survive the colonial era. German and then French authorities created a system of forced labor that badly disrupted village life and led to a series of famines between 1911 and 1933 that reduced the population by half. The survivors moved away from the harsh conditions into areas with improved transport and access, resulting in further depopulation of northeastern Gabon. By the 1930s, the forest was taking over the entire region. When Gabon won independence from France in 1960, the government relocated the last of the people living far from the administrative centers in a process known as *"regroupement."*

No extensive human activity has taken place in the tropical forests of northeast Gabon for nearly seventy years. Yet these forests are not primary, but a mixture of secondary forests near the old village sites, flooded forests along the rivers, and tall, mature forests on the hill slopes—almost a perfect mix for supporting a diverse community of plants and animals. Richard Barnes, who now studies forest elephants in West Africa for Wildlife Conservation International, believes that elephants actually prefer the secondary forests on abandoned villages and plantations, though they avoid roads and settled villages. People thus continue to shape the forest long after they have disappeared.

Gabon's forests, which form the basis for a competitive timber industry, remain intact largely because Africa's population boom seems to have missed the country entirely. In 1986, the Gabonese government stated that the country's population was 1,202,000 people, but the official figures are generally accepted as overestimates. The World Bank puts Gabon's population at no more than 800,000. The truth is that Gabon's population figures have been adjusted and readjusted so many times to fill so many political needs that nobody really knows how many people live here.

Gabon's population remains low because perhaps one quarter of the women in the country are sterile, due to parasites and a high incidence of venereal disease. Few other countries in Africa face such infertility problems. Indeed, Africa's fertility rates are the highest in the world. The booming population that comes with runaway fertility lies at the root of the frightening environmental statistics across Africa. Africa's population is growing exponentially, and population growth today dominates nearly all discussion of the future of conservation on the continent. The statistics reveal a stark contrast between Gabon and much of the rest of the continent: Africa loses 9 million acres of forest each year, and deforestation outstrips new tree planting by 29 to 1. It has been estimated that up to 90 percent of Africa's rangelands and 80 percent of its cropped land are affected by soil degradation. Unless conditions change soon, Africa's national parks and reserves may be surrounded on all sides by the crush of settlements and cultivated fields.

None of the usual doomsday environmental scenarios apply to Gabon. Yet the country is not what it seems to be on the conservationist's checklist—a country devoid of human population waiting to be declared a national park. Rather, it is a country of complex interactions between extractive industries such as oil, mining, and forest exploitation; rural poor existing at low densities and relying upon the forest for their livelihood; forest ecosystems relatively untouched by humans, resulting in large populations of forest wildlife; and a city-based human population demanding more resources from the forest to pay for an improved standard of living.

Gabon's population is growing only slowly, but cities like Libreville, the capital, and Port Gentil are booming as young people continue to move from the rural interior in search of work and economic opportunity. The rural areas have been forgotten, and those who remain in the villages earn pitiful wages. The government has habitually devoted less than 2 percent of its development budget to agriculture, so the countryside is in an alarming state of decay. Villages have been emptied of young people, leaving just the elders, who have no expectations to chase in the cities. They sit and wait for government support that will not arrive. As a result, elephants, gorillas, and other animals ruin unprotected crops, and the rural population continues to decrease. People rush to the cities looking for a chance to make it big, while others continue the process of moving rural villages nearer to roads, the railway, and other transport routes, leaving vast blocks of forest uninhabited.

With all that forest in the country, the Gabonese government has not had to think much about how to deal with the environment. In fact, with so few people, it is not clear if there is any reason to worry about environmental degradation: the country is an unbroken stretch of trees from one end to the other. If Gabon is to continue to develop, however, then those trees are going to have to pay for themselves, or at least so says the government. More importantly, so says the World Bank.

In other countries, pressure from banks and foreign governments to develop the timber industry in order to make debt payments spells disaster for the environment. The Gabonese forest, however, is blessed with a species of tree known locally as *okoumé (Aucoumea klaineana)*. The tree grows only in equatorial Africa within some 150 miles of the coast, and its range is centered on Gabon. Okoumé trees grow tall and straight, with a light gray, smooth bark and a spreading crown some 100 feet up in mature trees. Logs of this species can be peeled into lightweight, sturdy plywood—it is the preferred species in the construction of hydroplanes in the United States—and wood from okoumé has a wide range of construction uses. Okoumé trees also produce a pungent resin that is highly flammable and thus of great value in the rain forest. Gabon essentially controls the world market of this species, as few of the trees are found in neighboring countries. Along with okoumé, there are some sixty-five other species of tree that are considered commercially valuable in Gabon's forests.

Before the discovery and exploitation of oil reserves, logging was the major industry in Gabon, representing 80 percent of revenues in 1965. By 1983, income from forestry activities represented only 2 percent of Gabon's gross national product. Logging in Gabon is highly selective, as four of every five trees cut are okoumé, so the distribution of okoumé dictates the size and shape of the logging industry. The tree grows in scattered clumps rather than large, homogeneous stands—five acres of forest will likely have only three okoumé trees. While cutting these trees has an impact on the forest, it is much less than in a country like Malaysia, for example, where loggers may cut as many as seven trees per acre.

The selective logging in Gabon has direct and indirect effects on the environment: felling trees and constructing roads alters wildlife habitats, and the timber industry also opens up new areas for hunting and settlement. Gabon's Ministry of Waters and Forests, which supervises all forestry activities, has divided the country into two zones for exploitation. The first zone covers approximately 40 percent of Gabon and is the zone of easiest access; here timber can be transported by navigable rivers or the sea to processing plants or to foreign markets. Selective logging has been under way in this zone since the beginning of the century, and many areas have been logged two or three times at thirty-year intervals. Three of the five protected areas in Gabon are in this region, and the forests of all three have been selectively logged at least once.

The second zone covers the remainder of the country, though interest in exploiting timber extends only to the geographical limit of okoumé distribution. Much of the forest in this zone was inaccessible until the completion of the Transgabonese Railway line in 1986. One of the world's largest construction projects, requiring sixteen years of labor with fifty bridges, a tunnel, and 420 miles of track through the tropical rain forest, the railway cuts a diagonal swath through the forests from Libreville in the northwest to Franceville in the southeast, thus opening many previously isolated regions to timber exploitation. Constructing the railway cost billions of dollars, and it needs operating subsidies of over $50 million a year. The government issued logging permits for the second zone in 1970, when construction of the railway began, and the entire area is allocated to large, foreign-based forestry companies that can no longer work in the first zone, where only Gabonese-owned companies can get permits. With a continued slump in prices of oil and such commodities as coffee and cocoa, the government faces great pressure to boost other sectors of the economy; timber is particularly important both in terms of income for the government and business for the Transgabonese Railway system.

The presence of men and machines during timber extraction certainly disturbs the animals. Preliminary survey work suggests, however, that at least the larger animals, such as elephant and gorilla, move out of the area during logging but do not hesitate to return once the loggers leave. The long-term implications of these activities are not well known, though with elephants it may be that logging has little or no impact on their distribution, and that other factors such as plant fruiting cycles and the species composition of the forest may be more important. Light-gaps and clearings in the forest, created naturally when older trees fall, or by timber extraction, are rapidly colonized by herbaceous plants and seedlings of light-tolerant tree species. Many of these species are important food plants for elephants, gorillas, and mandrills, and the changes in vegetation following selective logging may favor these animals.

All this poses delicate questions for conservationists, who are more accustomed to attacking the timber industry. Researchers in Gabon can often be heard discussing, with no little anxiety, what to do if in fact research shows that selective logging is beneficial to forest wildlife. Without a doubt, more work is required. However, logging activities, as presented to potential donors of large conservation organizations, are almost always couched in terms of deforestation and destruction. In Gabon this is far from the case, though neither conservation policies nor programs have anything to do with the situation.

The same can be said about hunting. Workers at forestry camps hunt with guns and snares, and hunting often continues long after logging moves on to other areas, as newly built roads permit entry into previously inaccessible forests. Numerous small camps can be found along most old logging roads. These consist of a few huts, often a small bar, and a few living quarters. A fire is almost always burning, with bushmeat suspended on a platform of wooden sticks being smoked for transport into the capital. Such activity is not solely limited to the areas opened up by loggers in Gabon, but is common throughout the country. Villages depend on bushmeat as a source of protein, and as a source of income to purchase basic necessities— soap, kerosene, cooking utensils—as well as other items. When asked why he continued to hunt small game, a villager near Lopé in central Gabon replied, "I was going to university in Libreville, but I lost my financial support [provided by the government] and was forced to return to my village. I need clothing, food, batteries for my radio and flashlight. Where will I find the money out here for these things unless I have something to sell? There is nothing except the animals."

Such a response is not at all unusual, given the current economic problems facing Gabon. Most of the rural people in Gabon have been incorporated into a cash economy that relies almost entirely on imported items, and they are habituated to Western clothing and food, radios, television, watches, cars, and so on. As commodity prices have decreased, many farmers have abandoned their plantations because the effort of producing crops is no longer worth the prices they can get for them. They have always relied on bushmeat as a source of personal protein, but now are looking to it as a means of raising cash for taxes and basic necessities, and as a method of controlling crop pests. The demand for bushmeat in the cities, full of recent villagers who prefer wild meat to beef, pork, and chicken, is at an all-time high, and the cost per pound has risen accordingly. As much as 4 tons of bushmeat may enter Libreville, the major market, every month.

Studies of bushmeat use in West African countries are beginning to show not only that it is a major contributor to the economy, but that rural people make rational choices about hunting based on a variety of factors such as the price of ammunition, distances between villages, size of the animal, and the need for food and cash. They are not vicious killers setting out to destroy every wild thing in their path, as they have been portrayed. In Liberia, for example, the traded value of bushmeat was estimated to be on the order of $24 million (3 percent of GDP) and the subsistence use (at rural trade prices) was worth $42 million. This compares with the 1989 earnings of $20 million in tax revenue from exploitation of the forest for timber. Although Liberia, along with most other countries and donors such as the World Bank, tends to regard bushmeat as a common resource of no specific value, the costs to the state of substituting for lost bushmeat resources by importing beef or pork from abroad provides clear evidence of its real economic worth. This is a powerful argument for investing in a sustainable yield of bushmeat and the diversification of domestic meat production.

While wildlife use remains a hidden aspect of many African national economies, the potential costs of its loss or mismanagement are significant. In the current economic climate, forest products like bushmeat are critical. Commodities such as bushmeat, forest fruit, and traditional medical products provide highly valued subsistence goods at a low cost to the people who can least afford them.

Conservationists often miss this aspect of resource use in Africa. Many studies, not only of the bushmeat trade but of the general use of forest resources, have tended to stress species preservation. They result in such less than scientific statements as these, gleaned from a variety of consultants and their reports: "The situation is catastrophic . . . anyone can kill anything, anywhere, anyhow, anytime"; "All hunting should be banned for five years . . . rangers should be armed . . . better a dead poacher than a dead ranger"; "They eat everything that moves"; "If the loggers move into that region, there won't be a tree left or an animal breathing."

With improved technology, people are indeed moving into

the forest, but hysteria about loggers and poachers does little to illuminate the often subtle changes that are taking place, nor will it help the government of Gabon address the problems of wildlife conservation. The Transgabonese Railway has opened up new regions, allowing for more intensive use of resources, often with unknown consequences. Old forms of hunting with nets, fiber snares, crossbows, and homemade guns are being replaced by long-lasting wire snares and modern shotguns and rifles. The pattern should be a familiar one: it was improved firearms and the opening of the North American Plains by railroad that helped lead not only to the collapse of the bison populations, but to the end of the great horse culture of the American Indian.

The Gabonese government has a well-established set of laws to control the use of resources. Enforcement of these laws is vested in two departments, the General Directorate of Waters and Forests and the General Directorate of the Environment. There is a twofold problem: First, there is no framework which allows those people most dependent on the forest to participate in the policy-making and planning process; it is imposed from above. Inevitably, this means that the interaction between resource users and resource managers will be antagonistic. If a conservation strategy is intended to identify attainable objectives and to minimize conflicts of interest, then the opinions of everyone involved must be included. Second, those responsible for management are not given the resources necessary to do the job. Financial resources are so tight that no one can go into the field to gather the data necessary to make informed decisions. Most resource managers are stuck in their offices in Libreville, while those posted in the field lack transport to get them to the capital.

Recently, the Gabonese government has begun to realize the uniqueness of its natural resources, both in terms of the state of its tropical forest and the continental importance of specific wildlife populations, notably elephant, gorilla, and chimpanzee. This awareness has become a point of pride, and thus conservation has become what Richard Bell calls "an aesthetic decision." As a result, the government is paying more attention to environmental issues and it is actively seeking support from outside the country. The challenge is to ensure that such support takes the best possible form for Gabon.

Gabon generally lacks conservation expertise. Many decisions are based on models from East Africa, a reaction to East Africa's successful public relations campaign. In the Wonga-Wongue Presidential Reserve, south of Libreville, the government has attempted to introduce species from the East and southern African savannas such as zebra and wildebeest in the mistaken belief that only these animals represent Africa's heritage. Given the habitat differences between the two areas, these introductions have generally been failures.

In 1989, Jean Hubert Eyi-Mbeng was appointed director of Gabon's Department of Wildlife and Hunting. (His predecessor was removed after he was caught forging permits for the exportation of ivory—he was arrested while chairing an international meeting on elephant conservation in Central Africa.) Upon taking over the position, Eyi-Mbeng was confronted with all the problems of a department demoralized by corruption and lacking the funds and staff necessary to carry out its mission.

A soft-spoken, slight, gray-haired man, Eyi-Mbeng is most often to be found behind his desk, surrounded by piles of paper that seem to be taking over his cramped office. Eyi-Mbeng's growing awareness of Gabon's unique wildlife resources is hamstrung by a lack of high-level support. He voices the complaint that "it is not the rural people who need environmental education programs, they know all about it, but rather the decision makers who create policies in our government. We have a valuable resource here which can contribute to the country's development."

As if that wasn't enough, in 1990 riots broke out in Libreville following the mysterious death of an important opposition leader. Numerous buildings were burned, and rioters attempting to get at confiscated firearms being held in the offices of the Department of Wildlife and Hunting ended up burning the building to the ground. The department now has no office, only a limited staff, no vehicles for transport, and no past history, as all the files were lost in the fire. As Eyi-Mbeng said at the time, "Here I am responsible for Gabon's wildlife and I don't even have a telephone." Despite this turn of events, neither the government nor those aid agencies supporting conservation activities have made any effort to construct a new office or provide the institutional footing to manage the country's wildlife resources.

Although Gabon's capability to manage its wildlife resources is extremely limited, the European Community has been planning over the last four years to begin an ambitious project in the Lopé Faunal Reserve. The project, with the weighty title "Conservation and Sustainable Utilization of Forest Ecosystems in Central Africa," involves seven Central African countries and receives its funding under a regional perspective. Projects of this kind typically start slowly, as the process of actually getting funds into the field and a project under way is long and ponderous. The current EC project is no different.

As originally implemented, the EC contracted with the International Union for Conservation of Nature and Natural Resources (IUCN) to undertake the initial studies of what could be done regionally, and specifically within each of the seven Central African countries. The first phase consisted of hiring foreign consultants to work with the host country governments to describe the status of each country and develop a "model" project representing some facet of conservation (i.e. research, education, utilization, management). Each country then would receive help for a particular conservation technique, and the EC would get credit for supporting conservation in Africa's tropical forests, something for which it is under great pressure at home.

The sites in each country were identified early in the process; in Gabon, the EC chose the Lope Reserve. The consultant hired to develop the Lope project visited the site and proceeded to develop a scheme based on wildlife utilization and sustainable use around the reserve. It seems the only problem with his approach was that he didn't talk with anyone—not the villagers, not the local officials, not the central government. At a meeting in November 1988 involving the EC, IUCN, the Gabonese government, and various other aid organizations and technical experts, by chance held at the Lopé, the project was roundly criticized and redesigned.

The new project envisioned support for management of the Lopé Reserve, including a core area where logging would not be allowed, as well as an effort to direct benefits to the local communities surrounding the reserve. Progress, however, remains murky and highly secretive by virtue of the EC process. These projects are not designed with active participation by the rural communities from the planning stage onward, but are put out to bid to consulting companies based in Europe. These companies, by nature of the competitive process, do not like to disclose the details of their proposals for the project, lest a competitor steal a good idea. The proposals which will, or should, involve and benefit the rural communities and the country are, as a result, highly confidential. Questions to the Wildlife Department as well as the ministry regarding specific details, and exactly where the project stands, are met with shrugs.

A further difficulty stems from the regional nature of the EC program. To qualify for regional funds, all the country projects must move ahead at the same time—if there is a problem in Zaire, then the project in Gabon cannot move ahead. Such planning begins to sound like a structure to ensure jobs for the bureaucrats in Brussels and EC consulting firms, rather than successful conservation and development initiatives in Africa. Today, four years after the conceptualization of the program, there remains no sign of action on the ground. "We've had lots of European tourists," says a resident of Kazamabika village, within the Lopé Reserve. "They come and promise us all sorts of benefits because the reserve is here. We never see their promises, though. I think they make them so they can visit the animals. We all know the reserve is here for the Europeans— the animals just eat our crops. We are tired of waiting."

The project has taken so long to begin that loggers in the reserve, fearing a ban on their operations, have accelerated their cutting schedules. The result of the EC project to date is thus increased rates of logging in the reserve, exactly the opposite of the effect intended.

As long as these programs are geared to responding to the needs of constituencies in Europe and North America, and based on contracting with firms in those countries, the real needs will never be met. The EC project in the Lopé has a budget of approximately $520,000 per year over five years. The entire operating budget for the Wildlife Department has averaged $280,000 per year during the last three years, and the department must manage not only the Lopé but all other operations within the country. Simple economics tells us that such a program will not last unless institutional changes are made in how the government of Gabon manages its wildlife resources. Without policies that can help structure conservation plans, without strong institutions to implement policy decisions, and without relatively secure sources of long-term funding, support for the traditional field project approach to conservation in Gabon will remain problematical.

Lasting conservation in Gabon will be built on three pillars: institutional support to government agencies, private concerns, non-governmental organizations, and rural communities; training in environmental management; and public awareness and educational outreach to the general public, within the education system, and most importantly, to the decision makers. This process involves providing a wide range of information and technical assistance, along with low levels of financial support to allow those people working with natural resources to make their own decisions and act upon them.

Conservation must be institutionalized as part of the country's development, with basic strategies and programs replacing the showy five-year projects still being developed and implemented by aid agencies and international conservation organizations.

Governments and conservationists alike need to think in terms of twenty- to fifty-year strategies and to plan for periods of a decade or longer. The traditional approach among international conservation organizations, however, is to try to convince people that every situation is desperate, that every program is an emergency. Such a mind-set simply doesn't jibe with population changes that may take many generations to work themselves through, or with tropical timber harvesting that may rotate over periods of eighty years or more. The individuals and agencies responsible for managing a forest in this manner must take this time span into account; five-year timber-cutting concessions promote the "cut out–get out" methods currently employed.

Jean Hubert Eyi-Mbeng requires support from his government, both politically and monetarily, if he is to be successful in his job. The government has the ability—Gabon is a wealthy country by African standards—to support conservation activities as part of its development process. But without government support, be it for government action or decentralized rural control of wildlife management, technicians like Eyi-Mbeng and villagers like those living in Kazamabika will remain forever frustrated—forever waiting for the government, for the EC, and for the chance to take responsibility into their own hands. Without the institutional underpinnings, conservation in Africa will continue to be dominated by short-term projects with their high failure rates. Such efforts, with their "charismatic species," sites of "exceptional priority," and "baseline populations," may be lucrative for non-governmental organizations, aid agencies, and their constituencies, but do little toward long-term change. While Gabon's unique biological resources, its species diversity, and its unusual demographics grab the attention of outside organizations with an interest in conservation, it is the people, in both their government institutions and their rural communities, who require long-term support and attention.

CHAPTER XII

▼ ▼ ▼

WHO SAYS
AFRICANS DON'T
CARE?

*Better to let them do it imperfectly than to do it
perfectly yourself, for it is their country, their way
and your time is short.*

—T. E. Lawrence

A t about *1:30* P.M. on January 31, 1990, Gilbert Bangandombi-Kotali and four other laborers stopped
work for their midday break. Gilbert and his co-workers were
opening and improving rough bush tracks in the Manovo-
Gounda-St. Floris National Park in the northern part of the
Central African Republic (CAR), a region of savanna woodland and grassy river drainages which at one time held some of
the greatest concentrations of wildlife in West or Central
Africa. Broad floodplains supported communities of tsessebe,
kob, hartebeest, roan antelope, and buffalo in a migratory system covering both the CAR and southern Chad, an area larger
than the Serengeti. The woodlands held significant populations of elephants, black rhino, and giant eland.

Gilbert was well paid, so despite the hard labor and the heat
he was thankful for the job, as there is not much opportunity
for work in this part of the country, except hunting for meat
and ivory. Indeed, ivory hunting had become a much easier
and more attractive occupation as the hunters acquired modern methods. The traditional elephant hunters of these north-

ern savannas were among the bravest on the continent. They chased the elephants on horseback, using long spears with heavy metal points to slash at the elephants' hamstrings, finally bringing them down and killing them with repeated thrusts of their spears. More recently, however, civil wars in Chad and Sudan brought automatic weapons into the area, leading to widespread killing of both elephants and black rhino for ivory and horn, and later most other species for meat. Sudanese caravans of camels and horses entered Manovo-Gounda-St. Floris National Park for weeks at a time, hunting animals and smoking the meat before returning home, where war and famine had created a great demand for such meat. The situation became intolerable for the government of the CAR when the country's president, André Kolingba, visited the area and the hunters began shooting at his helicopter.

This event turned out to be a stroke of good luck, at least for those people, like Gilbert, who needed work. In an attempt to get control of the situation, the CAR turned to the European Community for money to improve the park's infrastructure and management, and to involve the local communities in this process. One obvious benefit was employment—and Gilbert and his friends were the beneficiaries.

Building roads in the hot sun is sweaty work, but on this day Gilbert and his comrades were near the Goro River, so they walked down to the riverbank to wash up and cool off. As they crouched by the water, a vehicle drew up along the dirt track they had been clearing. From down along the river's edge, deep in the tall grass, it was not possible to see who the visitors were. Suddenly, the afternoon silence was broken by the sound of gunfire. Gilbert knew he'd been hit, and he found himself on the ground. He dragged himself more than 30 yards before dying. Gilbert had been struck by two bullets, one in the upper leg and one in the chest, and he slowly bled to death. His comrades either ran or hid in the tall grass. As one reported later, "In the following silence three men, a white and two blacks, walked up to Gilbert's body and said, 'Well done.'"

Gilbert's mistake was that he was an African in an African national park. A white French expatriate, Jean Labourer, confessed to the murder, but many people believe he was taking the fall to protect his son, Mathieu, who is responsible for a tourist operation in the area. Mathieu Labourer had been touted as Tarzan in a *Paris-Match* article about his life. He was supposedly conducting an anti-poaching patrol. The weapon the Frenchman used was an American-made M-16 assault rifle, unofficially supplied through the U.S. Embassy for anti-poaching work. At a more basic level, however, Gilbert Bangandombi-Kotali was killed by the myth that the press, conservation groups, Western governments, and even African governments have built up around national parks, wildlife, and Africans. Any African in a park, so the story goes, must be a poacher. In the war to save Africa's vanishing wildlife, any poacher must be shot.

The irony here is that Gilbert was murdered while taking part in a process that has become the centerpiece of modern conservation efforts in Africa, a process aimed at overcoming the entrenched myths: providing direct benefits, including employment, to rural people living around and directly affected by protected areas. What happened after Gilbert died suggests that his life was not worth very much to those in charge of at least this particular rural development effort. The entire affair has been obscured by the bickering between the EC, the tourist operation, and the government of the CAR. Questions remain as to who was ultimately responsible for Gilbert's murder; although some of the EC staff have left the project as a result, no other action has been taken.

Africans have been giving their lives in the name of conservation since the birth of the first national park. Scouts from such little known places as the Vwaza Marsh Game Reserve in Malawi, as well as from famous parks like Parc National des Volcans in Rwanda or Kenya's Masai Mara National Reserve, have died in the line of duty. Most remain anonymous. Many people in Kenya believe that the death of African scouts at the hands of Somali poachers was not being taken seriously until the Somalis killed the European manager of the Galana Game Ranch in 1977. The resulting publicity forced the Kenyan government to reassess the situation. The death of a white wildlife manager or, more recently, white tourists, has been used to impress upon the public the dire situation facing African wildlife and the negative role Africans play. Africans employed as wildlife managers, just like the people in rural communities living near protected areas, have been marginalized by the conservation movement.

Africans and wildlife do not belong together; this remains a central paradigm of the myth of wild Africa. Yet Africans have more than demonstrated their interest in and understanding of the importance of conservation—aesthetically, practically, and culturally.

The argument made by some Western conservationists that Africans, on a continentwide scale, do not value the natural world around them does not stand up under scrutiny. Even by the most demanding Western measure of commitment to conservation—the extent of national parks and other protected areas—African governments compare favorably with any in the world. The 1990 edition of the *United Nations List of National Parks and Protected Areas* notes that there are over 88 million hectares of land set aside in 426 protected areas in sub-Saharan Africa. These lands make up almost half of all the protected areas in the tropics. African governments have set aside over 48 million hectares of land, or 55 percent of the total since independence. African governments spend an estimated $115 million each year on managing these areas, a figure that far outstrips the support provided by international conservation organizations. World Wildlife Fund, the largest non-governmental conservation organization, spends no more than $15 million on the continent.

African governments continue to make sacrifices in the name of conservation despite the staggering odds. Botswana has devoted almost 18 percent of its land area to wildlife, while in Tanzania the figure is over 13 percent. Actual expenditures on protected areas and wildlife as a percentage of these countries' total budgets range from 0.20 percent in Botswana to 0.45 percent in Tanzania. Zimbabwe allocates as much as 0.60 percent of its budget for these activities. By contrast, the United States has set aside about 8 percent of its land as protected areas (62 percent of it in Alaska) and spends about 0.15 percent of its total budget on protected area management and wildlife.

The commitment of African governments to conservation seems even stronger when seen in light of all of the other development issues they must confront, from famine to the need to improve education and increase employment opportunities. Africa has not only been described as a member of the Third World, but sometimes the Fourth or Fifth World due to developmental and environmental bankruptcy. Such condemnation seems unfair, given that the rationale that drives Africans and their governments to make certain choices (often choices that seem antithetical to conservation) is often exactly the same one that drives environmental policies in the United States.

The epigraph from T.E. Lawrence fits nicely with conservation in Africa, though Europeans and Americans are no more able to conduct "perfect" conservation than anyone else. Cutting old-growth timber in the Pacific Northwest with taxpayer dollars, for example, clearly demonstrates the importance placed on short-term economic payoffs—local timber jobs and the high market value for timber in the Far East—at the expense of long-term environmental and economic benefits, ranging from biological diversity and help to endangered species to salmon fisheries and the growing value of recreational activities. The pressure to keep the forests open for logging is as great or greater than that facing African governments trying to carry out wildlife conservation programs. Such pressure comes from people involved in the timber industry who, while they may be terribly hurt by the loss of their jobs, have vastly greater alternatives and economic resources than rural Africans.

The decision to drill for oil in the Arctic National Wildlife

Refuge rather than enforce conservation measures at home provides another telling example of our domestic environmental priorities. At the same time, we call for the halt to oil exploration in tropical forests and other sensitive ecosystems in countries like Gabon, and we cry out for bans on the tropical timber trade and the cutting of tropical forests. Given the high cost of development in African countries, the double standard is shockingly unfair unless we can help African governments to provide alternatives.

The industrialized nations use the vast majority of earth's available resources. These nations, with just one quarter of the world's population, use up 75 percent of the energy, 80 percent of all commercial fuels, and 85 percent of the timber. In one year, a single American uses the same amount of energy as three hundred Malians. Coupled with greater life expectancy in the United States, this means that each child born in this country will be as great a burden on the environment—as represented by energy use—as five hundred Malians. It is difficult to demand further sacrifices from Africans, given these figures.

On an individual level, Africans work to protect wildlife under conditions that conservationists in northern countries would not tolerate. Most protected areas are in the remotest parts of Africa. Wildlife managers are often expected to live without electricity or running water, with no regular access to schools or health facilities. They are often forgotten by the governments that employ them and the conservation organizations that raise money in their name. It is not unusual for pay to arrive late, if at all, nor is it unusual for all the park vehicles to be out of commission. Over time, equipment breaks down due to the lack of maintenance and investment, and uniforms wear out and are not replaced. Wildlife scouts walking in the bush without shoes are a common sight. Yet these Africans stay on—though frequently in violent conflict with people who share the same history, culture, and values. As long as Western conservationists continue to invest in young expatriate researchers who count animals for publication and advanced degrees, rather than investing in those responsible for the day-in, day-out management of protected areas, the results will never match the objectives.

This is where the breakdown in the Serengeti took place. Scientists, almost all expatriates, undertook basic research which had little applicability to problems facing the management staff. No one invested time and money in those who were destined to remain in the park, namely, the Tanzanians and the Tanzanian Department of National Parks. Concentration on the biological aspects of the park resulted in the inability of researchers and managers alike to deal with the immediate problems—those primarily involving the rural populations around the park. Only now, thirty years after the start of research in the Serengeti, is Tanzania being given the resources and support it needs to begin an active program to look into and address the human question.

Rural communities in Africa are fully capable of taking active, well-planned steps to protect their environment, despite popular misinformation to the contrary. Rural people not only interact daily with the environment, but rely upon it to supply most of their basic requirements. Such communities, however, often see wild animals from a different perspective than people who do not live in close proximity to them. It is easy to call for a halt to the killing of elephants from an office in Washington, D.C., or from an armchair in Iowa following the latest "Nature" special. It is another thing to tell this to villagers in Gabon who must abandon their fields and move their families because elephants have destroyed their crops and livelihoods. International conservationists claim wildlife as a world heritage and call for its protection. African governments in urban settings regard it as a national resource and put rules and regulations on its use. Rural people have traditionally seen wildlife as their own, and it plays an important role in local culture, diet, and economy.

Africans have developed complex participatory systems of

resource use and environmental management. In the traditional *chitemene* farming system of the Bemba in Zambia's Northern Province and throughout the miombo woodlands of Africa, villagers plant crops on cleared woodland plots fertilized by burning the branches collected from nearby trees. Farmers grow finger millet, maize, and sorghum for three years, and then abandon the plot so it can regenerate. As the forest cover returns, so do the animals, attracted to the young, tender plants that shoot up once the farmers move on.

Hunters in these rural communities, as Joshua Nyirenda was in Malawi, are professionals providing important resources, both in terms of cash and protein. They use appropriate technology and self-help—factors usually described as indicators of successful development. Any organized effort, whether it be conservation or rural development, that works with and seeks to learn from these systems, developed through trial and error over long periods of time, is much more likely to be successful than projects proposed from the outside, for a short duration of time, and from the top down.

Over the last century, African governments and international aid agencies have developed policies which have reduced the traditional systems of environmental management to little more than resource mining in preparation for an unknown future. Among the Bemba in northern Zambia, the government policy of emphasizing cash cropping of maize, cotton, sunflower, tobacco, and groundnuts has caused changes in the farming system, making it more reliant on external factors, less environmentally sound, and less nutritious. Anti-poaching laws have turned centuries-old practices of subsistence hunting into a crime, and have transformed wildlife from a valuable commodity to a nuisance which threatens crops, livestock, and the local people.

Most agricultural schemes imposed on Africa by various aid agencies have failed, although agriculture continues to form the foundation of development efforts on the continent. In contrast, the use of bushmeat in the West and Central African forests continues to provide for human needs without leading to widespread ecological destruction. Bushmeat is sold throughout the region at market prices. In Gabon, animals harvested in the forest are marked up by over 200 percent for sale in the cities, and the demand remains strong. Much of the economic return accrues directly back to the rural communities. There is little or no outside interference—few aid agencies could generate much domestic support for a program that funded bushpig hunting in the Congo—and in most situations the trade is not even officially recognized as part of the economy. In Liberia and elsewhere, however, as noted in Chapter XI, the contribution can be significant.

Many people in the international aid and conservation communities are now calling for more rigorous control of the bushmeat trade. Before such advice becomes practice, conservationists and economists need to examine the impact of the bushmeat trade on forest animals, the importance of the practice to rural communities, and the possible economic alternatives that might fill the gap that will be created if regulations are imposed. The current bushmeat trade in Africa may provide a better model for agricultural policy than the other way around, thus turning the usual development scenario on its head.

No one would argue that bushmeat alone will fill all the varied needs of rural Africans. Meeting those needs requires long-term investment, as does meeting the needs of Africa's park managers. The two are obviously intertwined, and are at the heart of the challenge facing conservation and development. Unfortunately, neither the economics of the bushmeat trade nor park management plans will provide the immediate results which international conservation organizations so often require as grist for their fund-raising mills.

Much of the news one hears about conservation in Africa portrays a continent in crisis. Increasing human population, decreasing agricultural production, loss of forest cover, and mounting debt all point to a bleak future. Even in the countries where conservationists are most active, the black rhino remains near extinction and the elephant population is crashing. It is this crisis mentality that fuels conservation, and pressures Western governments into setting aside funds for environmental activities. Encouraging wealthy governments to pay for global conservation is all well and good; the problems arise when the time comes to spend the money. Just like famine relief in Africa, the nature of the conservation crisis means that responses will be of short duration—usually five years or less—and then forgotten. Then the search is on for the next crisis.

Is there really a crisis, or is it just a creation of the Western media, attention-grabbing efforts by those whose livelihood depends on saving the last species? Elephants and rhinos, the most charismatic of all large mammals, provide perhaps the best illustration of these efforts. They have been described as the "bread and butter" of international conservation. Initiatives to save these species were built on the myth of wild Africa and now serve to perpetuate it.

The elephant population in Africa seems to be following a ten-year cycle, closely followed by rhinos. Concern over the elephant follows the inverse curve: each time the population hits a trough, human interest in the species peaks, and someone predicts the elephant's imminent demise—it's been happening since Roman times. The most recent peaks in the "elephant crisis" were 1979 and 1990, when researchers carried out continentwide counts of dubious validity. With the numbers to back them up (or so it seemed), conservation organizations called for huge donations and for new legislation to protect the remaining populations. The fact that such programs were not successful in 1979 did not stop the same thing from happening in 1990. Funds continue to flow into elephant studies, especially counts of the continental population and the effects of trade bans on poaching. Little money is made available to address the institutional needs of African governments and rural communities to manage elephant and other wildlife populations.

The elephant is often described as a flagship or keystone

species, one which has such fund-raising possibilities that it gains the money needed for a wide range of activities that by themselves would attract little attention. Yet the process also works in the opposite direction. Many of the more innovative programs, such as CAMPFIRE in Zimbabwe and ADMADE and LIRDP in Zambia, with their "go-slow" approaches and emphasis on community involvement, are included by the "elephant gurus"—those conservationists and aid officials who build careers on saving elephants—as elephant projects. Such a classification serves two purposes: first, it broadens the types of management tools used in conserving elephant populations, and thus looks good when it comes to defending the amount of money being spent; second, it increases the flow of cash to what appears to be elephant conservation. Thus, no one need go to the trouble of designing a new effort to soak up the huge amounts of money now being thrown at elephants. When the U.S. Congress pressured USAID to support elephant activities, the agency did little more than repackage its existing natural resource management efforts into elephant projects. Conservation organizations have done the same thing to demonstrate to the public their commitment to elephant conservation.

Rhinos are never far behind. It is almost as if the "rhino gurus," with all the excitement over elephants, are afraid that their cause will be lost in the outpouring of concern. Now that the elephant has been placed on Appendix I of CITES, and trade in ivory has dropped off, conservation organizations are turning back to the rhino, which is already on Appendix I.

In the spring of 1991, the international rhino campaign kicked into gear again, focusing primarily on the issue of the rhino horn trade. Headlines like "Last Chance for the Rhino?" are being bandied about once more, along with special overviews of the plight of the world's five rhino species. While the goal is noble, one might question the timing of the campaign: rhinos are in more or less the same position they were a year ago, with some populations, particularly in Asia, in terrible shape while others are stable or growing. A year ago, however, all anyone wanted to hear about was elephants, and before that it was the mountain gorillas. No doubt in a couple of months it will be another issue—perhaps the Serengeti.

Most conservation organizations maintain that these campaigns further the worthy goal of educating their public, the people who give them money to do conservation. Everyone who tries to carry out practical conservation programs in developing countries while also maintaining a large and generous core of supporters back home faces the same fundamental conflict: education quite often involves telling people something they do not want to hear, while fund raising almost always involves telling people only the things they most want to hear. The result is that these organizations give the public what it wants to hear in the hope of raising money, and pass it off as education.

This is not dishonesty as much as doing what it takes to survive. With a limited number of people willing to contribute to conservation, organizations tend to appeal to people's emotions with pictures of baby elephants or mountain gorillas, rather than presenting an intellectual discussion about the complexities of conservation in Africa, including the continued role of hunting and wildlife utilization. An interest in wildlife conservation usually begins with an emotional commitment to animals. Basic issues such as poverty, lack of employment opportunities, poor working conditions, lack of education or training, institutional needs, and the timeframe in which changes take place are all factors that rarely generate such commitment. They make for poor photo spreads, as do racks of bushmeat drying in the sun. On the other side, elephants and rhinos, good guys and bad guys, young expatriates working in the wilds of Africa, are the photogenic aspects of African conservation, so they grab the public's attention and raise money.

Conservation organizations are comprised of professionals who know that long-term, multi-faceted approaches are required to address the twin problems of wildlife management and rural development in Africa. They appreciate the variety of methods and approaches, and the importance of involving local people throughout the process. International conservation organizations have after all been leaders in implementing new conservation and development methodologies. They have not, however, been as willing to publicize this to their general membership.

A simplistic way of attempting to bridge this gap is the conservation organizations' newfound love for indigenous peoples and their affinity with nature. But indigenous people living in "harmony" with nature are as big a myth as the portrayal of Africans and wildlife. Faith in the environmentally-sensitive, rural African was built up through studies of rural peoples living at low population densities with a correspondingly low impact on the environment—much the same conditions the early European explorers found in parts of Africa, which led to the idea that there always had been few people on the continent.

Given the chance, indigenous peoples will exploit their environment to their advantage using whatever technology is available. Indigenous peoples are loved when they harvest fruits, grow vegetables, weave baskets, and carve wood. But few conservationists love the Maasai when they try to practice their traditional pastoral movements through the Ngorongoro Crater, the Serengeti, Masai Mara, or Amboseli; nor do they love Central Africa's BaAka pygmies when they kill an elephant for its bountiful supply of meat and its ivory. Then these people are little more than trespassers and poachers.

Conservation organizations now must make a greater effort to educate their constituencies. Fund raisers and educators are experts in getting messages across to large numbers of people. Up until now, however, it has been easier to pass on the myths so deeply ingrained in us rather than to make the effort to understand these complex relationships. In the process we have dug ourselves in deeper, reinforcing by our own propaganda the myths that marginalize Africans from the land and from their own heritage. Africans will remain on their land long after northern conservationists have gone home, and they must be allowed to make the decisions that directly affect their livelihood.

If outside support for conservation in Africa has been based on a set of assumptions that are little more than myth, what should be done now? There are few short- or medium-term answers which will change how Western governments or international organizations approach conservation issues in Africa, and it is not possible to turn back the clock and start over again. National parks and other protected areas have an important role to play on the continent, and governments, as well as individuals, have demonstrated their commitment to these forms of land use through direct investment, through the loss of land set aside as wildlife habitat which might otherwise generate income from alternative uses, and through loss of life, as Gilbert Bangandombi-Kotali's family discovered.

Rural communities will support wildlife conservation only when they become active participants in the process. Conservationists, their methods, and even the rural communities will have to change dramatically before this can happen. The myths upon which conservation assumptions rest have developed over hundreds of years, and they influence not only governments and international conservation organizations but the Africans themselves.

The evolution away from the myth of wild Africa is under way. Terms like "ecodevelopment" and "sustainable development" have entered the lexicon as people recognize that conservation must become a more integral part of a country's development program. Conservationists have just begun the crucial process of addressing issues ranging from national policy, institutional reform, and investment, to local-level factors such as real needs, self-help, and community participation. Long, frustrating experience, as well as a dose of common sense, has convinced conservation organizations that protected areas and laws alone cannot protect wildlife in the long run without the acquiescence of their human neighbors. Rural people bear significant costs from living with wildlife, yet they have been progressively excluded from the decision-making process about it.

At almost all levels Zimbabwe has been the most progressive in integrating its wildlife resources as a part of the country's national development program. The programs in Zimbabwe demonstrate the wide range of interventions necessary to manage wildlife populations. At the national policy level, Zimbabwe introduced the 1975 Parks and Wildlife Act, giving private landowners the responsibility for the conservation and use of wildlife on their lands, including community proprietorship. Such action is an important step toward decentralizing the decision-making process, moving it further down to the level of those who have historically suffered the greatest costs of living with wildlife.

Actions such as these, along with wildlife utilization programs, are often taken by the international conservation community to mean the end of national parks. This has hardly been the case in Zimbabwe, where people regard wildlife as part of their national heritage, and where protected areas conserve species and their habitats in tandem with greater participation from neighboring communities. Policy questions about wildlife do not present either/or choices but rather complex decisions, which balance the intangible value of protecting wildlife in a national park with real economic needs, such as community-based wildlife utilization. Efforts to define the value of wildlife solely in economic terms are just another form of simplifying these complex relationships. Wildlife conservation must take both economic and aesthetic value into account.

Zimbabwe's approach to wildlife management offers a graphic illustration of the two sides of conservation. The Department of National Parks and Wildlife Management manages the parks while also assisting rural communities in using their wildlife resources. In the parks, as illustrated earlier, the department responded to illegal hunting of rhinos in the Zambezi Valley by employing conventional methods used by conservationists over the last fifty years: intensified law enforcement, rhino relocation to safer areas, and so on. The program has been a success, but at great expense; it reveals the real cost of traditional conservation based on preserving aesthetic values, and the infrastructure necessary to support it.

Outside national parks, Zimbabwe continues to move ahead with the CAMPFIRE program, empowering rural communities to make decisions about the management of communally owned natural resources. Despite its growing pains, this program is addressing problems that arise from communal ownership of natural resources, problems now being experienced throughout Africa. Its focus on the conservation and management of wildlife, forestry, grazing, and water is enabling rural communities to obtain direct financial benefits from the exploitation of these resources. Rural communities in Zimbabwe have started to come to the Department of National Parks and Wildlife Management and request their help. The transformation of the department from a law enforcement agency to one that provides technical assistance is among the most important moves that can be made in the wildlife sector within African governments. Authoritarian, top-down enforcement breeds discontent; help and technical assistance promote cooperation and collaboration.

The importance of Africans carrying out conservation for themselves extends all the way up to national policies. Many of Zimbabwe's environmental policies, for example, are embodied in a document called the "National Environmental Strategy." Similar strategies in other parts of the developing world traditionally have been funded by international conservation organizations and aid agencies that bring in expatriate consultants to coordinate the process of putting such a document together. The consultants usually become the primary authors—they almost always find it easier to do something themselves than to try to motivate other people to do it. In Zimbabwe, this was not the case. Zimbabweans developed their strategy with local private and public support, and thus it became a truly "national" conservation strategy.

Zimbabwe's "National Environmental Strategy" is hardly a sleek or sophisticated-looking document. A similar environmental strategy for neighboring Zambia, on the other hand, was funded by aid agencies and produced by consultants. It is a glossy publication, with color photos, maps, and graphs. Unfortunately, style is often confused with substance. "I wouldn't take it [the Zimbabwe document] too seriously," said one of the consultants developing Botswana's national conservation strategy. "Look at the quality of the paper it's printed on, a rather amateur production. Nobody is going to pay much attention to it."

The unspoken message is that Zimbabwe's environmental strategy is unimportant because it was created by Africans. This simply extends the colonial dogma that Africans cannot be trusted to conserve their wildlife resources. The persistence of this attitude is leading conservation to a dead end. Wildlife conservation on the continent hinges on ensuring that Africans—government decision makers and technicians, private entrepreneurs and rural communities—take on responsibility for themselves. Rural Africans rely on their natural surroundings for their livelihood, and they have always been willing to make sacrifices in order to manage it. Ensuring their involvement in modern conservation, however, means taking their needs seriously.

No one has the blueprint for transforming one hundred years of conservation practice in Africa. As a start, some of the fundamental elements must be reexamined. Timeframes, for example, must change. Successful conservation will not be accomplished within the three to five years covered in most projects. With everything working in its favor, CAMPFIRE languished for eight years, and still is struggling to overcome entrenched interests and patterns of behavior. The Nazinga Wildlife Utilization Project has struggled for twelve years to develop a program of rational utilization in the savannas of south-central Burkina Faso. What these programs have in common are long-term commitments to the people and the areas in which they operate. Strategies and programs must replace simple projects; fifty years is not an unrealistic time-frame when the goal is a profound change in the behavior of institutions and individuals.

Conservation needs a new cast of characters, drawn from both government institutions and the rural communities. Empowering Africans to be the decision makers in conservation has come to mean giving the rural communities rather than the central government control over communal resources. While an important step, the process cannot stop there. In reality, conservation has gone so far that, while governments pass and attempt to enforce laws and pay for basic institutional costs, much of the control over funds and decisions still rests with expatriate advisers, aid agencies, and international conservation organizations. This control is wildly out of proportion to the amount of money these organizations invest, but they have the power of world opinion behind them.

The international institutions concerned with conservation would be more effective if they invested in technical assistance and training for Africans rather than Western-based consultant companies and researchers. Government institutions responsible for training, scientific research, and wildlife management do need urgent help to build up their capabilities. Yet most of these institutions seem unwilling to relinquish their hold on the responsibility for managing natural resources, in large part because they lack effective policies or management skills.

It is time for the torch to be passed on. Africans must become the "doers" in wildlife conservation, with the help of African governments, international conservation organizations, and aid agencies. Empowerment and participation must take place at all levels within a country and include all aspects of conservation: design, implementation, management, and benefits. The closed bidding system of the EC, for example, does not ensure participation by either the government or the rural communities in Gabon, nor do visiting EC delegates promising benefits from wildlife to villagers. These people don't need to be told. They are intimately acquainted with the benefits from wildlife, as well as the costs.

Conservation cannot be done "to" or even "for" or "with" Africans. Conservation must be done by Africans. Conservation is as much a process of adaptive management, to use Richard Bell's phrase in a slightly broader context, as is rural development. There are no instructions. It is a system of trial and error, with few means of predicting the outcome, and one learns not just from the successes but from the failures as well. The right to fail and to succeed must be handed over to the inhabitants of the continent. The West has been at it for over one hundred years in Africa—building upon a myth—and conservation based on myth is bound to fail.

Niare Kadiatou works in the village of Kouroussale, some 40 miles from the Malian capital of Bamako. She is involved in helping women's cooperatives grow vegetables for food and market. Before her village project was implemented, Niare pointed out to the women that the main constraint they would face would be wandering livestock getting into their gardens and destroying the crops. She made two suggestions: either tie up the animals or hire a young boy to look after them. The village women didn't want to do either, saying their animals were not used to being tied up and it was too expensive to hire somebody to watch over them. They were, however, very keen to start the project. Three weeks after the project started, the vegetable were growing nicely. Then, one afternoon, the village women approached Niare saying that animals had gotten into the gardens and destroyed much of the crop. Without despairing, Niare encouraged the women to start anew. They did, and the following week animals were again in the gardens. Again, the village women started over. After a third incursion, they finally decided to take action. Feelings were running high.

As one village woman said, "We have duplicated our labor and time for nothing. In this way we will produce nothing by the end of the season."

The women then decided to solve the problem of animals getting into their gardens. At a meeting they developed the following strategy: an enclosed holding pen would be built near the public garden; any animal found in the public garden would be caught and put in the enclosure with a fine of approximately $30 to the owner; after two weeks, the captured animal would be sold if the fine went unpaid, and these funds, minus the fine, would be given to the animal's owner; no interventions (read "by men") would be accepted.

Although the women were initially against protecting their gardens, through this trial-and-error process they arrived at a solution. As a result, the gardens were not only protected from the animals, but manure from the holding pen became available as fertilizer. When people are motivated by an activity, they will find the solutions to the different problems they experience. They don't need, nor will they always accept, someone else's solution.

Despite the calls of crisis in Africa, the future remains positive. Africa holds the greatest assemblage of large mammals on earth, and wildlands and habitat abound. Africa is the cradle of the human race: fossilized remains go back 5 million years, and there is evidence suggesting the human form as far back as 10 million years ago. Haskell Ward argues in *African Development Reconsidered* that Africa has always demanded from the human species a respect for the continent's physical and biological systems as a condition for survival. Wisely, Africans accepted that condition and organized their patterns of life to accommodate increasing drought in the north, accelerating wetness near the Equator, fragile soils throughout most of the continent, and a rich diversity of flora and fauna. Shifting patterns of living are the norm.

The African spirit—the capacity not just to survive but to survive with buoyancy and a huge reserve of goodwill—represents a tangible asset that conservationists must build upon. Investment must be increasingly in human development. While the myth of wild Africa formerly kept people out of the picture, especially those who suffered and lost the most, it is these same people who offer the greatest hope for the future. The Victorian social reformer John Ruskin noted that "the wealth of a country is in its good men and women and nothing else." Pride and determination to succeed are among the most powerful motivating factors in any society. Africans do care about wildlife. They live with it every day. They have been labeled as the problem; they are in fact the solution.

AFTERWORD

▼ ▼ ▼

Ex Africa semper aliquid novi
There is always something new out of Africa.
　　　　　　　　　　　—Pliny the Elder

The social, economic, and political changes in Africa in the four years since the publication of the first edition of this book amply illustrate the modern relevance of Pliny's ancient wisdom. From the joyous, peaceful revolution in South Africa to the nightmarish violence in Rwanda and Burundi, from Namibia to Eritrea, the political map of Africa has changed as dramatically as at any time since the overthrow of the colonial powers. Some countries, as defined by a functioning central government, have ceased to exist. Zaire stands as a hollow shell, not a nation but a series of separate entities serving local economies.

While some states have disintegrated, others have emerged in new and vibrant forms. Communities and governments are tailoring democracy to fit African realities. To a degree unheard of even four years ago, many rural Africans control their own affairs, and can pressure the highest levels of government. The birth of new democracies in Africa holds the promise of vesting the responsibility for conservation with rural communities, where it belongs. With democratic reforms come powerful African voices as well as international donors and business interests preaching the gospel of economic growth and free trade. Yet, a wholehearted embrace of development—defined as quantitative growth in size of the economy rather than qualitative improvement in people's lives—may prove ruinous. Less developed countries cannot grow their way out of economic hardship, contrary to standard development theory, because economic growth, fueled by an ever more rapid depletion of natural resources, is not the solution but the problem. The challenge for Africa, indeed for all regions of the world, is to reconfigure economic structures and community values so that people can improve the quality of their lives without the constant accumulation of material wealth. In Africa, the first step in that process—for which no one, least of all the developed nations, has any instructions—is to give rural people a voice. Even that small change will be tortuous, and, for conservationists, agonizing. Democracy allows Africans to decide what they want, and they do not always want the same things as conservationists.

Gabon serves as a case in point. Before the recent democratic changes which have transformed Gabon from a one-party state to a multi-party democracy, people living in rural areas often did not bother to complain about animals, notably elephants, destroying their gardens. The elephants were in the gardens—the village of Nioungou, for example (see Chapter XI) no longer exists because marauding animals forced the villagers to move away—but people knew the government would pay no attention. Following the creation of parliament, however, the members of that body became responsible to their electorate, and complaints poured in. The government responded to these complaints by requesting aid to buy guns and train wildlife agency staff to shoot elephants. Conservationists explained that they could not supply arms or training for the wildlife agency staff to kill elephants, because the European and American public would not support such actions.

The halting, tenuous emergence of rural Africans as effective advocates for their rights lies at the heart of the changes we have sought to document in this book. Conservation in Africa, once the exclusive province of Europeans and Americans, increasingly carries an indelibly African stamp. This transformation of conservation from a largely colonial to a fundamentally local endeavor bears close analysis. While popular perceptions of African conservation continue to ignore local people, the transfer of power provides reason for hope in an otherwise grim era of burgeoning human populations, stagnant economies, and widespread social unrest.

Simple justice demands that we recognize the primacy of Africans in conserving their natural heritage. The continued resistance of many people outside Africa to admit this seemingly self-evident notion stems in large part from the deep misperceptions about Africa and Africans. The recognition that Africans are willing and able to take the lead in conservation efforts on the continent would be an enormous change in attitude, and yet is just the first step on a difficult and uncertain path. This book provides no more than tentative suggestions for crafting a more effective and equitable style of conservation. Today's African conservationists will face the same inevitable and intractable conflicts between people and animals as did their predecessors, and with fewer resources and less time.

Alternatives to the traditional, Western-dominated conservation of the past half-century have begun to emerge, as is seen in examples from Zimbabwe, Zambia, Botswana, Tanzania, and elsewhere. The urgency of these efforts has increased over the past four years, but the innovative approaches that will carry conservation forward cannot be drawn up on a blackboard or written down in a consultant's report. They will emerge by trial and error, as Africans seek to balance their deep concern for the natural world with their compassion for the needy. Once conservationists and their supporters embrace the notion of African-centered conservation, then Africa can become a laboratory for new methods, radical techniques, and good science, as well as a place where the age-old verities of conservation—national parks, anti-poaching units, and the like—can be retooled for a new generation.

The inclusion of science in our list of the essentials for successful conservation may seem surprising, given the critical comments on basic ecological research in East Africa in Chapter V. Some readers took that criticism as a blanket dismissal of all science as irrelevant to conservation. That was not our intention. Strictly from a conservation perspective, much of the research conducted from the 1960s to the mid-1970s left a great deal to be desired. Today, however, more and more scientists are turning to the emerging, applied specialty of conservation biology. This shift bodes well for expanded cooperation between ecologists of all stripes and wildlife managers.

The discussion of science in Chapter V highlights one particularly influential book, entitled *Serengeti: Dynamics of an Ecosystem,* edited by A. R. E. Sinclair and Michael Norton-Griffiths. Nothing captures the changing role of science in conservation better than the title of the second edition of that book, published in 1995. *Serengeti II: Dynamics, Management, and Conservation of an Ecosystem,* edited by Sinclair and Peter Arcese, contains outstanding research papers, as did the first volume, but now much of that research is explicitly relevant to conservation. Nearly a third of the book's chapters focus exclusively on conservation and management of the Serengeti ecosystem, and several examine human needs, economic structures, and conservation policies. Even Myles Turner, warden of Serengeti National Park from 1956 to 1972 and implacable foe of researchers, would be pleased.

One of the contributors to *Serengeti II* is Holly Dublin, who continues to rank among the most interesting conservation biologists working in Africa today. Dublin's chapter focuses on the role of elephants and fire in vegetation dynamics in the Serengeti. Some of her most intriguing research, however, is on the effects of the international ban on the ivory trade. The ban (see Chapter IV) dominated the debate over conservation in Africa in the late 1980s and early 1990s. Both the ban and the furor surrounding it remain the touchstone for international perceptions about conservation in Africa today.

Supporters of the ban, particularly outside of Africa, believed that halting the ivory trade was the quick-fix solution to the problem of elephant poaching. Dublin's study, *Four Years After the CITES Ban: Illegal Killing of Elephants, Ivory Trade and Ivory Stockpiles,* which she conducted in 1994 with wildlife trade specialist Tom Milliken and ecologist Richard F. W. Barnes, reveals the futility of searching for such a simple answer. Dublin and her colleagues looked at nine countries (Cameroon, Gabon, Ivory Coast, Kenya, Malawi, Nigeria, Tanzania, Zambia, Zimbabwe) and found it nearly impossible to tease apart the effects of the ban itself from the effects of other, related developments such as new legislation, changing attitudes toward wildlife, and fluctuating wildlife department budgets.

Only one thing is certain: many people on both sides of the issue make grand claims on the basis of rather scanty information. The most common is that the ivory ban has resulted in a reduction of the number of elephants being poached in Africa. Yet, as noted in Chapter IV, monitoring the mortality of elephants across Africa involves as much guesswork as science, so any continent-wide assessment of the success or failure of the ivory ban can be little more than an ideological assertion. The table below illustrates how anyone can quote such tenuous figures for their own purpose:

Estimated elephant numbers in states voting against the ban 1989 and 1995:

Country	Elephants 1989	Elephants 1995*
Botswana	68,000	80,174
Malawi	2,800	2,087
South Africa	7,800	10,010
Zambia	32,000	33,004
Zimbabwe	52,000	81,855
Congo	42,000	32,563
Gabon	74,000	82,012
Sub-total	278,600	321,705
All other range states	330,400	221,770
Total elephants	609,000	543,475
% in voting against	46%	59%

from Ivory Trade Review Group 1989, I. Douglas-Hamilton (section 1.1, table 8)
* from Said, M.Y. *et al.* 1995, IUCN including definite, probable and possible estimates

In sum, when the ivory ban went into effect in 1989, the seven countries listed here—all of which opposed the ban—accounted for an estimated 278,600 elephants or 46% of the total estimated continental population. In 1995, according to updated figures produced by the IUCN African Elephant Specialist Group, the overall number of elephants fell by 65,525. That is, Africa lost over 65,000 elephants since the enactment of the ivory ban. The number of elephants in those states that originally voted against the ban actually increased by about 43,000, while those in states that voted for the ban decreased by over 108,000.

What does all this mean? Does it mean that those range states that voted against the ban had it right in the first place, that active management and utilization of elephants for the benefit of local communities and national governments is the most effective way to protect the animals and build up herds?

Does it mean that those countries taking a protectionist view cannot adequately protect their elephants, and that non-consumptive use activities are not adequate to pay for elephant conservation? Or do these figures show that the loss of 65,000 elephants over the last six years is much less than were being lost during the days of the ivory trade and it can be concluded that the ban is successful?

In fact, these numbers support only one conclusion: that numbers are not enough. Given the range of quality in counts due to the capacity and technical ability of different wildlife departments throughout the continent, the differences in habitat—from open desert and grasslands to dense forest and bush—and the difficulties in reaching areas where elephants live, it is impossible to say with any certainty not only how many elephants exist, but whether they are increasing or decreasing. Even with accurate census figures, however, an informed judgment on the success or failure of the ivory ban requires detailed information on illegal hunting, law enforcement, national budgets, and local attitudes. As *Four Years After the CITES Ban* notes with some frustration, such data are rarely available.

The international community clearly hoped that the imposition of the ban on the ivory trade would stop the poaching of elephants. According to the ivory study, poaching dropped in the two years immediately following the ban but has picked up in the past two years, though for the most part poaching levels remain below the pre-ban levels. Poaching for ivory continues in all range states, and is a significant problem in Zaire's Garamba National Park, and in Angola, Mozambique, Chad, Sudan, and Nigeria. Neither conservation organizations nor CITES instituted a monitoring program to ascertain whether or not the ban was successful. As a result, the imposition of the ban on the ivory trade became little more than an uncontrolled test of a hypothesis from which no conclusions could possibly be drawn.

The debate over the ivory ban led to huge increases in antipoaching budgets, which made the greatest contribution to protecting elephants. The data compiled in *Four Years After the CITES Ban* reveal the trend is now going the other way. Antipoaching budgets have shrunk in real terms, sometimes dramatically — 97% in some protected areas in Tanzania, and nearly a 90% drop in operational spending in Zimbabwe. Conservationists and park managers generally agree that elephant conservation requires the expenditure of at least $200 for each square kilometer of park land. In 1993, three-quarters of the protected areas in the ivory study were allocating less than $5/km² for law enforcement activities, and only one was spending more than $100/km². Another rule of thumb holds that elephant conservation requires one trained and equipped park ranger for every twenty square kilometers, but less than 10% of the areas that Dublin and her colleagues examined have that much manpower available.

The ivory ban succeeded, however, in shutting down the major international ivory markets. Ivory markets in Europe and the United States have vanished, while Japan, the largest consumer of ivory prior to the ban, has been depleting the ivory held in its stocks when the ban went into effect. The continuing poaching for ivory suggests that some former markets may still be alive and that other, new markets may be forming, particularly in South Korea and Taiwan. African government stockpiles of ivory continue to grow from confiscations and from animals killed because they were raiding crops or otherwise threatening human life. The pressure to find an equitable solution to the stockpile problem under CITES will increase and test the durability of the ban itself.

Despite the lack of evidence, some conservationists have declared the ivory problem solved, and some donors who were full of promises leading up to the CITES meeting that resulted in the ban now have other priorities. Such simplistic declarations of victory do not help the elephants, but they have enormous public relations value. The far more cautious judgments of *Four Years After the CITES Ban* hardly won many friends. The report has created a great deal of ill feeling, including attempts to get the report withdrawn, criticism in the press, and personal attacks on the authors.

Some of the threats to elephants come from forces completely beyond the scope of the ivory ban. In southern Africa, particularly Zimbabwe, the increase in elephant poaching is tied directly to a dramatic upsurge in rhino poaching. Over the past several years, hunters have decimated the black rhino population to feed the vibrant Asian pharmaceutical market for rhino horn. When the rhino population dwindled to a mere handful, the poachers turned their weapons on the still-thriving elephant herds. Zimbabwe's communal lands have seen an increase in elephant poaching, particularly in areas which once supported significant numbers of rhinos and are near international borders.

The reports from Zimbabwe are especially troubling, given that CAMPFIRE, the country's innovative wildlife management and rural development effort, was designed in part to reduce illegal hunting on the part of local communities by enabling people to gain direct benefits from having elephants and other animals on their land. Some of the increase in poaching in Zimbabwe, however, may be due to better reporting by those communities. Many people once tolerated poachers on their land and did not bother to inform authorities when they found an elephant carcass. Now, motivated by a greater sense of ownership over their wild resources, and recognizing that every elephant shot by a poacher means one fewer that the community can use to attract tourists or sell to a safari hunter, rural communities willingly help park rangers catch poachers.

CAMPFIRE may have had a perverse success, in that the growing elephant herds—the nationwide population is up to roughly 70,000—mean an increasing number of ever-bolder elephants. In some places elephants have become pests, the oversize equivalent of the deer munching tomatoes in a suburban backyard. In the past, a crop-raiding elephant meant a plea for a ranger to come shoot it in the name of problem animal control, or PAC. Now, fewer people want the elephant killed and more just want it moved or fenced out of their gardens. The drop in the number of elephants killed for PAC partially compensates for, and perhaps even outweighs, the increase in elephant poaching.

Elephants are only the most visible animals to benefit from CAMPFIRE, which remains one of the most fascinating and influential programs in all of Africa. Officials of both public and private natural resource management and development agencies from across the continent now regularly travel the communal lands in search of the keys to locally based conservation. Of course, CAMPFIRE has no master plan, not even a plan easily transferable to neighboring countries like Botswana and Namibia, each of which has created its own program. But CAMPFIRE, which began as an experiment, has become a movement in rural Zimbabwe.

The evolution of CAMPFIRE over the past four or five years illustrates the problems and potential of linking conservation and rural development. The program now looks far beyond herds of game or crop-raiding elephants, to broader questions of the control people can exercise over their own futures. Until the introduction of CAMPFIRE, communal people were not empowered to make decisions about the way they—or others—used their natural resources.

The people behind CAMPFIRE always recognized its broader significance, but only in the past few years has it become clear that such a comprehensive effort could actually work. Today, 24 of Zimbabwe's 56 districts have adopted CAMPFIRE, and more than 360,000 households are directly involved with wildlife management. In 1980, only the government focused on wild animals, and then only in officially protected areas, which cover just 12 percent of the countryside. Wildlife now runs on fully a third of the country, and the entire increase has taken place outside of protected areas.

Four years ago, the question was whether CAMPFIRE

would survive. The question today is not survival but what form the program will take, and how effective it will be. CAMPFIRE has grown so deep in many rural communities that its political opponents—some of whom occupy high positions in government—cannot hope to uproot it. Those opponents, however, may still be able to twist and weaken CAMPFIRE, leaving communal lands literally strewn with Potemkin villages with the appearance but not the reality of control over their own lives.

The reason for the unease of some politicians, and the enthusiasm of others, lies in the role of CAMPFIRE as an exercise in democracy, a forum for a wide range of issues including representation, economic participation, and the governance of communal areas. More simply, some of the conflicts now surfacing within revolve around who gets the money the project generates. The fact that people are fighting over resources may not be entirely detrimental to CAMPFIRE, to the extent those fights reflect not a shortage but rather a new-found value in the resources themselves. CAMPFIRE focuses as much on the nature of rural communities and collective decision making as on the technical challenges of sustainable use of wildlife.

Rural communities are beginning to appreciate the finite nature of resources and have begun to control immigration into their areas. In the past, many rural communities encouraged immigration in an attempt to increase their political voice. These same communities now recognize the importance of elected representatives who truly understand their needs. Indeed, several members of Zimbabwe's parliament came up through the ranks of CAMPFIRE.

CAMPFIRE and the many similar efforts it has spawned rest on the notion that a long-term strategy for biodiversity conservation must include the sustainable use of wild species as a key component. The idea dates back many years, but research interest into the ecological implications of sustainable use has picked up considerably. People will use wild resources, so the debate must focus on how and when to use which species, and how best to insure that such use is not destructive.

Nearly all the available ecological evidence suggests that once human beings begin exploiting a particular part of any ecosystem, that ecosystem quickly loses some portion of its previous stock of biological diversity. But how much of a loss is too much? How fast is too fast? And most importantly, is there some magical breakeven point beyond which we dare not go, an equilibrium where the gain in human welfare bought by the use of a wild species precisely balances the loss of biodiversity? Unfortunately, neither ecologists nor philosophers have yet been able to provide answers to these questions, which may hold the key to the future of much of the Earth's natural wealth.

When human activities overshoot the equilibrium, the result can be catastrophic. In hindsight, the western arm of the Rift Valley, including parts of eastern Zaire, Burundi, Rwanda, and western Uganda, has long been a tinderbox waiting for a match. The region's rich, volcanic soils support huge numbers of herbivores, which attracted early conservationists intent on creating national parks and more than willing to ignore another consequence of fertile soils: an exploding human population. In Rwanda, the growing population squeezed farmsteads so small they could no longer support even a single family. The inevitable conflict turned into genocide when extremist Hutus in the government attacked moderate Hutus and Tutsis in an effort to gain control over the country's shrinking land resources. Up to one million people have been killed and another one million or more live as refugees.

Human tragedy often begets ecological disaster. In Zaire, refugees plunder Parc National des Virunga for meat and fuelwood—by one estimate, 100 tons of wood every day. Sustainable use of resources becomes idle fantasy in such circumstances. Rwanda's Parc National des Akagera, once a jewel, all but ceased to exist as it was invaded by Rwandans looking for land to graze livestock and for animals to hunt. Although some park guards in Parc National des Volcans, home of the mountain gorillas, heroically remained on the job, many others fled. (World

Wildlife Fund recognized the efforts of those who remained by awarding them the $50,000 J. Paul Getty Wildlife Conservation Prize, which will cover back pay and supplies.) The mountain gorillas have suffered from poaching as well as from the setting of land mines in some areas of the park. More importantly, tourism, which was rapidly becoming one of the most important sources of income for the Rwandan government, has collapsed. The real losers in the collapse of tourism are the communities that were benefiting from the money brought in by visitors. Rwanda will not soon, and in fact may never again, command the trust and confidence of the market necessary to attract people to see the mountain gorillas.

Even if the civil wars can be calmed, racial hatreds contained, and refugees repatriated, conservationists will face a humbling paradox. The productivity of the land means that human population densities will increase, and people will use the land intensively. Under these circumstances conservationists and planners cannot create buffer zones of reduced and managed use around parks and protected areas. Protected areas will be surrounded by seas of human settlement. At the same time, this productive land also supports assemblages of unique plants and animals, thus placing the region high on any list of conservation priorities.

Traditional integrated conservation and development models likely will not work in Rwanda or its equally crowded and troubled neighbors. Bringing together conservation and development requires time to educate surrounding communities, and time has run out. Here conservation and development remain at loggerheads, and conservationists must accept that there are going to be hard edges between parks and people. National parks now take on added significance—an ironic twist, given the history of how the parks came to be established in the first place. The mountains of the western arm of the Rift Valley provide the watershed for the millions of people who farm and raise livestock. The continued denuding of the forests will likely lead to a loss in the capacity of the soils to manage the waterflow. Siltation on the Rift Valley lakes could cause a loss in the productivity of the fisheries, leading to further impoverishment of the resource base. The protected areas in this region act as the bank for the future. They hold the water, act as a repository for wildlife, and may one day provide income through tourism. But the land is finite. Even if these areas were turned over to the people for farming and grazing, they would only buy time for a short while, and then the problem would reemerge. The next time there will be nowhere to turn.

While integrated conservation and development may wither in Rwanda, it flourishes in diverse forms in southern Africa. In northwestern Namibia, the rugged region known as Kaokoland supports an estimated 50,000 people, most notably the Himba, a pastoral group of people practicing their traditional livelihood of raising cattle, goats, and sheep. These semi-nomadic people move throughout the area to find water and pastures. All of this land is communal and administered by the state, and it has no formal conservation status.

Since 1982, a Namibian NGO has worked to gain the local communities' active participation in the fight against illegal hunting. The program has been operating now for fourteen years, and is in an important respect the inverse of CAMP-FIRE. While CAMPFIRE assumes that communities will not share their lands with wild animals unless they see immediate benefits, the project in Namibia holds out the promise of future benefits to the communities for conservation efforts now. As wildlife populations grow, then the communities will begin to benefit through harvesting and tourism.

In 1995, the government of Namibia gave rural communities permission to derive income directly from the area's natural resources. Today, communities are beginning to harvest wildlife, market it, and reinvest the proceeds back into the community. Direct community involvement in natural resource management over a fourteen year period in Kaokoland is now marked by increasing wildlife populations, a growing awareness that wildlife is an important component of the ecosystem, and direct revenues returning to the community.

The volcanic region of the western Rift Valley, with its well-watered mountains and rich agricultural lowlands, and the dry, desolate homeland of the Himba are the two ends of a spectrum that covers all of Africa. Each unique situation requires carefully fitted approaches and responses. Conservation in Africa cannot be written out and followed like a road map; it is a journey full of dead ends and rough roads. The remarkably persistent myth of wild Africa, however, creates the expectation that simple solutions lie just around the next bend. They do not. Conservationists will not know what they will find until they travel the road ahead. As always, Africans know the way best.

Jonathan S. Adams
Silver Spring, Maryland

Thomas O. McShane
Gland, Switzerland

March, 1996

BIBLIOGRAPHY
▼ ▼ ▼

Ake, Claude. "Why Is Africa Not Developing?" *West Africa*, June 15, 1985, 1212–14.

Akeley, Carl E. *In Brightest Africa*. New York: Doubleday, Page, and Co., 1923.

Anderson, David, and Richard Grove. "The Scramble for Eden: Past, Present, and Future in African Conservation." In *Conservation in Africa: People, Policies and Practice*, edited by David Anderson and Richard Grove. Cambridge: Cambridge University Press, 1987, 1–12.

Anstey, Simon. *Wildlife Utilization in Liberia*. WWF/FDA Wildlife Survey Report, 1991.

Asibey, E. O. A., Child. "Wildlife Management for Rural Development in sub-Saharan Africa." *Unasylva*, 161, vol. 41 (1990).

Ayittey, George B. N. "Why Africa Can't Feed Itself." *International Health and Development*, Summer 1989.

Baker, Samuel White. *Albert Nyanza, Great Basin of the Nile*. London: Macmillan and Co., 1866.

Barbier, Edward, and Timothy Swanson. "Ivory: The Case Against the Ban." *New Scientist*, November 17, 1990, 52–54.

Barnes, R. F. W., K. L. Barnes, M. P. T. Alers, and A. Blom. "Man Determines the Distribution of Elephants in the Rain Forests of

Northeastern Gabon." *African Journal of Ecology*, 29 (1991): 54–63.

Bell, Richard. "Conservation with a Human Face: Conflict and Reconciliation in African Land Use Planning." In *Conservation in Africa: People, Policies and Practice*, edited by Anderson and Grove, 79–102.

———, and Erica McShane-Caluzi, eds. *Conservation and Wildlife Management in Africa*. Proceedings of a workshop organized by the U.S. Peace Corps. Kasungu National Park, Malawi: United States Peace Corps, 1984.

Bentsen, Cheryl. *Maasai Days*. New York: Summit Books, 1989.

Bierman, John. *Dark Safari*. New York: Alfred A. Knopf, 1990.

Blixen-Finecke, Baron Bror von. *African Hunter*, edited by Peter Capstick, translated by F. H. Lyon. New York: St. Martin's Press, 1986 (first published 1938).

Boardman, Robert. *International Organization and the Conservation of Nature*. Bloomington, Ind.: University of Indiana Press, 1981.

Boseman, Paul, and Anthony Hall Martin. *Elephants of Africa*. Johannesburg: Struik, 1988.

Boshe, John I. "Wildlife Conservation in the Ngorongoro Conservation Area, Tanzania: Social and Ecological Implications of Increasing Pastoralist and Declining Per Capita Livestock Populations." Paper presented at the Fifth International Theriological Congress, Rome, August 22–29, 1989.

Bull, Bartle. *Safari*. New York: Viking Press, 1988.

Burton, Richard F. *Lake Regions of Central Africa*. London: Longman, Green, Longman, & Roberts, 1860.

———. *First Footsteps in East Africa*. Mineola, N.Y.: Dover Publications, 1987 (first published 1856).

Buxton, Edward North. *Two African Trips*. London: Edward Stanford, 1902.

Carter, L.A. "Into Your Hand: Cultural Impacts on African Wildlife." In *Voices from Africa*, edited by D.M. Lewis and L.A. Carter.

Chase, Alston. "A Small Circle of Friends: How the Conservation Elite Gets the Job Done." *Ouside Magazine*, May 1988.

Colby, Michael. *Environmental Management in Development: The Evolution of Paradigms*. Washington, D.C.: The International Bank for Reconstruction and Development/The World Bank, 1990.

Crosby, Alfred W. *Ecological Imperialism: The Biological Expansion of Europe, 900–1900.* Cambridge: Cambridge University Press, 1990.

Crouse, Debby. "Up Close with Gorillas." *International Wildlife,* November–December 1988, 5–11.

Cumming, D. H. M. "Wildlife Products and the Market Place: A View from Southern Africa." Paper presented at the 2nd International Game Ranching Symposium. Edmonton, Canada, June 4–8, 1990.

———. "Wildlife Conservation in African Parks." In *Voices from Africa,* edited Lewis and Carter.

Cumming, Roualeyn Gordon. *Five Years of a Hunter's Life in the Far Interior of South Africa.* London: John Murray, 1850.

Curtin, Philip D. *The Image of Africa.* Madison, Wisc.: University of Wisconsin Press, 1973.

Dinesen, Isak. *Out of Africa.* New York: Vintage Books, 1972 (first published 1938).

Douglas-Hamilton, Iain, & Associates. "Identification Study for the Conservation and Sustainable Use of the Natural Resources in the Kenyan Portion of the Mara-Serengeti Ecosystem." Report to the European Development Fund of the European Economic Community, 1988.

Douglas-Hamilton, Iain, and Oria Douglas Hamilton. *Among the Elephants.* Harmondsworth, Middlesex: Penguin Books, 1978.

Du Chaillu, Paul B. *Explorations and Adventures in Equatorial Africa.* New York: Harper, 1861.

Ford, John. *The Role of Trypanosomiases in African Ecology: A Study of the Tsetse Fly Problem.* Oxford: Oxford University Press, 1971.

Fossey, Dian. "The Imperiled Mountain Gorilla." *National Geographic,* April 1981, 501–23.

———. *Gorillas in the Mist.* Boston: Houghton Mifflin, 1983.

Graham, Alistair D. *The Gardeners of Eden.* London: Allen and Unwin, 1973.

Grove, Richard. "Early Themes in African Conservation: The Cape in the Nineteenth Century." In *Conservation in Africa: People, Policies and Practice,* edited Anderson and Grove, 21–40.

Grzimek, Bernhard. *No Room for Wild Animals,* translated by R. H. Stevens. London: Thames and Hudson, 1956.

——, and Michael Grzimek. *Serengeti Shall Not Die,* translated by E. L. and D. Rewald. New York: E. P. Dutton, 1960.

Harms, Robert. *Games Against Nature.* Cambridge: Cambridge University Press, 1987.

Hayes, Harold T. P. *The Last Place on Earth.* New York: Stein and Day, 1983.

——. *The Dark Romance of Diane Fossey.* New York: Simon and Schuster, 1990.

Hunter, J. A. *Hunter.* New York: Harper and Brothers, 1952.

Huxley, Julian. *Africa View.* London: Chatto and Windus, 1931.

——. *The Conservation of Wild Life and Natural Habitats in Central and East Africa. Report on a Mission Accomplished for UNESCO, July–September 1961.* New York: United Nations Educational, Scientific, and Cultural Organization, 1961.

Hyden, Goran. *Beyond Ujamaa in Tanzania.* Berkeley and Los Angeles: University of California Press, 1980.

——. *No Shortcuts to Progress.* Berkeley and Los Angeles: University of California Press, 1983.

The IUCN Directory of Afrotropical Protected Areas. Gland, Switzerland: International Union for Conservation of Nature and Natural Resources, 1987.

Jansen, D. J. "Sustainable Wildlife Utilization in the Zambezi Valley of Zimbabwe: Economic, Ecological, and Political Tradeoffs." Unpublished research paper. Harare, Zimbabwe, April 1990.

Jeal, Tim. *Livingstone.* New York: G. P. Putnam's Sons, 1973.

Kanoute, Asetou. "African Women and the Natural Resources of the Wildlands: Linking Conservation Projects to Development Activities." Report to World Wildlife Fund. Washington, D.C., 1990.

Kinloch, Bruce. *Shamba Raiders: Memories of a Game Warden.* Southampton: Ashford Press, 1988.

Leader-Williams, N., and S. D. Albon. "Allocation of Resources for Conservation." *Nature,* 336 (December 1988): 533–35.

Lee, Douglass B. "Okavango Delta, Old Africa's Last Refuge." *National Geographic,* December 1990, 39–69.

Lewis, David Levering. *The Race to Fashoda.* New York: Weidenfeld and Nicolson, 1987.

Lewis, D.M. and L.A. Carter, eds., *Voices from Africa.* Washington, D.C.: World Wildlife Fund, in press.

Lewis, Ethelreda, ed., *Trader Horn: Being the Life and Works of Alfred Aloysius Horn*. New York: Simon and Schuster, 1927.

Livingstone, David. *Missionary Travels and Researches in South Africa*. London: John Murray, 1857.

MacKenzie, John M. *The Empire of Nature: Hunting, Conservation, and British Imperialism*. Manchester: Manchester University Press, 1988.

Marks, Stuart A. *Large Mammals and a Brave People*. Seattle: University of Washington Press, 1976.

———. *The Imperial Lion: Human Dimensions of Wildlife Management in Central Africa*. Boulder, Colo.: Westview Press, 1984.

Marnham, Patrick. *Fantastic Invasion: Dispatches from Africa*. London: Penguin Books, 1987.

Martin, R. B. "Communal Areas Management Programme for Indigenous Resources (CAMPFIRE)." Unpublished research paper, Harare, Zimbabwe, April 1986.

———. "The Status of Projects Involving Wildlife in Rural Development in Zimbabwe." Yearly report. Harare, Zimbabwe: Department of National Parks and Wild Life Management, 1989.

Matowanyika, Joseph Z. Z. "Cast Out of Eden: Peasants versus Wildlife Policy in Savannah Africa." *Alternatives*, 16 (1989): 30–39.

Matthiessen, Peter. *The Tree Where Man Was Born*. New York: E. P. Dutton, 1983.

McNeely, J. A., and Kenton Miller, eds., *National Parks, Conservation and Development*. Washington, D.C.: Smithsonian Institution Press, 1984.

Montgomery, Sy. *Walking with the Great Apes*. Boston: Houghton Mifflin, 1991.

Moorehead, Alan. *The White Nile*. New York: Harper and Brothers, 1960.

Moss, Cynthia. *Elephant Memories*. New York: William Morrow, 1988.

Mudimbe, V. Y. *The Invention of Africa*. Bloomington, Ind.: University of Indiana Press, 1988.

Nash, Roderick. *Wilderness and the American Mind*. New Haven: Yale University Press, 1967.

1990 United Nations List of National Parks and Protected Areas. Gland,

Switzerland: International Union for Conservation of Nature and Natural Resources, 1990.

Norton-Griffiths, Michael. *Counting Animals.* 2nd edn. Nairobi: African Wildlife Leadership Foundation, 1978.

Our Common Future. Report of the World Commission on Environment and Development. Oxford: Oxford University Press, 1987.

Owens, Mark, and Delia Owens. "Kalahari Migration—A Secret Walk to Water." *International Wildlife,* 13, no. 5 (September/October 1983): 32–35.

————. *Cry of the Kalahari.* Boston: Houghton Mifflin, 1984.

Park, Mungo. *Travels into the Interior of Africa.* London: Eland Books, 1986 (first published 1799).

Parker, Ian, and Mohamed Amin. *Ivory Crisis.* London: Chatto and Windus, 1983.

Parkipuny, Moringe S. Ole, and Dhyani J. Berger. "Sustainable Utilization and Management of Resources in the Maasai Rangelands." In *Voices from Africa,* edited Lewis and Carter.

Pennington, Hilary. "A Living Trust: Tanzanian Attitudes Towards Wildlife and Conservation." Unpublished dissertation, Yale University, 1983.

Poole, Joyce H., and Jorgen B. Thomsen. "Elephants Are Not Beetles: Implications of the Ivory Trade for the Survival of the African Elephant." *Oryx,* 23, no. 4 (October 1989): 188–98.

Repetto, Robert. *The Global Possible.* New Haven: Yale University Press, 1985.

Rice, Edward. *Captain Sir Richard Francis Burton.* New York: Charles Scribner's Sons, 1990.

Ritvo, Harriet. *Animal Estate: The English and Creatures in the Victorian Age.* Cambridge, Mass.: Harvard University Press, 1987.

Robinson, Ronald, and John Gallagher. *Africa and the Victorians.* New York: St. Martin's Press, 1961.

Rodney, Walter. *How Europe Underdeveloped Africa.* Washington, D.C.: Howard University Press, 1982.

Roosevelt, Theodore. *African Game Trails,* edited by Peter Capstick. New York: St. Martin's Press, 1988 (first published 1910).

Rosenblum, Mort, and Doug Williamson. *Squandering Eden.* San Diego: Harcourt Brace Jovanovich, 1987.

Saitoti, Tepilit Ole. *The Worlds of a Maasai Warrior.* New York: Random House, 1986; Berkeley: University of Calif. Press, 1988.

Schaller, George B. *The Mountain Gorilla: Ecology and Behavior.* Chicago: University of Chicago Press, 1988 (first published 1963).

―――. *Year of the Gorilla.* Chicago: University of Chicago Press, 1964.

Shoumatoff, Alex. *African Madness.* New York: Vintage Books, 1990.

Sinclair, A. R. E., and M. Norton-Griffiths, eds. *Serengeti: Dynamics of an Ecosystem.* Chicago: University of Chicago Press, 1979.

Soulé, Michael E., ed. *Conservation Biology.* Sunderland, Mass.: Sinauer Associates, Inc., 1986.

Spear, Thomas. "The Environment: White Man's Burden." *Christian Science Monitor,* November 30, 1990.

Stanley, Henry M. *How I Found Livingstone.* New York: Charles Scribner's Sons, 1872.

―――. *Through the Dark Continent.* Mineola, N.Y.: Dover Publications, 1988 (first published 1899).

Stigand, Chauncey Hugh. *Hunting the Elephant in Africa,* edited by Peter Capstick. New York: St. Martin's Press, 1986 (first published 1913).

"Sustainable Wildlife Utilization: The Role of Wildlife Management Areas." Proceedings of a workshop organized by the Kalahari Conservation Society in conjunction with the Department of Wildlife and National Parks. Gabarone, Botswana, November 21–22, 1988.

Taylor, R. D. "Ecologists' Report for 1989 Nyaminyami Wildlife Management Trust Annual General Meeting." Unpublished research report, Harare, Zimbabwe, February 1990.

―――. "Socio-Economic Aspects of Meat Production from Impala Harvested in a Zimbabwean Communal Land." Unpublished research report, Harare, Zimbabwe, 1990.

Thomson, Joseph. *Through Masai Land.* London, 1883.

Tinbergen, Niko. *Social Behaviour in Animals.* Frome, Dorset: Butler & Tanner, 1969.

Turner, Myles. *My Serengeti Years.* New York: W. W. Norton, 1987.

Vansina, Jan. *Paths in the Rainforest: Toward a History of Political Tradition in Equatorial Africa.* London: James Currey, 1990.

Vedder, Amy, and William Weber. "The Mountain Gorilla Project." In *Living with Wildlife,* edited by Agnes Kiss. Washington, D.C.:

The International Bank for Reconstruction and Development/ The World Bank, 1990, 83–95.

Ward, Haskell. *African Development Reconsidered: New Perspectives form the Continent*. New York: Pheps-Stokes Institute, 1989.

Warford, J. J. *Natural Resource Management and Economic Development*. Washington, D.C.: The International Bank for Reconstruction and Development/The World Bank, 1986.

Watt, Ian. *Conrad in the Nineteenth Century*. Berkeley and Los Angeles: University of California Press, 1979.

Weber, A. William. "Conservation of the Virunga Gorillas: A Socio-Economic Perspective on Habitat and Wildlife Preservation in Rwanda." Unpublished Dissertation, University of Wisconsin, Madison, 1981.

———. "Socioecologic Factors in the Conservation of Afromontane Forest Reserves." In *Primate Conservation in Tropical Rain Forests*, edited by Clive W. Marsh and R. Mittermeier. New York: Alan R. Liss, 1987, 205–29.

Weber, and A. Vedder. "Population Dynamics of the Virunga Gorillas." *Biological Conservation*, 26 (1983): 341–66.

Williamson, D. T., J. Williamson, and K. T. Ngwamotsoko. "Wildebeest Migration in the Kalahari." *African Journal of Ecology*, 26, no. 4(December 1988): 269–80.

Worster, Donald. *Nature's Economy*. Cambridge: Cambridge University Press, 1987.

SUPPLEMENTARY BIBLIOGRAPHY

Davidson, Basil. *The Black Man's Burden: Africa and the Curse of the Nation State*. New York: Times Books, 1992.

Noss, Reed F., and Allen Y. Cooperrider. *Saving Nature's Legacy: Protecting and Restoring Biodiversity*. Washington, D.C.: Island Press, 1994.

Sinclair, A. R. E., and Peter Arcese, eds. *Serengeti II: Dynamics, Management, and Conservation of an Ecosystem*. Chicago: University of Chicago Press, 1995.

Wells, Michael, and Katrina Brandon. *People and Parks: Linking Protected Area Management with Local Communities*. Washington, D.C.: The World Bank, 1992.

INDEX

▼ ▼ ▼